Dr Brown
Sept. 1996

The Korean War began by interrupting the American adjustment to peace following World War Two, and ended not only without a victory but with a United States loss of life and suffering comparable to Vietnam. Even today, nearly four times as many American MIAs from the Korean War remain unaccounted for as from Vietnam.

Ensign Charles F. Cole, graduated from Cornell University in 1950, and was also in the first Naval ROTC class to be commissioned. Cole and his classmates anticipated two years of peace-time duty to repay their obligation. Instead, within a few weeks of graduation, they were swept into the Navy's frantic preparation to re-equip a Navy whose war-time strength and proficiency had been decimated by military cutbacks. The skeleton Navy force on duty in both Atlantic and Pacific fleets, was quickly augmented by those 1950 NROTC Ensigns and the recall of World War II Reservists. The former provided the large number of Ensigns needed by an expanded Navy. The latter, who still retained their World War II skills, provided the expertise needed to man the ships coming out of mothballs.

Cole is unstinting in his praise for the returning Reservists. He and his fellow classmates are an emphatic affirmation of the value of the NROTC program envisioned by Dr. (Captain) Arthur Adams and named in honor of Admiral James Holloway. Without those NROTC Ensigns and the returning Reservists, the United States Navy's participation in the first year of the Korean War would have been minimal at best.

Cole served eighteen months on the USS *Ozbourn* off the Korean Coast. Underwater Demolition Teams began during World War II to help ensure the safety of forces landing on the various Atlantic and Pacific beaches. This type of unconventional warfare was in its infancy when Cole took his Navy demolition training in 1951.

D11005399

Ensign Charles F. Cole
1950

About the Author:

Charles F. Cole received his PhD in Ichthyology from Cornell University in 1957 and spent the next thirty-seven years teaching before retiring as a professor from Ohio State University. Active in the Naval Reserve, and serving as a faculty advisor to ROTC units, Commander Cole also served as commanding officer of several Reserve units before retiring. He and his wife, Emma Jean, presently live in Worthington, Ohio. Although now retired from teaching, Cole is still active in professional organizations.

KOREA REMEMBERED:
ENOUGH OF A WAR

The USS *Ozbourn's* First Korean Tour, 1950-1951

by

Charles F. Cole, CDR USNR-Ret.

YUCCA TREE PRESS

KOREA REMEMBERED: Enough of a War, the USS Ozbourn's First Korean Tour, 1950-1951. Copyright 1995 by Charles F. Cole. All rights reserved. No part of this book may be reproduced in any form or by any electronic or mechanical means, including information storage and retrieval systems without permission, in writing, from the publisher except by a reviewer who may quote brief passages in a review. Yucca Tree Press, 2130 Hixon Drive, Las Cruces, New Mexico 88005.

First Printing   1995

Library of Congress Cataloging in Publication Data.

Cole, Charles F.

   KOREA REMEMBERED: Enough of a War, The USS Ozbourn's First Korean Tour, 1950-1951
        1. Korean Conflict - U.S. Navy. 2. U. S. Navy - Korean Conflict. 3. USS Ozbourn.   4. Naval Reserve Officer Training Program.   5. U.S. Navy - SEALS.   6. U.S. Navy - Underwater Demolition Teams.
        I. Charles F. Cole. II. Title.

Library of Congress Catalog Card Number: 95-060802

ISBN: 1-881325-13-X

DEDICATION

To the officers and enlisted men who served with me in Under-water Demolition Team #4, those on board the USS *Ozbourn*, and the recalled Naval Reservists who made the difference.

To Dr. Arthur S. Adams and Rear Admiral James Holloway, USN, for their foresight in creating the modern Naval Reserve Officer Training Program (NROTC).

But most of all, to Robert Gillespie, HMSN, and the 33,500 other United States servicemen who gave their lives in combat during the Korean War in order that South Korea could remain a nation.

ACKNOWLEDGMENTS

The assistance, advice, and counsel of the following caught and corrected many of the errors and flawed memories of the author: Captain Charles O. Akers, USN-ret; Captain Ronald Fredrickson, USNR-ret; Captain Philip Gubbins, USN-ret; Robert Hodgson; Kenneth Jones; Captain Frank Kaine, USN-ret; Captain Barr Palmer, USN-ret; Captain Leslie Skowronek, USN; Captain James Tregurtha, USN-ret; Commander Robert Whitten, USNR-ret; Dr. Langley Wood; and Joseph Worthington. I am also indebted to John S. Blonsick for his many additions. Although we shared a room on the *Ozbourn*, Jack's version of events and mine disagree frequently, which is the nature of old memories when committed to paper. All remaining errors are mine alone.

The friendly assistance of Janie Matson, of Yucca Tree Press, has been invaluable and I am particularly in her debt for seeing a book buried in a rough manuscript and then helping it emerge.

I am deeply indebted to my wife, Emma-Jean, for her continued tolerance of the late-night clacking of a dot-matrix printer as it produced yet another version. Finally, I am indebted to those with whom I shared the events described in the following text. We were involved in a strange, heart-rending war; the cost in lives and the emerging meaning of the events we shared will remain with us to our individual ends. God bless us all.

TABLE OF CONTENTS

ILLUSTRATIONS

MAPS

PREFACE

The Korean War began by interrupting the American adjustment to peace following World War Two, and ended not only without a victory but with a United States loss of life and suffering comparable to Vietnam. Even today nearly four times as many American MIAs from the Korean War remain unaccounted for as from Vietnam.

The United States response to the invasion by North Korea began with strong political support, even with the weight of international indignation as well as a United Nations (UN) umbrella of sanctions to justify it. Regardless of its beginning, the Korean War ended with an unhappy, stalemated cease-fire along a Demilitarized Zone (DMZ) approximating the 38th Parallel, almost exactly where combat had begun. Although the three-year war restored political integrity to South Korea, it also propelled world attention into the Cold War and gave logic to a massive international arms race. Within ten years of the Korean War's finish, Vietnam emerged as our next blood bath and replaced, in the American mind, unhappy memories of Korea with others better remembered but scarcely more painful.

From an American perspective, the war's first year was fought not only by those regulars already on active duty but also by large numbers of recalled reservists from each of the services. Unanticipated by anyone, this sudden war made demands on the military resources of the United States that could only be resolved by a massive recall of reservists and National Guard. They, and the regulars, bore the brunt of the first year while those drafted or enlisting arrived later. To add to world anxiety, during that first year, was the belief held by many that Korea signaled the start of a war with the Soviet Union–World War Three. By the end of the first year, that fear had dissipated and the massive battles surging up and down the peninsula had largely ceased. Instead, the war turned into bloody, but stalemated, trench warfare more characteristic of World War One. By April 1951, General Douglas MacArthur had been fired and American enthusiasm for 'Truman's War' had nearly evaporated. It lasted for two more bloody years while we waited for a political solution from the Peace Tent in Panmunjom.

More than forty years later, a Demilitarized Zone (DMZ) approximating the initial border at the 38th Parallel remains as that stalemated solution. It remains an unsolved war with armed camps on either side of a troubled line splitting the Korean Peninsula.

Following Korea, our preoccupation with the Cold War and our Soviet antagonists reduced every conflict to a single cause and kept us from seeing additional reasons for the many other antagonisms around the world. In 1991, President Bush and the United States Congress, responded to later UN Resolutions and authorized an armed intervention to restore Kuwait. Inevitably reservists and National Guard were recalled and the resulting family upheavals brought back vivid memories of 1950-51. Although Desert Storm seemed solely a response to naked aggression, it also contained elements of conflict for natural resources, ethnic diversity, and religious intolerance–issues which remain unresolved elsewhere in the world. If we become involved, we will require a military of both active and reserve components. If so, we must keep in place succeeding generations of qualified reservists willing to follow those who served during Korea and Desert Storm.

This book is dedicated not only to those Naval Reservists whom I knew during that first year in Korea, but also to those Regulars on active duty during the brief peace from 1945 to 1950. The Korean War consumed both in varying ways.

Now back to 1944, the war in the Pacific and the Tinian invasion. The two wars are related by decisions, people, equipment, tactics, and locations.

PROLOGUE

TINIAN AND PRIVATE OZBOURN

The goals of the invasion of the Marianas Islands–Saipan, Tinian and Guam–were to provide advanced bases for the Navy and the Army Air Force, a place from which B-29 bombers could reach Japan. On 24 July 1944, Marines landed on Tinian in what General Holland M. 'Howling Mad' Smith, USMC, declared to be "the perfect amphibious operation in the Pacific War," which didn't mean at no cost. On 30 July, Private Joseph William Ozbourn and four other Marines moved forward against Japanese dugouts along a tree line. Just as Ozbourn was about to throw a live grenade, a Japanese grenade exploded nearby severely wounding all five. Ozbourn's wounds prevented him from throwing his grenade and instead of dropping it amongst the others, he chose to fall on top of it sacrificing his own life to save his comrades. Others died as well. On 13 August, Senator Leverett Saltonstall (R-Massachusetts) lost his son, Sergeant Peter Saltonstall, USMCR. When the mopping up was finally over three months later, American dead totaled 389.

For heroism above and beyond the call of duty, Ozbourn was awarded the Congressional Medal of Honor posthumously and the USS *Ozbourn* (DD-846) was commissioned in his memory nearly two years later. Tinian soon became a huge air facility and, from it, nearly a year later, a B-29 named *Enola Gay* departed with the atomic bomb to be dropped at Hiroshima. Soon afterward, the Pacific War ended with the surrender in Tokyo Bay in September 1945, just as I entered my Senior year in Beaver High School.

PART I

THE BEGINNING

STRATEGIC ISSUES

Following the end of World War Two, American attention was focused on rebuilding Europe, but the Pacific Rim also contained difficult problems – a Japan to be occupied as well as defended from Soviet aggression; a liberated, but now divided, Korea separated into two sovereign nations; a Chinese Civil War won by Communists in late 1949 but with one more item on their agenda, the take-over of Formosa (Taiwan); a liberated Formosa occupied in 1949 by armies and leaders escaping from mainland China who vowed to return the war to the mainland; instability in Indo-China as the French attempted to reestablish their colonies after the defeat of Japan; the development of Communist-based resistance to the French; an insurrection underway in the Philippines by the HUKs[1] opposing the American-supported government and similar problems in the former Dutch East Indies. Though these might not all be American foreign policy issues, each had the potential for American involvement and any American involvement could easily grow into a serious commitment.

United States foreign policy in the Far East under the Truman Administration seemed drifting toward a post-war isolationism, and was under scrutiny and attack by the 'China Block' which included those in the US Senate who blamed the State Department for the US failure to prevent the loss of

Mainland China to the Communists. Senator Joseph McCarthy and others contended that China had fallen because the State Department had been "soft on communism." Their contention was that we had not won the Pacific War only to lose everything to Communism. If anything, the Far East was more unstable than Europe and it certainly was much less understood by the American public.

On 12 January 1950, Secretary of State Dean Acheson spoke to the National Press Club and described Formosa and South Korea as outside United States strategic interests. This comment was not surprising given the withdrawal of our occupation forces from Korea in 1949. Acheson's remarks have since been interpreted an explicit invitation to North Korea to invade South Korea. When US occupation forces left in 1949, we provided South Korea with limited defensive weapons and then promised President Syngman Rhee additional support. North Korea, under the leadership of Kim Il Sung, on the other hand, was well-supplied with Russian T-34 tanks, aircraft, and other offensive weapons during the early months of 1950.

Further, North Korea had inferred from US behavior that they could effect a forceful unification if they wished and that the US would not respond. What was the level and extent of Russian involvement in the North Korean decision to invade is only now being unraveled, but the United States was neither expected, nor prepared, to intervene. Once war began, the fundamental international question in the summer of 1950 became—"Is Korea the start of World War Three and will Russia escalate the Korean War elsewhere in the Far East as well as Europe?" No one doubted their involvement in Korea; what happened next became the real concern.[2]

Because of budget cuts, greatly reduced combat readiness and an excessive, but misplaced, reliance on the atomic bomb, US potential for conventional armed response anywhere in the world had become very limited. Any response, except nuclear, to an attack in Europe, or in the Far East, seemed beyond US control. Further, in 1950, most Americans assumed that any attack by a communist country occurred only because they were puppet states operating under close Russian tutelage.

South Korea (Republic of Korea or ROK) under Syngman Rhee was just as intent on Korean reunification as was the

North under Kim Il Sung. Each side asked impossible conditions from the other and both accepted armed aggression as the ultimate solution. Unfortunately, Rhee had only limited defensive weapons that were unequal to the task. The US had promised to provide additional military support but, by June 1950, it had not yet done so. From January 1950, onward, the stage was being set for the Korean War as supplies moved into North Korea. While both sides had intent, only the North had acquired the capability.

Start of the War

The Korean War commenced at 4:00 a.m., Sunday 25 June 1950 (Korean time) or 3:00 p.m. (Eastern Daylight Time), Saturday 24 June. Six and a half hours later, 9:26 p.m. Saturday (EDT), the United States Ambassador to South Korea, John Muccio, provided Washington with the first news of the attack. All US citizens in Korea needed to be protected or evacuated, no matter what decision might be made regarding the defense of South Korea.

On Sunday, 25 June, President Truman ordered the Seventh Fleet northward from the Philippines to Sasebo on Kyushu Island, southern Japan, there to report to the operational control of Admiral C. Turner Joy, Commander, Naval Forces, Far East (ComNavFE). From Sasebo, ships could then be deployed to Korea to begin evacuating US citizens. President Truman flew back to Washington from Missouri on Sunday afternoon to attend a 7:30 p.m. dinner meeting of his top military and State advisors. At the same time, the UN Security Council met to consider the invasion.

Earlier in June, Jacob Malik, Soviet delegate to the UN Security Council, had begun boycotting meetings of the Council. He had walked out because he had been unable to replace Nationalist China with Red China in the permanent seat on the Security Council. As the delegate of a permanent member of the Security Council, he was empowered to block any Resolution before the Council simply by exercising the veto given to each of the four permanent members: Nationalist China, United States, United Kingdom, and USSR. At 6:00 p.m., Sunday, after four hours deliberation, the UN Security Council

voted, 9 to 0 (3 abstentions; 1 absent—USSR), in favor of the
first resolution asking for withdrawal of troops and a cessation
of hostilities.

By Monday, 26 June, the situation had clearly worsened.
That evening Truman met again with his advisors. Because the
North Koreans had ignored the Security Council's Resolution,
the US asked for a second Security Council resolution sanction-
ing UN armed intervention. The second UN Resolution, passed
on 27 June, asked that member nations provide such assistance
as needed to repel the attack and to restore peace and security.

With passage of the second Security Council resolution
authorizing military intervention, President Truman announced
his decision to provide US air and sea support to South Korea.[3]
In his speech to the American radio audience, he went beyond
Korea and linked US intervention in Korea with a concurrent
need for neutralization of the Straits of Formosa. The US
administration believed that a Mainland China-to-Formosa invasion *and* the North Korean invasion were but two parts of a
single battle plan. Neutralizing the Straits of Formosa *and*
supporting South Korea would become the US response to any
Soviet encouraged, if not controlled, plan to take over Formosa
and Korea. Whether invasions of Formosa and Korea were
ever planned as linked operations is still not known. Truman
also announced increased assistance to the Philippines as well
as to French Indochina in order to stabilize the entire region.
His action was highly acceptable to the US Congress, to the
American and European press and to the American public. The
US was returning to meet its Pacific obligations.

On the same day, the House extended the draft for one year
and authorized the President to call up reservists from all services;[4] the Senate passed both measures on Wednesday. President Truman avoided the political stigma of asking Congress
for a declaration of war by beginning the practice of a Congressional Resolution, which was later followed for Vietnam and
Desert Storm. Truman also picked up a phrase first used by a
China Block adversary, Senator William Knowland (R-Califor-
nia), to describe our response. It wasn't to be a war but a 'police
action.' Among those of us present during the Korean War, it
was never 'Truman's police action,' except in grim jest, nor was
it ever the 'Korean Conflict'; it was simply the 'Korean War,'

declared or not.[5] Efforts appearing to sugarcoat the war infuriated US service personnel involved–it was enough of a war for anyone.

Truman's linkage of Korea and Formosa partially softened political anger coming from the 'China Block.' However, on Wednesday, Senator Robert A. Taft (R-Ohio) argued that the Administration was responsible on two counts for the invasion of South Korea: first, its failure to supply South Korea with adequate defensive arms, and second, because of Dean Acheson's speech on 12 January. He then agreed with the Administration's actions. There was no need for a declaration of war–Congressional concurrence was initially sufficient and the American press and public fully supported the intervention. Such enthusiasm would not last the year.

Neither action by the Security Council nor that in Washington made any impact on fighting in Korea and the situation continued to deteriorate. On Thursday, 29 June, General MacArthur flew to Korea to inspect the battlefield. Upon his return to Japan, he recommended to the President that thirty-three thousand American ground combat troops be sent to Korea. On 30 June, in response to the request, President Truman released two of the four divisions stationed in Japan for combat duty in Korea. My Beaver Scout Troop buddy, Howard Johns, were soon be moved from garrison duty in Japan. He and his friends were used to slow down the North Korean advance until we and others got there. They were not ready for combat and Howard's summer would be spent slowly retreating southward into the small rectangle of land which was to become known as the Pusan Perimeter.

The Navy began to move in the Western Pacific. Although Seventh Fleet movements had initially been toward Sasebo in southern Kyushu, once there they would be within range of Russian bombers. Senior officers in the Pacific Fleet remembered too well the results of the Japanese bombing of Pearl Harbor and no one dared concentrate a fleet within range of Russian bombers able to deliver nuclear weapons. Accordingly, the coalescing UN fleet was redirected to Buckner Bay, Okinawa. That this war would ultimately become limited to the Korean Peninsula and that Japan and Manchuria would become sanctuaries for each of the respective combatants was not to be assumed by either side until well into 1951.

The Seventh Fleet arrived in Buckner Bay and was joined by the British carrier, HMS *Triumph*, their cruiser HMS *Belfast* and two British destroyers, *Consort* and *Cossack*. Once this joint fleet was assembled, some were assigned to a carrier striking force while other ships went to support and blockade duties. Although Truman's 'Police Action' had begun in Korea, an armed invasion of Formosa also had to be prevented and a neutralizing patrol of the Straits of Formosa by air and sea forces was also begun. The initial Formosa patrol also included American submarines.[6]

By early August, when Russia had still not overtly interfered, Sasebo was gradually transformed into the major staging area for ships operating off Korea.

Available Naval Forces and Their Missions

As June 1950 began, the US Navy had duties in European waters as well as in the Western Pacific. The two-ocean Navy had been functioning with a Pacific Fleet and an Atlantic Fleet since before World War Two and only rarely were ships moved from one Fleet to the other. As a result, characteristic Fleet differences emerged; the Atlantic Fleet seemed more formal, even stuffy, while the Pacific was less so, perhaps having kept its 'get on with it' attitude from the Pacific war.

The Atlantic Fleet, involved in newly developing NATO commitments, required ships to move back and forth from fleet concentrations at Newport, Rhode Island, and from the Norfolk, Virginia, area to assignments in Europe and the Mediterranean. The NATO Treaty signed in April 1949, had come at the end of a string of European crises from the Soviet takeover of Czechoslovakia in 1946 to the Berlin Airlift in 1948-9. US political attention remained focused on events in Europe as it had through the war years and the very real Russian potential for aggression into western Europe was becoming more ominous as time passed.

Ships of the Pacific Fleet rotated to the Western Pacific for tours up to six months or more from their home ports in Pearl Harbor, San Diego, Long Beach, San Francisco, and the Seattle area. Each ship had officers and crew with experience extending back to the Asiatic Squadron prior to the war but many others had limited fleet experience. Each ship was badly under-manned and unready for wartime steaming.

Duty in the Pacific Fleet had a different quality. The Pacific Ocean seemed an American lake and the Navy was servicing an American Empire or, if not that, at least it was dealing either with European colonies or with countries having recent colonial backgrounds. Finally, crossing the Pacific Ocean routinely took even a destroyer fifteen or more days. This long trip created for everyone a huge emotional gap between the Unite States and some other world later to become known as WestPac.

Vessels in both Fleets operated under the administrative and technical supervision of their own Fleet Type Commanders but for operational control were placed under Fleet, Force or Task Group Commanders. Commander Cruisers and Destroyers Pacific Fleet (ComCruDesPac) was Type Commander in charge of management, doctrine development and planning for Pacific cruisers and destroyers; ComPhibPac for amphibious ships and related units; and ComSubPac for support of submarines. Commander-in-Chief, Pacific Fleet (CINCPacFlt) controlled all of the Pacific Fleet from Pearl Harbor.

In early June 1950, two groups of US naval vessels were present in the Western Pacific: Naval Forces Far East and the

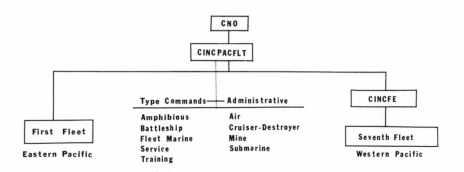

Figure 1: Organizational chart of the Commander-in-Chief, Pacific Fleet (CINCPacFlt).

Seventh Fleet. Naval Forces Far East (NavFE) was commanded by Vice Admiral C. Turner Joy, (ComNavFE), and included
all amphibious and support ships assigned to the occupation of
Japan. ComNavFE reported directly to General Douglas Mac-
Arthur, Commander-in-Chief, Far East (CINCFE).

NavFE's Amphibious Force was limited to an amphibious
command ship, two attack transports, an LST, and a fleet tug.
NavFE had no ships able to refuel or rearm a carrier task force
while at sea. NavFE's Support Force included: USS *Juneau*, a
light anti-aircraft cruiser, four destroyers, and six wooden-
hulled mine-sweepers. These ships were part of the combined
forces occupying post-war Japan and conducted patrols between Korea and Japan to reduce smuggling into Japan. They
also made port visits in Japan showing the flag as well as patrolling around Hokkaido, the northernmost island then being
contested by the Russians. British ships of the Far East Station
were also assigned to occupation duty in Japan and they included an aircraft carrier, two cruisers, two destroyers, and three
frigates. In addition, several Australian ships were also assigned
to duty in Japan.

In June 1950, the Seventh Fleet, commanded by Vice
Admiral A. D. Struble, was also in the Western Pacific. Its ships
were distributed from Sangley Point and Subic Bay in the Philippines to Hong Kong. They consisted of one aircraft carrier,
Valley Forge, one heavy cruiser, and eight destroyers. In March
1950, the Seventh Fleet had conducted joint maneuvers with
similar British naval units from Far East Station, Hong Kong.
The Seventh Fleet provided a US presence in the Far East, stabilized the Philippines against the communist-inspired HUK
insurgency, worried about a Chinese invasion of Formosa, or
vice-versa, and observed the break-up of the far east elements
of the Dutch, French, and British Empires. Each location
represented a potential trouble spot that often needed the
stabilizing presence of a port visit.

I was commissioned as an Ensign, USN, on June 12, 1950,
and was assigned to the USS *Ozbourn*. Destroyer Squadron 11
(CAPT J. R. Clark, USN, commanding) consisted of two Divisions (111 and 112), four destroyers each. Division 111 contained: *Wiltsie*, *Theodore E. Chandler*, *Hamner*, and *Chevalier*.
Wiltsie carried ComDesRon 11 on board as well as my class-
mate, ENS Jim Tregurtha. Destroyer Division 112 included:

Ozbourn, Frank Knox, Hollister, and *McKean.* Our Division 112 had earlier returned from a typical WestPac tour which would then be followed by leave, yard-time, transfers, fleet exercises, and, finally, a work-up for the return to WestPac. Our 'Des Dog,' was ComDesDiv 112 or Commander, Destroyer Division 112. Radio voice calls were assigned to various units for phonetic and clarity purposes and not because they inherently meant anything. Still, our Division Commander's voice call—'Mobilize Dog'—never seemed sufficiently respectful. On the other hand, our ship's call was 'Fireball' and that seemed like something we had yet to earn.

Other elements of the Pacific Fleet were scattered from Bremerton, Washington, south to San Diego, and west to Pearl Harbor. All were significantly undermanned and only those in the forward areas in WestPac came close to being ready for wartime operations.

Endnotes:

[1] The Hukbong Bayan Laban sa Hapon (HUK) were guerrilla fighters originally formed to fight the Japanese. After 1946 and the creation of an independent Philippine Republic, they became peasant Communists dedicated to the overthrow of the republic. *Lands and People*, Vol. 2, Lexicon Press (1977: 331).

[2] Spurr (1988:13), etc. for details from the North Korean perspective.

[3] Whelan (1990:100-150) and Boetticher (1992) for details of the sequence of meetings in far greater detail than needed here. See also, Acheson (1969) and others.

[4] Alexander (1986:42).

[5] See Summers (1992) for a comparison of the political processes by which the US entered Korea, Vietnam, and Desert Storm. Summers makes a strong argument for development of the political support that a formal declaration of war entails.

[6] See Schratz (1989) for details. Submarine operations off Russian ports and the Chinese coast were apparently still classified when Cagle and Manson (1957) was written. They do not discuss submarine operations, but Field (1960) does.

THE AMERICAN DESTROYER

Destroyers had been part of the US Navy since before the turn of the century and they were gradually being modified or redesigned as obsolescence and funding dictated. Five classes of destroyers had been designed and built between 1938 and 1946 but only three—'Fletcher,' 'Sumner,' and 'Gearing'—predominated by 1950. In June 1950, some 347 US destroyers were either on active duty or were in mothballs.[1] Those in mothballs could be recommissioned but that process would take six months or longer, and much depended upon the need for shipyard time for modernization of radar and other electronic equipment, as well as the state of armament and engines. In early June, the Navy had some fifty-seven destroyers in the Pacific Fleet, twelve of which were already in WestPac.

There was a more desperate need for qualified officers and men if the ships already in commission were to operate under combat conditions. Active duty personnel could be transferred from shore assignments but there were only so many qualified people on active duty and, as a result, wartime allowances would be met only by an immediate recall of reservists. Further, as mothballed ships were being brought back, assembling skilled people and training a crew might add six months beyond yard time before the ship was ready for combat. At the beginning of the Korean War, the *Ozbourn* had approximately one hundred eighty enlisted and eight officers on board. This was not even close to her wartime complement of three hundred fifty. The war might not permit the time needed to bring crews to wartime levels and provide for ships coming out of mothballs.

Beginning in 1930, eight relatively small classes of destroyers were constructed to replace the by then obsolete two hundred and sixty five American destroyers ('four-pipers' and 'flush-decks') constructed during World War One. Despite their obsolescence, one hundred were transferred to Great Britain for convoy duty. Others were converted into attack transports (APDs) to transport Marines and Underwater Demolition Teams during World War Two. Naval construction preceding US entry into World War Two centered on three classes of destroyers. Ninety-six 'Benson' class, sixty-four 'Ellyson' class, and one hundred seventy-five 'Fletcher' class destroyers dominated the destroyer fleet of World War Two.[2] Of these three, Fletcher class destroyers predominated by the end of the Pacific war. By 1950, seventy-eight Fletcher destroyers remained essentially as constructed although many were in mothballs and most had seen considerable use during the war. They would be recalled for the Korean War but it was the destroyers of the next generation—Sumner and Gearing classes—that would predominate in Korea.

Sumners and Gearings

Sumners and Gearings, produced late in World War Two, were designed to overcome the handling deficiencies of the Fletcher class and to provide internal passageways. They were also needed to control Japanese suicide air attacks. Kamikaze attacks began during the Philippine landings in December 1944 and lasted through the Okinawa campaign in April 1945. Fletcher class destroyers seemed unable to stop persistent aircraft. Thus, air and anti-submarine defense replaced the classic nighttime gun and torpedo battles as the primary destroyer activity. During the Okinawa offensive, twelve US destroyers were sunk by kamikazes; the 40mm and 20mm guns and single five-inch mounts on Fletchers were not heavy enough to stop suicide attacks. Sumner and Gearing destroyers were designed to meet the challenges of their 1944-45 adversaries, but not for the jet aircraft and fast submarines of the 1950s.

By the end of World War Two, seventy Sumner and one hundred and three Gearing destroyers had been built. In 1950, fifty-three Sumner and one hundred and one Gearing destroyers were available, either in commission or in mothballs. A Sumner destroyer was larger and more stable than a Fletcher. Displacing 2,200 tons, the Sumner destroyer was 376 feet long, 40 feet wide, and had a draft of 19 feet. Each carried three dual, closed five-inch 38 gun mounts as main armament and secondary anti-air armament. Several Sumner class destroyers had been completed in time to serve late in the Pacific Campaign and in Europe.

USS Ozbourn As A Gearing

Ozbourn had been commissioned 5 March 1946 and her first commanding officer was CDR Bernard 'Barney' Smith, USN. *Ozbourn* reported for duty August 1946. She departed San Diego, 6 January 1947, on her first deployment to WestPac with DesDiv 111 and returned to the West Coast October 1947. On 1 October 1948, off the coast of China on her next WestPac deployment, she collided with USS *Theodore E. Chandler* (DD-717) during a torpedo exercise. She lost her bow and two sailors were killed. Although her commanding officer, who had replaced Smith, protested the impending maneuver and was ultimately exonerated, nonetheless, he went to an early death convinced the losses had been his fault. In the summer of 1949, she had accompanied the USS *Springfield* on a midshipmen cruise to Panama and later around the Galapagos Islands. I saw her from the deck of the *Springfield* while we crossed the Equator and were initiated into the Royal Order of Shellbacks. I did not see her again until 5 July 1950.

Ozbourn was a Gearing. They were begun in late 1944 and none was completed before the war's end. Essentially they were 'stretched Sumners,' longer by only fourteen feet added between the stacks, and only slightly heavier, displacing 2,425 tons. Gearings were difficult to separate either visually or in terms of performance—except in range—from Sumners. Their peacetime complement was 257 officers and men; wartime allowance, 350. A black tripod mast characterized both Gearing and Sumner destroyers in Korea. Virtually every destroyer on active duty and serving in Korea in 1950-51 had been through similar shipyard modifications since the war. All Gearings had been constructed during the last year of the war, none had more than four years of fleet duty and none had seen combat prior to Korea.

Gearings had four oil-fired boilers, two in each fireroom. They could make up to twenty-seven knots with only two boilers on line and under wartime conditions, used one boiler in each fireroom. Traveling with 'the plant split,' required both firerooms to be manned, but made her more combat-worthy. Two additional boilers, for speeds up to thirty knots, required up to a half hour before they were hot enough to provide superheated steam to the turbines.

By July 1950, *Ozbourn* still had Mark 15 torpedoes in a five-tube trainable torpedo mount located between the two stacks on the deckhouse. Despite her collision with *Chandler*, torpedo attacks remained part of our mission. A torpedo attack made by a squadron of destroyers at thirty knots has all the glamour of a cavalry charge, but against alert surface vessels equipped with radar-controlled guns, we might have been more successful making a real cavalry attack. Our primary task was to defend the carriers against aircraft and submarines. Whether we might also be called upon to face attacks from ships depended upon the Soviet and Red Chinese intentions; this remained unknown in the summer of 1950.

Until someone told us more about the capability of the enemy, even who that might be, torpedoes were at the ready. In the fleet, torpedoes were already being changed into anti-submarine devices, but our torpedomen had no option but to keep on pulling, cleaning, fussing, and fidgeting with ours. We hoped never to be where we would need them. Normally during General Quarters, our two Chief Torpedomen (TMC), DeWitt and Higgins, served as forward three-inch battery control officers defending the ship against aircraft. If we were firing torpedoes, or were attacking a submarine with depth charges, they would be in charge of the torpedo tubes and the depth-charge racks and K-guns.

We even had small arms on *Ozbourn*. They seemed unnecessary on a ship operating in a carrier task force but they might be needed aboard an armed whaleboat sent inshore after a downed pilot. They might even be needed by boarding parties or to repel boarders if we anchored at night off an enemy coast. Nonetheless, small arms were tightly locked in the 'small arms locker' which contained Garand M-1 rifles, carbines, Thompson 45-caliber sub-machine guns, as well as 45-caliber pistols. Hand-held pyrotechnic launchers were usually on the bridge for recognition signals to passing Navy patrol bombers.

Passage about the ship during the daylight and normal weather conditions at sea could be handled by walking out on the weather or main deck or up a ladder and along the 01-level. If you needed to get out on the main or weather deck just forward of the wardroom, a dogged hatch could be opened to permit passage forward either to the two forward five-inch mounts or to the deck gear controlling release of the anchor. Usually, these hatches were dogged shut because the bow was swept with waves and spray while underway. Under more normal circumstances, if the seas were down and ships' work finished, officers and chiefs might stand around on the fore-deck. On a cruiser, this area seemed huge and somewhat like a formal garden in which to stroll. On a destroyer, it was often unsafe and dangerous. If officers sometimes lounged on the foredeck, on *Ozbourn* the crew owned the fantail as well as midship's passage.

Midship's passage ran athwartship and split the main deck house into a forward and an after section. It also set off sick bay and the laundry located forward, from the ship's office and the supply office located aft. Off the supply office was the broom closet-sized ship's library. 'Midship's' was the closest thing to *Ozbourn*'s 'downtown.' It became a halfway house where those from forward crew's berthing met those from after spaces. A large windlass for handling mooring lines was also present and usually became a seat from which one could watch the passing ocean while smoking a cigarette. The chow line also began there and then snaked along the port weatherdeck if clear, or in the passageway forward past sickbay, if it was bad out. Time passed in a tedium of four hour watches, meals, movies, and more watches for crew as well as officers. The door to the laundry was always open and often was the rumor-hub for the latest scuttlebutt. If the laundrymen did not know, the yeomen across in ship's office might, but they usually kept it to them-selves.

During darkness, or in heavy weather, one moved forward or aft in the ship only along the passage inside the main deckhouse that ran from a ladder to after crew's compartment forward, past the ship's store and then to the athwartship's passageway. Thence forward past a small sickbay, two scuttles with vertical ladders to the two firerooms, a ladder up to the next deck (01 level) to CIC, Radio Room and, ultimately, up to the Bridge. It passed the crew's galley, the officer's galley and ended at the door to the wardroom.

Crew members coming forward as far as the galley could either go down a ladder to their own messing spaces and then forward to the forward berthing space, or they could go out to the weatherdeck or up the ladder toward the bridge, but never into the wardroom except in an emergency. Off the forward crew's berthing space was Sonar, continuously manned for antisubmarine and mine detection when underway.

If an enlisted man needed to enter the wardroom, he knew to be respectful because he was in 'officer's country,' thus: knock, enter cap in hand, state your question, get your answer and get out. The wardroom was equipped with a leather-covered sofa and a long table covered with a green felt cloth. The table had the capacity of handling dinners with white linen or becoming the operating table during either combat or appendix operations; the operating room light overhead reminded you of that point during dinner.

Breakfast in the wardroom was continuously available up to 0800 when everyone left for quarters. Lunch and supper had two servings; the first, more boisterous, was mostly junior officers but also accommodated oncoming watch-standers. The second settings, at 1200 and 1800, were for the ship's captain, the division commander to his right, and any of the rest of us, in descending order of rank, ensigns at the bottom, plus any off-coming watch standers.

Discussions were usually limited to what interested the captain and division commander, called 'Commodore' when you spoke to him. Their opinions prevailed and any opposing personal opinions were kindly kept to yourself. Politics, religion, money, women, and other misadventures were best left to the junior end of the early serving. Except for an occasional cup of coffee or meetings, the wardroom was off-limits for lounging until after working hours.

When seas became rough, out came the cherrywood fiddle-boards that attached to the wardroom table and formed little wood-sided boxes for keeping plates and silverware on the table. Generally meals were excellent. Bacon and eggs or French toast for breakfast and a huge noon meal followed by something similar for supper. When I left *Ozbourn*, I had gained fifteen pounds—too much to eat and too few ways to work it off.

Just forward of the wardroom on the starboard side was a stateroom equipped to handle two officers—typically, department heads. On the port side was a larger room—the captain's stateroom. Most new junior officers were quartered in the forward officers' quarters, one deck below, or in after officers' with the executive officer and chief engineer. One reached forward officers' by a passageway leading forward from the wardroom, past the skipper's room on the left and the senior officer's cabin on the right, around the base of Mount 52 and then down a ladder. This was also our route up and out should any emergency occur.

There were more staterooms in after officers' quarters but as newest ensign I was assigned an upper bunk in forward officers' quarters along with 'Pay,' the ship's Supply Officer. Up forward we paid close attention to changes in weather and sea state because heavy seas converted a sound night's sleep into an all-night tag match with the mattress as one tried to keep from falling out and still stay asleep. The trick was to stay asleep while holding on to the bouncing bed frame and remaining wedged between the bulkhead and the restraining bar. I would finally figure out once again how to get into a locked position and then drop off. Yet, even when everything was at its worst, my bunk was still a safe haven and a home in which to escape.

On the port side and just forward of officers' country was chief petty officers' mess and bunkroom. Although it might have been a short-cut, no chief would ever use the ladder leading into the wardroom. Except for General Quarters, when they left their space, like other enlisted personnel, they went through the enlisted berthing compartment. During GQ, everyone got out quickly before the sailor responsible for securing that part of the ship slammed shut and dogged down the steel hatch. Remaining below trapped you below the maindeck. *Ozbourn* was to be my home from early July 1950 to January 1952.

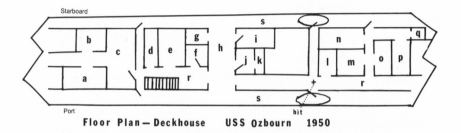

Floor Plan — Deckhouse   USS Ozbourn   1950

Figure 2: Diagram of the main-deck structures of the USS *Ozbourn* as of 1950-51 (not to scale). a: Commanding Officer's cabin; b: Abbott and Hadley's room; c: wardroom; d: wardroom galley; e: crew's galley; f: sick-bay; g: ship's laundry; h: mid-ship's passage; i: ship's office; j: supply office; k: library; l: ship's store; m: chief engineer's room; n: executive officer's room; o: Jarrett and Thornhill's room; p: Blonsick and Cole's room; q: after-officers' "head"; r: inside passage; s: weather deck-main deck. Portside boat, motor whaleboat; starboardside boat, captain's gig.

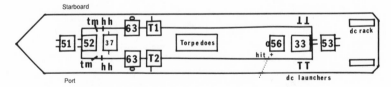

Armament and Fire Control Systems   1950

Figure 3: Armament and Fire Control Systems - 1950 (not to scale). Three main batteries: dual 5-inch 38 caliber Mounts 51, 52, and 53, normally controlled by Director Mark 37. Two 3-inch 50 caliber single mounts, Mounts 31 (starboard) and 32 (Port). One dual 3-inch 50 caliber Mounts 33 aft and centerline, normally controlled by Directors 31 and 32, and aft by Mount 56. Two depth-charge racks astern and two depth-charge launchers (T) on port and starboard sides aft. Five trainable torpedo tubes on 01 level between two stacks. On 01 deck level just aft of Mount 52, one 20mm machine gun and a hedgehog launcher on either side.

Endnotes:

[1] *Jane's Fighting Ships for 1950-51*. This volume, from a series published yearly, and provides an accurate listing of all ships currently in commission by class and type for each Navy in the world.

[2] An essay by CAPT John Moore, RN, "Torpedo Boats, Destroyers, Escort Destroyers and Frigates," in *Jane's American Fighting Ships of the 20th Century* (1991:148).

BEAVER VALLEY

After the War

World War Two had ended just as my senior year in Beaver High School began. The 1945 edition of our high school yearbook the previous spring, listed thirteen members of the class of 1945 who had joined the armed forces during their junior and senior years; in addition, it recognized the seven male and two female teachers who had also enlisted. It also honored the fifteen Beaver High School graduates killed during the war, beginning with Richard McClure, Class of '30 and ending with John Baker, Class of '43.

My seventeenth birthday, August 3, 1945, occurred on nearly the same day as the bombing of Hiroshima. That September, my classmates and I entered our senior year in high school with the world at peace. Suddenly, upon graduation, our options were to go to work or to college; military service was not inevitable. We also realized that peace had suddenly separated us from the challenge endured by our high school friends only one or two years older. They all had served, and some of them had been wounded or even killed. Strangely, some of us felt left out.

Our 1946 yearbook pictured six veterans who returned to complete high school with us. Something awesome was finished and mysteriously it was something in which we would never play a part. If any of my classmates saw a long-term strategic need for the military in 1946, they never told me. The teachers had returned, the older guys on the block were back and, somehow, sole possession of the atomic bomb seemed to replace the need for any significant standing armed forces. We had no potential enemies in 1946. No one was around except victors and vanquished.

By graduation in May 1946, relief had overtaken the sense of being left out. Everything was swept up in a euphoric discovery of peace and prosperity after an absence of seventeen years. The boys were coming back, and, those entering colleges and universities directly from high schools in Autumn 1946 were continually reminded both of sacrifice and patriotism. We seemed a humble minority in the flood of returning ex-GIs who shared our classes.

A few of my high school friends did choose the service, and most for the typical reasons. They didn't know what to do with themselves; they wanted to learn a trade, or they wanted to get covered by the World War Two GI Bill before it expired December 31, 1947. Although the war was then only one year behind us, rapid demobilization had created a need for seamen recruits to keep ships moving and for privates for occupation duty in Japan and Germany. Jack Bayes and I had walked to school daily for years and as seniors we considered going in for the GI Bill. We even went together to the Recruiting Center in Pittsburgh to take pre-enlistment physicals. I backed out. Jack joined the Marines and, by 1948, he had GI Bill money for college.

Others stayed home and worked in the steel mills. Some chose Navy or Marine Reserve Units or the National Guard to add to their pay from the mills. Howard Johns, a friend from my scout troop, enlisted in the Army. After he completed basic, Howard stopped to say goodbye to dad before leaving for garrison duty in Japan. He, like many others, had heard how great the barracks life was in Japan, particularly when compared to work in the mills. For some, going in the service became a chance to mature away from home; for others, it was the GI Bill. Some must have even been trying to capture the feeling we had missed—what service to country had been like in 1941-45.

Instead of joining, I applied for college. Shortly after being admitted to Cornell University, I heard about a new Naval ROTC Program which would pay full tuition, fees, books and a monthly stipend in exchange for only two years on active duty as an Ensign. Cornell was going to be very expensive and the NROTC program seemed too good to pass up. Although I decided to apply, it wasn't just the money. With parental approval, it also seemed my time to serve, and anyway, who could get hurt on a ship during peacetime?

Cornell University

Four years later, it was June 1950, and I had just returned home from graduation. Most of my life had been spent in Beaver, a small town of some five thousand, twenty-five miles northwest of Pittsburgh. Beaver, just downstream from the confluence of the Beaver and the Ohio Rivers, is the county-seat of Beaver County. The term, 'Beaver Valley,' refers collectively to the steel towns of Aliquippa, Ambridge, Beaver Falls, Midland, and Monaca as well as to the residential towns of Beaver, Bridgewater, Freedom, New Brighton, and Rochester. Beaver Valley had been my family's home since the early 1800s.

I graduated from Cornell University with a degree in zoology and was commissioned as an Ensign, USN, on 12 June. Mother, Dad, my sister Susan, and Emma-Jean Way, my future wife, as well as four of my five aunts, were all present for the ceremonies. After commissioning, I was saluted for the first time by Chief Martinez to whom I paid the traditional dollar bill. He smiled, returned the dollar to my mother. Suddenly, college was over.

Seven of us who had just received our Ensign, USN, commissions earned at Cornell had done so under the Navy's new NROTC or Holloway Plan and were now slated for an obligatory two years active duty. Across the nation at forty nine other colleges and universities approximately five hundred other newly commissioned Ensigns faced the same obligation.[1,2]

In contrast to the Navy's hope, in 1946 most of us that entered the Navy's NROTC Class of 1950 were more interested in the size of their scholarships than in any prospects of a naval career. We each had received four years of full tuition, fees, and books, in addition to fifty dollars per month, in exchange for three summer midshipmen cruises and two years on active duty. I felt somewhat guilty knowing I did not intend to start a naval career but nonetheless left the Ithaca campus with nearly a month of commissioning leave before reporting for active duty.

All spring, each of us wondered where we would spend those two years. In late May, I received orders to join the USS *Ozbourn* (DD-846), one of eight destroyers then assigned to Destroyer Squadron 11 and home-ported in San Diego. Our three midshipmen cruises had given us some sense of what the Navy was going to be like, and I viewed this assignment with some concern. During our 1949 midshipman cruise on the USS *Springfield* (CL-66) I learned that *Ozbourn*, also sailing with us, had earlier been in a night-time collision with another destroyer in the China Sea and had lost her bow as well as several sailors. As I had viewed her from the deck of the cruiser, USS *Springfield*, she now seemed able to keep out of the way but I did not view her as an auspicious assignment.

On the other hand, my Cornell dairy science friend, Jim Tregurtha, had been assigned to USS *Wiltsie*, also in Destroyer Squadron 11 and thus also home-ported in San Diego. Our experience, limited to three midshipmen cruises, told us that Pacific Fleet destroyers spent most of their time tied up to buoys. Although I expected to get to know a lot about San Diego, at least in the beginning I would know Jim. Both of us had every intention of getting in and getting out of the Navy. Jim was looking forward to a career in food and milk technology. After graduate school at either Cornell or Wisconsin, he wanted to become a college professor. I had considered both Cornell and the University of Michigan for graduate school but had decided to try to come back to Ithaca, earn my doctorate, and teach in some college. By the time I came off active duty, I hoped Emma-Jean and I would be married and it would be graduate school for us as it had been for the married vets from World War Two. Many of these vets had become my friends, even mentors, and they were now just beginning to complete their own graduate degrees. But first, for me, the Navy.

I had gone to Cornell thinking I would become an ornithologist and ultimately work in a museum studying birds—the Navy scholarship program would help pay expenses. Unfortunately, the undergraduate program in ornithology was in the College of Agriculture. Because I had no farming background, were I to get a degree from the College of Agriculture, I would have to spend three undergraduate summers working on farms. I could either farm or cruise, but there was no acceptable combination of both. I could only resolve this by changing my major to zoology and transferring to the College of Arts and Sciences. There I was fortunate to have Professor Edward C. Raney as my advisor. Without much further thought, I moved from birds to fishes. Ed was already a nationally known ichthyologist and was developing his own 'school' of MS and PhD graduate students. Ed had also been a Lieutenant Commander during the war and had briefly commanded a destroyer escort. His own naval experience and understanding of the military were of great help. In fact, many of the Cornell faculty had served but he especially seemed to understand why I could be pursuing a regular naval commission and simultaneously becoming interested in his own field. Somehow it made sense that someone could become a real naval officer and still make use of a degree in marine fishes and oceanography. You couldn't learn that at Annapolis. Because we would soon be competing with graduating Annapolis midshipmen, we spent some time comparing ourselves with them.

The NROTC program could also lead to a Marine Second Lieutenant's commission. After riding ships for two summers, I became convinced that being a Marine Second Lieutenant had to be more exciting than getting seasick on a ship. This meant applying during my junior year and if selected, spending my final summer cruise with the Marines. Early the next morning I knocked and entered Dr. Raney's office to try my new goal on him. Always blunt and never mincing words, he abruptly advised that while I might indeed make it in the Marines, I would, no doubt, waste my two years of active duty serving somewhere in Panama as officer-in-charge of surplus pup tents. At least, if I went to sea, I could be learning about the ocean. That made sense, particularly because I had already been to Panama on my first midshipman cruise and thought I remembered seeing that pile of tents. His scenario seemed far more likely, and certainly described something far less heroic than becoming a Marine Second Lieutenant and winning recognition and medals at the next Iwo Jima. I was so impressed that he was interested and had taken the time to discuss it that I changed my mind again and stayed with the Navy.

In retrospect, not everyone in the NROTC Class of 1950 received similar advice. Our Midshipmen Class was soon to provide the Korean War with its fair share of Marine Second Lieutenants whose duties were far different and whose casualty rates considerably higher than Dr. Raney had envisioned for me. After returning to Cornell to became his graduate student, I reminded him that he had once saved my life. He had no memory of the incident. This has always caused me to wonder what unsuspected impact I have on students, and they on me, and what major life decisions they may have made using my own off-the-cuff comments.

After Graduation

College days were behind me, and I had arrived in Beaver with nearly a month of leave. Summer was pleasant and things were quiet with nothing much going on except, swimming, movies, playing golf, mowing the yard, family, and seeing Emma-Jean. Mother's big request was a photograph of me in my new dress whites. Ernie Casteel had just bought the local photography studio; his daughter, Ernestine, and I had graduated from Beaver High School in 1946. Everybody knew everybody in Beaver. Ernie took the picture.

During June, the *Beaver Valley Times* was filled with other college graduation notices. Mary Copeland had graduated from Syracuse University; she usually sat two or three seats behind me in any alphabetized seating in high school. Even Roger Netherland made the *Times*. After graduation from Annapolis in 1947 and a tour on a destroyer, Roger was now finishing carrier qualifications at Pensacola, Florida. Following carrier qualifications, he would be off for four months of advanced training in Texas. While we were in high school, I knew Roger only as freshmen know seniors. He was president of his senior class, as well as a football star. He even dated the spectacular cheerleader who lived across the street from us. After a year at Pennsylvania State Roger had transferred to the Naval Academy at Annapolis, Maryland. A brief thought of applying to the

Naval Academy evaporated when I realized that if Roger represented the qualifications needed, I would never get there. I would never become a naval aviator and fly F4Fs, or become a submariner and win medals. Satisfied with that personal self-assessment, I then moved on to other ambitions, alternating between becoming an engineer like my father or something like a forester or an ornithologist. It was ornithology that, ultimately, led me to Cornell.

My major interest during this month's leave was Emma-Jean Way. We had met at a Valentine Day Dance in 1946. Her family also lived in Beaver and we were to be an off-and-on thing for years. By June 1950, she was between her sophomore and junior years in the dietetics program at Penn State and had just begun a summer job working the telephone switchboard at a construction company in nearby Rochester. Dad always rearranged his car pool when I was home so the family car was free. I used it each afternoon during the week to bring her home.

About 5:00 p.m. on Monday, 26 June, I was driving down Third Street en route to Rochester. Just before reaching the P&LE train station, I heard a news report—North Korea had attacked South Korea! The exact time and place burned into my memory much as had Pearl Harbor nine years prior on Sunday, 7 December. This time I would not clip war photographs and maps out of the *Pittsburgh Press*; this had personal written on it. That evening, the *Beaver Valley Times* carried the headline "World Warily Watches New War," but it also included details of a local milk strike, a horse show for Crippled Children the previous weekend, and plans for the Rochester town picnic. Life would go on in the Beaver Valley at the same time it would change for many of us.

The North Koreans had begun their attack at 4:00 a.m. Korean time Sunday 25 June which was 3:00 p.m. Saturday afternoon in Beaver. The *Beaver Valley Times* did not publish on Sunday, thus nearly two days elapsed before I read anything about it. For the next two days, newspapers had headlines but few details. On 27 June, the *Times* reported an air battle between United States (US) and North Korean (NK) planes over Seoul. On 28 June, it reported that US air and naval units were in action. By 29 June, Kimpo Air Field outside Seoul had been

recaptured and the line now had been 'stabilized,' or so the
Times thought. By 30 June, General Douglas MacArthur had
received authorization to use "certain supporting ground
troops." Meanwhile Beaver County continued plans for its
August Sesqui-centennial celebration representing one hundred
and fifty years of progress and change.

On Wednesday, 28 June, Dad and I drove to Pittsburgh to
see the Pirates play a night game with the Reds at Forbes Field.
The Pirates beat the Reds six to five but my mind was not on
baseball. We sat back of first base and I kept wondering what
was ahead? Somehow this couldn't be how World War Three
was supposed to start, but that feeling kept returning. I never
asked Dad what was going through his mind. Time was flying
and soon I would be leaving for California.

On Thursday, 29 June, I received the first hint of trouble. A
telegram from the Bureau of Personnel shortened my leave by
requiring me on board no later than 1200 5 July. That evening,
Jim Tregurtha called from New Jersey; his orders had also been
changed. Until then it had not occurred to either of us that our
entire squadron might be deploying to the Western Pacific
(WestPac). That raised the anxiety level around the dining
room telephone as the family listened in. Since Jim and I had
already planned to travel together by train, we decided to leave
a few days earlier.

On Friday, while Jim was en route, a telegram from *Ozbourn*'s commanding officer advised that *Ozbourn* was now in
San Francisco. Now, was I supposed to go to San Diego as my
orders specified or would *Ozbourn* still be in San Francisco on
the 5th when I had to report in? Without much thought, I
decided to go first to San Diego with Jim. Then, if *Ozbourn*
really wasn't there, I could take a train to San Francisco and still
meet the deadline. By now, Jim and I were too late to get sleep-
er space on trains going west.

The family met Jim in Pittsburgh on Friday night. Saturday
morning, 30 June, after an early breakfast, he and I took our
foot lockers full of new uniforms and clean underwear and
climbed on a New York Central train—first stop Chicago, last
stop San Diego.

When Jim and I climbed on the train the morning of 30
June, we were probably the first people leaving Beaver en route

to the Korean War. Few in town seemed to know much about Korea or why it was happening. In addition to being ignorant as well as scared, I was also worried about how ready we, as a nation, were.

During the first two years of President Truman's elected term (1948 to 1950), defense budgets had been unmercifully slashed. The President and his Secretary of Defense, Louis Johnson, as well as Congress, saw no need for a large standing Army, nor any need for much of a Navy. There had even been a debate in Congress over whether to continue the US Marine Corps. Naval appropriations in 1946-47 had been $4.1 billion, but for 1947-48 were dropped to $3.3 billion rising only slightly to $3.7 billion in 1948-49. Total Navy and Marine Corps personnel on active duty in 1948 had declined to 395,000 (Navy) and 83,700 in the Marine Corps.[3]

The Truman administration and Secretary Johnson continued defense reductions well into 1950. The federal debate on a defense mission for carriers versus a role for Air Force bombers, the necessity for the Marine Corps and other issues had been playing out in Congress and in the national press for most of the year. Officers and enlisted men with whom we had been in contact during our 1948 and 1949 midshipmen cruises often spoke bluntly of their fading enthusiasm for the Navy as a career and their messages had not been lost on us. By June 1950, as a nation, we didn't seem ready for much.

At least another Beaverite, Howard Johns, was safe through pulling guard duty in Japan. Despite my optimistic assessment, Howard and others in the four Army Divisions then in Japan would soon be moved to Korea and used up slowing down the advance until reinforcements arrived. His summer would be spent slowing the retreat into the Pusan Perimeter, mine in getting there in time to be of assistance. How, when or where, I wasn't sure.

Endnotes:

[1] The Holloway Plan, named after Rear Admiral James Holloway, was developed in 1945, by Dr., and then Captain, Arthur Adams, to augment the Naval Academy's production of officers for regular service following World

War Two. Dr. Adams, later Provost at Cornell, revamped the pre-war
NROTC which had been training reserve officers into a program to produce
regulars and, thus, solve the Navy's post-war need for more Ensigns than
Annapolis could produce each year.

[2] Schneider (1987), and a 10 pp., unpublished manuscript entitled "History of the Naval ROTC Unit and Department of Naval Science, The Ohio
State University"; author unknown, approximately 1970.

[3] *Jane's Fighting Ships for 1948* (1948:331).

THE ADVENTURE BEGINS

Off to San Diego

As Jim and I boarded that train in Beaver, I remembered watching those others who left five and six years earlier. Now, it was my turn. We settled in for the trip to Chicago. Once there my Aunt Izzy met us and took us out for supper. Afterwards we climbed on a Santa Fe train going west. Once in Los Angeles we would then change for San Diego, trailing our foot lockers after us. In Chicago, we could not find sleeping accommodations which meant sitting up for the next forty or more hours en route to California in a hot, old, red fuzzy-seated coach with no air conditioning.

Nearly our entire car was composed of newly enlisted sailors from South Carolina, Georgia, and elsewhere in the South all going west to San Diego for boot training. Some called us 'Ensign,' some called us 'Red' since we both then had red hair, and others called us 'Jim and Pete,' acceptable nicknames. My father had begun calling me 'Pete' as a small child and it had stuck, but this was not the place to use it. It would take a little time in boot camp for them to learn how to talk to officers, but Jim and I weren't about to spend the whole trip west starting their boot training early. The conductor was very interested in having us take charge of them and save his car for another trip west. We figured that was his task and our gang might as well

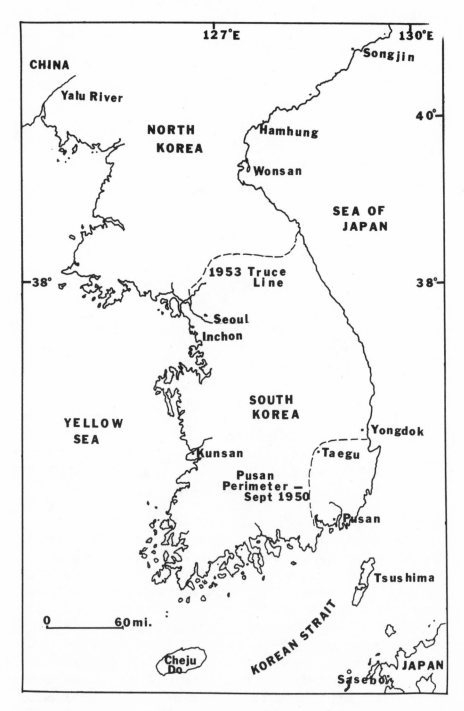

Figure 4: Korea, 1950-1953.

enjoy themselves. The rest of the train was just as unusual as our car; we were clearly riding west on the Santa Fe 'Cattle Train.' Our car also had at least four women with several children. They apparently couldn't afford the dining car and existed on sandwiches and pop from the butcher on the train. We even stopped for an hour while they put out a fire in the engine. During that time Tregurtha and I watched a poker game in the aisle.

Jim spent part of the trip sleeping under the seats on spread-out Chicago papers. Somewhere amidst the sports pages and the real estate advertising, he lost his St. Jude's medal, not an auspicious thing for a Catholic starting a long trip. By the time we reached Lincoln, Nebraska, we were pretty well beat. The train was short of everything; I wondered if railroad equipment was not already being assembled for troop trains. Just after we left Lincoln, a compartment became available and we took it with two other guys. Jim and I got the lower bunk. As we entered the sleeping car, we disturbed another bunch of seamen recruits shooting craps. Seeing us, they busted up the game and vanished down the passageway. Had they waited, they would have seen two Ensigns crashing into a single berth, an uncomfortable and inauspicious beginning to our respective naval careers. We changed trains in Los Angeles and ended the trip at the San Diego station, a short distance from fleet landing.

We both checked in with harbor operations and Jim easily found *Wiltsie* tied up to Broadway Pier. *Ozbourn*, on the other hand, was not there. Instead, it was still north of San Francisco in the Mare Island Naval Shipyard at Vallejo, just as I had been told it would be. For some obscure reason, I had stupidly come to San Diego to meet a ship temporarily in San Francisco, and now I had only five minutes to catch the last train of the day going north. I was thinking about this while standing at its steps with both our baggage claims. When I looked around, Tregurtha had vanished. Finally, when the train began to move and still no Jim, I gave our chits to a porter standing on the platform. "Give them to the first short, red-haired ensign you see," I yelled and stepped on board. Either I caught *Ozbourn* before she left or I'd face a hodge-podge of rides across the Pacific chasing her; maybe I'd even get into trouble for missing movement.

Jim arrived just as *Wiltsie* was making final preparations for departure for the Western Pacific (WestPac), along with the others in our squadron. The seven destroyers, minus *Ozbourn*, sailed 6 July and were off Korea later in July. This fifty-five-hundred-mile trip was usually broken by a stop in Pearl Harbor, fifteen-hundred miles into the voyage. The steaming range for our destroyers was only forty-five hundred miles which meant each would require at least one refueling. At best, even doing the entire fifty-five hundred miles at fifteen knots, the crossing would take nearly sixteen days.

For me, finding *Ozbourn* quickly became the only important thing. There was nothing to do but get to San Francisco. On the way across country, Jim and I had both agreed to keep in touch; we were both apprehensive. Now I was on a train going to Korea—or rather first to San Francisco. I had lost my foot-locker in San Diego and then had even given both our claim chits to someone I didn't know. I checked in at the Commandant Twelfth Naval District, San Francisco at 1030 on 5 July and arrived at *Ozbourn* about an hour and a half late.

There had been no need to rush because *Ozbourn* was in for boiler repair. I had arrived without my foot-locker and had no spare uniforms, nothing. For the next several days, daily I returned to San Francisco and haunted the train depot until my foot-locker arrived. Somehow, things had worked out on the train platform in San Diego. *Ozbourn* still had a problem to solve, but at least I had clean clothes. Nearly two busy months would pass before I ever saw *Wiltsie* or Jim.

As each Ensign from the NROTC Class of 1950 arrived on board his first duty station, old questions resurfaced. One was whether we would be treated equitably with our Annapolis counterparts. The second was, did we deserve to be? There had always seemed something unique and separate about the service academies which could be likened to seminaries producing priests. Those going to West Point or Annapolis seemed to be people taking vows to a message uniformly preached day in and day out—'duty, honor, country.' We NROTC Ensigns weren't disloyal and I scarcely objected to their 'duty, honor, country' message but on the civilian campuses we heard a great diversity of other messages and goals. People chose the Naval Academy somewhat as novitiates might choose a religious order knowing they wanted and would get a Navy-dominated education equipping them primarily for careers as naval officers. They were strongly motivated and self-selected to serve and, during the first decade of comparison, they would prove twice as likely to remain in the Navy as would Regular NROTC graduates. In the future that would change.

Unlike Annapolis, American universities had many missions. Every department had faculty advisers planning something different for each of its graduates. It was unthinkable that a civilian university would espouse a single mission—'train regular naval officers'—as Annapolis was able to do; it was antithetical to the very purpose of universities. Occasionally, a real scholar emerges as the highest product of the best universities, but, failing that, most universities settle for creating a whole stream of graduates with a diversity of majors and a host of different things stuffed into their heads. Whether the Navy had prepared itself to deal with this diversity amongst its regular officer corps was unclear to us.

During the process of joining the NROTC Program, we had been told we were to be treated as equals to graduates of the US Naval Academy, and that the road to becoming admiral was to be equitable for all. Were this not true, the Holloway Plan would fail, skewered on its own rhetoric. Some of us believed the rhetoric and others knew better, believing instead that the only career path leading to admiral's stars began solely with graduation from the US Naval Academy. Most of us didn't care but, as our own midshipmen years had passed, the value of an Annapolis ring on a junior officer—'ring knockers'—would often be apparent. We were also learning the value of the 'old school tie' from our own college alumni; who you knew and where you went to school did matter in the future.

On most ships, when the commanding officer talked to one of his ensigns about *the football team*, they both meant Annapolis and not Ohio State or Duke. Only infrequently might you and your skipper have gone to Berkeley or would he have been an NROTC at Cornell. You might even be fraternity brothers but that would be even more rare. The simple idea that we were there primarily because the Navy needed, not only wanted, another source for its career junior officers had escaped us. The junior officers we had seen on our summer cruises seemed to have come exclusively from Annapolis. We were different.

Finally, although Korea was to change all of our agendas, none of us had much of a notion as to what a career in the peacetime Navy even meant. For that matter, neither did our NROTC instructors, most of whom had come on active duty during a war and were learning about peace along with us. We all knew and respected what they had done during the war, but our own tours had to be different. Moreover, as we watched what the US Navy did while we were on midshipmen cruises, few saw much about which to be enthused. Operating funds had been increasingly curtailed by Congress. President Truman and Secretary of Defense Louis Johnson were pushing for even lower military budgets. Barring a few catastrophes—the Berlin Blockade and a few other European problems plus the Chinese Civil War—no serious crises had confronted us from 1946 to 1950, or so it had seemed from a college campus. Further, during our midshipmen cruises, we saw capable officers and enlisted people getting out while those less qualified stayed in. Even the battleship *Missouri*, site of the Japanese surrender, had run aground in Chesapeake Bay in 1950. The selling job up to June 1950 had become progressively worse and few of us saw career paths within the Regular Navy for those with degrees in zoology or dairy science from such places as Purdue, Penn State, and Cornell. Finally, as we arrived on our new stations at start of the Korean War, the entire process resembled more a sandlot pick-up baseball game with lives at stake than a well-planned-for response to aggression. It would remain as hard to be impressed by the Navy at the beginning of the war as it had been in the last years of peace. Somehow I had expected wars to be better organized.

And so, along with the Korean War, we began our competition with the Annapolis graduates with whom we shared our first duty station. Even though our commissions were Regular, because we were not graduates of the Naval Academy—ungraciously called the 'Canoe Club on the Severn'—we expected to be excluded from the brotherhood and the rites and privileges thereof. Despite what we had been told by our respective Professors of Naval Science at time of our commissionings, we did not expect to compete successfully in any future selection for flight, submarine, or other service schools, nor survive well at promotion time when competing against the Annapolis ring. No one I knew even intended to try. ENS Jerry Solomon, Annapolis Class of 1950, had arrived on board *Ozbourn* only several weeks before me. ENS Jack Blonsick, University of Mississippi NROTC, joined us in Japan in August. Whether the NROTC Ensign or the US Naval Academy Ensign was the better prepared was about to be tested by using the three of us as *Ozbourn*'s guinea pigs.

Preparations to Leave California

During July 1950, San Francisco retained the glamour it always holds for departing sailors and I could get there easily by bus. With little to do on board, I spent every hour possible away from Vallejo and walked the city for hours, enjoying the sights, going through bookstores, and unconsciously storing up ready-to-wear memories for use on a long sea voyage. San Francisco created a sense of pleasure for me that still remains; I have good memories of its cable cars, hills, cool bright sunny weather, and passing time. Unfortunately, it was also lonely doing it by yourself. Just finding a girl to talk to was hard; I was homesick.

I had been expecting *Ozbourn* to depart late in July and to arrive in Pearl about 1 August; that plan didn't fit in with reality. Things were getting worse in Korea faster than we realized. Sitting isolated in a shipyard, we were not really aware of the build-up of US forces either in Korea or, for that matter, in the continental United States. All we could tell was that the shipyard seemed in a great hurry to finish our boiler work and get us to sea. Had we been in San Diego watching other elements of the fleet and the Marines leaving, our outlook might have been different.

Ozbourn's problem began when a senior petty officer, BT1 (Boiler Tender First Class), failed to ensure that there was sufficient water level in one of the four boilers. Consequently the dry boiler tubes melted, knocking out the boiler. Without all boilers operational, we could not produce enough superheated steam to reach the more than thirty-knot speed needed for us to keep up with aircraft carriers during flight operations. There was no sense in leaving until the boiler was repaired; all four had to be available. This and the story about *Ozbourn* losing her bow in a collision seemed part of an unhappy pattern; maybe I also had lost my St. Jude's medal on the trip west even though Presbyterians don't use them.

While the yard repaired the damage, we held a court-martial for the BT1, and I was assigned to it as a junior member. This, too, was very different from learning about naval justice in a class. I was helping to make a decision that would affect someone's future and that of his family as well. We found him guilty, and our boiler tender had his stripes taken away, reducing him to third class, which reduced his pay and allowances. I hoped justice had resulted. Perhaps that court-martial symbolized some of the peacetime Navy's rust being chipped off; it was not yet clear how much metal remained beneath. This was as true of officers and men as of ships.

The United States was then only five years away from having had the most magnificent, best organized fleet ever known, but I worried that we had dropped a long way during those five years. It was not clear what demands were to be made when we got to WestPac. No one knew what would be asked nor how well each might respond given five years of peacetime inattention. Three problems had to be solved quickly: ships that worked, people trained to take them to sea, and a filled supply line to keep them operational.

The Navy obviously still had hundreds of relatively new ships laid up in mothballs which could easily be restored to operating condition, but it remained to be seen whether they had paid like attention to 'mothballing' people. Waging the start of this war fell on those already on active duty. They had to complete whatever tasks were assigned until sufficient reservists could cross the Pacific in a combat-ready state to bring a ship to wartime status. Although many sailors had joined the Reserves in 1945 as a condition of their discharge, few did so contemplating either a career in the reserves or ever being recalled to active duty. We were fortunate that their skills were still relatively fresh, and back they came.

When I reported on board on 5 July, rumor had it that we would leave in eight days for San Diego where we would remain until 1 August when we would leave for Pearl Harbor. That relieved me somewhat. Until then I thought we were in a rush. Dickson Pratt, a fraternity brother, lived in Honolulu and we would be there for his sister's wedding to a West Pointer. Along with such serious planning, there were shots, physicals, getting moved into a room, and finding my clothes that had to be dealt with.

By Sunday, 8 July, I knew even more. It now looked as if we would leave for San Diego on 12 July. With that, and having found my clothes, things were falling into a pattern. I had even been located by Bruce Gray, another fraternity brother who had participated in the Philippine landings as an infantryman in 1944. Bruce had just arrived from Ithaca in his surplus open-topped Army command car which was perfect for touring the Bay area. On Saturday Jerry Solomon joined us as we drove up and down San Francisco's hills looking for something to do. I even remembered that radio's "One Man's Family" had been written about San Francisco and had seemed so real that I half-expected to see Father Barbour and Margaret standing on some corner. Sunday evenings in Beaver had not been complete without their visit. We obviously didn't see them. After wasting good liberty time touring hills, Jerry left us to see what was happening at the Top of the Mark, the Mark Hopkins' famous bar.

Bruce and I ended our big day at a roller-rink. We seemed to be doing very well until I realized that my skating partner meant she would be returning to Lincoln *High School* and not Lincoln *University*—wherever that was. We were having fun and at least, I'd found a girl to talk to. Nonetheless, a skating rink was not the place to meet mature, sophisticated women, and I needed to work on the social side of being an officer and a gentleman.

On Sunday, I played tennis with Jack Warden, our senior ensign who had been on board for a year. Later LTJG John Bond and I went out for supper in Vallejo. John was from Texas and was also new, having just arrived a week before me. I still had little to do except to get used to rooming with the Paymaster and Supply Officer, LTJG Robert Jordan, and hang up my uniforms.

I'd been on board only a few days when Lieutenant Commander Walter Ousey, the executive officer, discovered me and began hinting that he would soon become sick of me doing nothing but sitting in the wardroom and drinking coffee, or playing at the tennis court. He started me on the indoctrination course required of all new officers assigned destroyers in Cruiser-Destroyer Force, Pacific Fleet (CruDesPac)—my first exposure to a Navy correspondence course. The questions required talents used in a scavenger hunt and sounded like something from a midshipman cruise lecture; it was important stuff but not very interesting. However, as I looked around the wardroom during meals, I began to sense the personalities, what their jobs were, who did or couldn't do what, and how to keep from embarrassing myself.

Our July mess bill would only be $15.00 because so many ate ashore; my share of our supplies already on board cost me an additional $21.77. I was beginning to see what sailors meant by 'three hots and a flop.' There was a comfortable reliability to everything and things happened on time as predicted by the Ship's Plan of the Day. I ought to be able to live like a king on this ship and save a bundle besides; maybe I could save enough to fund graduate school when I got out.

An unmarried junior officer only needed money for food, dates, and clothes; those that had experimented with owning cars cautioned against it. Cars were hard to deal with when a ship left home port; meeting girls with cars was a far better solution. We had nice discussions about going far away to strange places and then, suddenly, back came the realization that this impending cruise would be different from a midshipmen cruise.

Back home in Beaver, by Monday 10 July, the *Beaver Valley Times* was full of the war. Headlines started with "Planes, Artillery Halt.." and "Call for draftees, reservists...." Combat units on the west coast were being moved; Senator Walter George (D-Georgia) estimated one hundred thousand troops were needed and the first draft call since January 1949 would be issued within ten days. A few days later, Beaver County's four draft boards announced they were back in full operation to pick up those between eighteen and twenty-six who had failed to register or had failed to provide an address change. I had registered in 1946 but then had left Beaver without providing them with my latest address change—USS *Ozbourn*. ENS Jack Blonsick would later be drafted by his Board but the skipper would not let him go home.

Shortly after arriving on board, I bought a San Francisco newspaper with headlines about North Korean torpedo boats attacking the cruiser *Juneau* off the coast of Korea. On 27 June, *Juneau* had left Kagoshima, Japan, to oppose any NK landings on the South Korean coast. On 28 June she was investigating reports of landings on Kojo Do and on 29-30 June, she fired the war's first shore bombardment missions. On 2 July, while *Juneau* was with HMS *Jamaica* and HMS *Black Swan*, they engaged four torpedo boats escorting ten NK trawlers moving south on the east coast just below the 38th Parallel.[1] A chill came over me as I read the headlines and wondered how large this thing would become.

For those of us on *Ozbourn*, news about Korea before we left California was limited to newspapers; we had a radio in the wardroom but no one used it to listen to the news. I also saw a newsreel clip of MacArthur's 29 June inspection of Korea during a movie in San Francisco, but what we learned about Korea was pretty limited. The captain and several officers also had magazine subscriptions. Their old *Time* magazines began in the wardroom but usually ended up in the officer's head as light reading. Neither the captain or anyone else left the ship for briefings on what was happening and, accordingly, we passed very little on to the crew about where we were going or what our deployment might be like. No one really knew how broad this might become. Planning seemed to be limited to everyone getting out there as quickly as possible and doing whatever you could. We were in the 'Chinese fire-drill' planning mode and that was no compliment.

We left Vallejo for sea trials Thursday, 13 July, and on our return we reloaded ammunition before going back to the shipyard. We sailed again Saturday morning, 15 July, but this time, to deliver a technician to USS *Henrico*, an attack transport loaded with Marines underway for Korea. *Henrico* had broken

down north of Los Angeles and had returned to the yard at
Vallejo for repairs before continuing to WestPac. "Doug is not
going to like that," but we gave little thought as to why Mac-
Arthur needed Marines.

As we left San Francisco Bay, I realized I had last passed
under the Golden Gate Bridge on board *Springfield* only a year
previously on my last midshipman cruise. Much had happened
since. This time we were really doing something important, and
yet, as we turned into the cold fog to deliver the technician to
the transport, the gentle Pacific swells began to roll in from
starboard, and reality and apprehension returned. What at first
was to be a heroic and memorable experience on my new duty
station was gradually become unbearable; I was getting seasick.
From experience, I knew that I would recover if I only could lie
down and sleep or if somehow I could be up on the weatherdeck looking at the horizon. I chose bed. About 0345, someone
awoke me to relieve the watch in Combat Information Center
(CIC).

There were then three officer watch stations on destroyers
while underway in normal peacetime steaming: Officer of the
Deck (OOD), Junior Officer of the Deck (JOOD) and CIC
Watch Officer. My initial at-sea watches were spent in CIC
where little happened at night when you were operating alone.
CIC on a destroyer, about the size of a small living room, was
painted black and contained at least five radio speakers, the
two main radar units (surface search and air search), plus
several radar repeaters, back-lighted status and plotting boards,
a horizontal glass maneuvering board, and a dead-reckoning
tracer unit. In addition, five or more radarmen or designated
strikers were either moving around plotting things, making
coffee, quietly watching radar scopes, or just staring at the
clock. Two main voice radio circuits would be monitored when
we were operating with other ships. In addition, we could bring
up several aircraft radio nets. When operating by ourselves,
there was little radio traffic and the speakers hummed monoto-
nously in your ear. Nothing much happened in CIC from 0400
to 0800 and you had to force the clock's hands around while you
felt the ship gently rolling under your feet.

When a destroyer was underway alone, the CIC watch officer had only to keep awake, read official publications, keep the

enlisted men alert and himself in the same condition, and learn a little about what the radio and radar capabilities were. Later, during night watches, I tried passing time by studying oceanography. I gave it up when caught by the division commander who informed the captain that he considered such behavior to be both unprofessional and prejudicial to good order, or some such.

CIC was usually a boring place, dimly lit, and smelly with the typical electronic smell overlaid on top of normal ship fumes. As you watched the deck roll, saw chairs move, and wondered where the horizon was and why you weren't seasick, you gradually became so. I did very well until about 0600 in the middle of my first morning watch (0400 to 0800). Suddenly it was getting quite warm. When I realized it was more than that, I had to leave. I excused myself and fought my way out to the weather deck via a door leading first into a radar room. Another door later and I was standing outside in a light fog and the cold air cleared my head. It was becoming light and you could see the rollers passing—in from starboard, and then, while the ship rolled, out to port. Once outside where I was all alone, I knew everything would be just fine, but as I was walking next to the starboard three-inch gun mount, I lost whatever was left of the previous night's supper. Most people expect sailors to vomit to leeward. I didn't have time to figure out where that was and instead grabbed the only container handy—a telephone talker's helmet stored in a rack as part of the mount's battle equipment. Inevitably, someone would put it on in a hurry during next day's General Quarters drill. On board ship, you get sick, you clean up afterwards—who would stoop to puke in someone else's helmet? I had, but I didn't have a choice. After a few minutes, I stopped sweating, felt better, replaced the fouled helmet and returned to CIC to resume the remaining two hours of that miserable watch. I never returned to clean up my mess.

Later in the day I heard some sailor bitching about some SOB puking in his helmet and I knew in my heart he was saying it loud enough for me to hear. I have always wondered why I did that. Nearly every time we returned to sea I felt squeamish for the first day or so but I never again lost dinner, at least not on *Ozbourn*. Usually, I started every trip with a good case of the trots coupled with a need to sleep a lot, but no more puking.

After delivering the technician to the *Henrico*, we continued on to San Diego arriving Sunday, 16 July, and tied up to one of the many now-empty moorings in the harbor. Liberty commenced quickly for those officers and crew with families in the area. At that point we had thirteen officers on board, ten of whom were married and nine with families in the San Diego area. Jerry Solomon, Jack Worden, and I, all unmarried Ensigns, became keepers of the ship.

I got off briefly, saw a movie, looked for and then finally bought a second set of dress khakis (tropical worsted cost thirty-five dollars; gabardines, sixty dollars). I had one set from commissioning and not knowing what we'd be wearing in the 'forward area,' nor where the nearest dry cleaner would be, two sets seemed the minimum. All this fluff went into letters home; I was becoming sensitive as to how people at home might be interpreting my letters and used more paper on the cost of meals and clothing than on the cost of lives, including my own. World War Three still seemed inevitable.

On Monday, we had a short gunfire-control drill before beginning our scheduled five-inch gunnery shoot at the shore bombardment range on nearby San Clemente Island on Tuesday and Wednesday. Our shore bombardment practice was interspersed with five-inch aerial gunnery shoots as we tried to hit passing canvas sleeves towed by tractor aircraft. Cutting the towing cable or coming too close to the plane didn't count. Slow moving target sleeves loafing along on a known horizontal track—nobody flew that way against destroyers except tractor planes with targets but, even at that, we weren't very good. By then I was put to use as check-sight observer on Mount 51 and felt required to write home about our woeful ineptitude. A check-sight observer can stop firing if the ship is about to shoot down friendly aircraft, or if our shells seem likely to hit other ships. We did neither, but we also missed most of the sleeves. When we were finished on Thursday, we returned to San Francisco.

By then I had been graduated to an official place on the Ship's Watch, Quarters and Station Bill to something called Gunnery Liaison Officer for Machine Gun Batteries; I now was part of the system. That put me back in CIC during General Quarters where I stood looking at a radar scope while someone else plotted incoming air-raids by writing on the backside of a plastic screen off to my left. I was linked by sound-powered telephones to the captain on the bridge, our three three-inch battery control officers, an officer on the bridge who controlled the 20mm machine guns, and a radar technician somewhere whose task was to keep the radars on the three-inch Directors functioning. I was to sort out all the radar information on attacking aircraft and then assign air targets to the various batteries during an air raid. It was procedure from the final days of World War Two and I wondered whether somewhere off Okinawa we might not still find left-over Kamikazes lurking around. It all seemed very unreal. Although that was what I was supposed to do, it seemed inconceivable that I would ever have to do it. Instead, I worried more about having sufficient uniforms.

During that last week, all officers and watch standers were issued long, wool-lined, water-repellent pants and parkas for bridge work. The fur-lined boots and winter helmets were to come next. We appeared to be getting ready for winter patrol duty in the Bering Sea off Alaska, or so it seemed. After seeing all this winter gear, I placed an order home for woolen socks and a woolen sweater.

Back in San Francisco, we were told to expect several ship riders in transit to WestPac assignments. We were also expecting another new NROTC Ensign, but it was a month later before 'Smiling Jack' Blonsick arrived. Jack and I had been midshipmen on *Springfield* the previous summer. I knew every NROTC Class of '50 Ensign whose last name began with B, C or D.

In the midst of all the planning for movement and departure for WestPac, we had another summary court-martial for a seaman who was trying to get kicked out of the Navy. He had already deliberately missed one of our recent sailings and this one earned him his trip out of the Navy on a Bad Conduct Discharge.

When we arrived back in San Francisco, everyone wanting it got an early, if an abbreviated, liberty expiring on board at 0200 Saturday, 22 July. At 0400, after carefully counting the drunks and making an accurate muster, we departed for WestPac. None of the crew seemed to have the slightest idea where

Korea was, why we were going, or what the hell we would do there. I had just completed a course covering recent events in Southeast Asia, and at least knew where Korea was, but otherwise, I was nearly as ignorant as the rest of my shipmates. Cornell University had made the mistake of allowing me to choose an elective course to get prepared for the wrong war.

Summing up July 1950, I had found the ship, received my first pay, been given something to do, when or if, any shooting started, had bought another pair of shoes, now owned a back-up khaki uniform, had bought a camera and film, and purchased several books I hadn't yet read. I was ready for anything, even war. We were tardy, things had gotten worse without us but we were finally on our way west. Behind us was USS *Mt. Katmai* (AE-16).

Endnotes:

[1]Cagle and Manson (1957:282-290) for further details.

THE TRIP WEST

We expected to rejoin *Frank Knox, Hollister* and *McKean* either in a port in southern Japan or somewhere off Korea. Once the Division was reassembled, *Ozbourn* would again become flagship, but even the Division Commander and staff had already sailed leaving us to catch up as we could. I had growing apprehension about Korea and felt World War Three was unfolding. Furthermore, I had not forgotten *Ozbourn* had been in a collision and lost her bow several years earlier. Was I on a jinxed ship with a new bow and replaced boiler tubes that was carrying us into some further 'first-to-die' disaster? It might even be October and November 1941 all over again and we were part of the Pacific fleet moving west from San Francisco into an oncoming maelstrom. Somebody else's *deja-vu* was replaying itself for the Pacific Fleet and they had unintentionally included me. The long trip from Pearl Harbor to Japan would give me plenty of time to feel alone.

Although I was unaware of it, we were part of a massive westward stream of troops, attack transports, aircraft carriers, auxiliaries, repair ships, oilers, ammunition ships, cruisers, and destroyers. Each combatant ship going west escorted something else. The four destroyers in Division 111 had even escorted two submarines from Pearl to WestPac. From where I stood, it was only *Ozbourn* and USS *Mt. Katmai* (AE-16), an ammunition ship, and nothing more. *Mt. Katmai* was off to her first war as well.

We briefly stopped in Pearl Harbor to refuel and Dick Pratt came on board while *Ozbourn* went alongside the fuel docks. Dick was the fraternity brother who lived in Honolulu and he had also just graduated from Cornell. Two years earlier, he and his family had entertained a group of us midshipmen cruising on the aircraft carrier, USS *Boxer*, during our visit to Honolulu. Dick had been in the Navy briefly at the end of the war and fully expected to be recalled. We stood on deck reliving our "good old days at Cornell," now some six weeks in the past, until *Ozbourn* had completed taking on fuel. Upon completion, he and I shook hands and Dick ran down the gangway as mooring lines were being singled up and then brought on board. Following the long sound of her whistle, *Ozbourn* backed smartly from the dock and we were again underway. Once we had cleared the channel, it was "engines all ahead standard, make turns for fifteen knots." We were on our way to a war with our friend, *Mt. Katmai*.

The following days were uneventful and even peaceful as we transited the remainder of the Pacific Ocean. Normal watch standing was interrupted several times a day by fire drills and by General Quarters needed to sharpen the crew and break in new officers. We watched as *Mt. Katmai* set the pace; we passed the International Date Line on 30 July.

Under normal circumstances, we junior officers would have attended several short courses in San Diego before we left. The Fleet Training Center had CIC Officer, Anti-submarine Warfare (ASW) Officer, Ship Handling, Fire Fighting Courses of one to four weeks long but there was no time for that. Instead whatever we learned, we learned on the job. As part of that process, on the way over, I was shifted from CIC to the bridge for watch standing as Junior Officer of the Deck. On one bridge watch shortly after midnight, I was given the conn and spent the next two hours trying to keep *Ozbourn* two thousand yards dead ahead of our ammunition ship by increasing or reducing turns on our twin screws. It was dulling work and required effort to stay alert. However, because I was JOOD, if I made it to 0200, I would be required to inspect the ship. That was something that would likely end with an inspection of the crew's galley where a piece of pie might be found if the bakers were still up. A wise officer never presumed on the bakers' good-will but it could happen.

Finally 0200 arrived. After getting permission to conduct an inspection of the ship, I left the bridge to the OOD and the other watch standers. I made my way aft to the signal bridge and then down a ladder where I stopped at the torpedo tube mount between the smoke stacks and then studied the dark ocean. There I realized why I had been specifically asked to inspect the captain's gig and the motor whaleboat. We had been wallowing with a following sea that had picked up and I had to make certain our two boats were properly secured in their davits.

As I made the lonely trip aft on the 01 level on a ship with no lights showing, I suddenly realized how big the waves had become. They were walking ponderously up from behind the ship and, as I watched them, lit only by dim starlight, they moved along our side with their crests rising into peaks, then collapsing and breaking over into spray. It was inspiring when, suddenly, the entire sea surface exploded into bright beads and flashes of blues and purples fading and rising with each wave—all caused by luminescent plankton. It was spellbinding, yet absolutely frightening; an incredible, spooky water show as far as I could see and seen by no one else. I suddenly felt as if I were the only person alive in the entire world. Whether the two boats were properly stored I had no idea; I forgot about the pie, ran back in relief to the company on the bridge, made up some lame excuse to the OOD about having completed the inspection and was pleased beyond belief again to hear the whispered talk of the helmsman, lee helmsmen, quartermaster, boatswain of the watch, the port and starboard lookouts, and the Officer of the Deck as we passed the rest of the watch in the red light-lit pilot house keeping station on our ammunition ship. The remainder of the watch passed quickly.

Life on Board

Destroyer duty might be considered glamourous but it also required an adjustment to the confinement of a smaller ship. There was no flight deck on which to walk after flight operations nor broad cruiser decks to circle as you might on a cruise

ship, and, because officers stayed out of enlisted berthing areas
unless you were there for a reason, as well as vice versa, you
couldn't walk far inside. I was limited to pacing up and down
the main deck—something safe to do only during daylight
provided seas were calm. A final haven was always an escape to
the bunk where I could read or just shut my eyes and mentally
be somewhere else—even roller rinks in San Francisco would
have to make do.

Reading was always a great help in 'getting away.' Most
people at sea read a lot. Unfortunately, *Ozbourn*'s library was
about the size of a small broom closet and contained little more
than dog-eared paperback novels; every sailor had one in the
back pocket of his dungarees and, when they were finished, they
recycled them back to the broom closet. The trick was to find a
book store when ashore and then stock up, or better still, find a
base library, or one on the destroyer tender, and borrow ahead
of a trip. Then the problem became one of where to keep
things.

I had been assigned to one of the three junior officer forward bunk-rooms. Each room had two tiered bunks each running fore-and-aft, two narrow lockers for hanging uniforms, a
chair that unless restrained was given to wandering around the
room in tune with the roll of the ship, a desk with four drawers,
two for each occupant for socks, etc., a sink, and mirror. Each
bunk had a reading light and a shelf at the foot of the bed for
books as well as removable aluminum retainers to keep you
from falling out in rough seas. Although more private, upper
bunks were less desirable. Small steam pipes above them were
insulated with asbestos lagging covered with painted canvas
while the rest of the overhead seemed to be insulated with
fiber-glass. We also had a dual five-inch mount overhead. Any
time it was fired, asbestos and little glass slivers dropped into
the sheets. When the room temperature was nearly one
hundred degrees and you were sweaty, it was yet another
annoyance, although scarcely one to bring up to a Marine trying
to stay alive ashore.

Furthermore, officers were lucky compared to the crew.
They lived in compartments with forty or more sailors, each of
whom had a bunk, three in a tier, a tiny aluminum locker and
access to a communal bin in which to store sea-bags and pea

coats. Our accommodations were palatial by comparison. Even so, sailors familiar with earlier destroyers thought this one quite luxurious.

Our wardroom mess bills on *Ozbourn* were still fifteen dollars per month. I had been spending sixty dollars a month for meals at the fraternity just two months before. My monthly midshipman's check almost covered it and I usually peeled potatoes to pay the balance. On board *Ozbourn*, every officer was required to belong to the wardroom mess and to pay his share of the cost of rations. They were bought not only from ships' supplies but could also be augmented by purchases made ashore.

When the ship was tied up to a pier or swinging at a mooring in the harbor, only duty officers remained on board for evening meal although they might be joined, just before pay day, by one or two unmarried Ensigns who were broke. In the States, the unmarried officers took weekend duty watches so married officers could be home; overseas, reverse was to be the pay-back. If a married officer had the duty during the week, his family would often come on board for supper and the movie. Once we left for WestPac, mess bills returned to normal. Good though the wardroom meals might or might not be, there was no place else for officers to eat.

An unmarried Ensign was paid two hundred ten dollars, plus a subsistence allowance of thirty dollars per month. If an officer was qualified and assigned flight duty, submarine duty, Underwater Demolition Team, Explosive Ordnance Disposal, or hard-hat diving he received an additional one hundred dollars per month. The same duty was worth fifty dollars if you were enlisted. Except for uniforms and liberty expenses, a junior officer could save money living on a ship. It was the junior officers or young enlisted men with families who were in serious financial trouble. How they dealt with the expense of moving a family from one assignment to the next or how a wife traveled to meet the ship somewhere in the Far East or even just in California was beyond me.

After a month on board, I felt I had learned most of the protocol and what was expected of me. Chiefs occasionally came to the wardroom for meetings with division officers because there was no other place on board to sit down and talk

CAPT Bernard Roeder, USN ('Mobilize Dog') (*r.*) peering aft. CDR Charles O. Akers, USN ('Charley') (*r.*) looking ahead during entry into Pearl Harbor, April 1951.

left: ENS Charles Jarrett in Hong Kong, November 15, 1950.

LTs Don Abbott (*l.*) and John Hadley enjoying liberty at Victoria Peak, Hong Kong, November 12, 1950.

left: ENS John Blonsick at Keelung, December 11, 1950 while the USS *Ozbourn* was refueling from the USS *Guadalope*.
right: Moriarty at Victoria Peak, Hong Kong, November 12, 1950.

privately. Being invited to Chiefs' Quarters for a cup of coffee was an honor rarely bestowed on lowly ensigns. It happened only once to me. All too soon, the trip west was over—we had reached Japan.

Suddenly — Japan

On Friday, 4 August, we arrived at Yokosuka Naval Base near Yokohama. While crossing the Pacific, our weather had generally been both calm and cool; in Japan it was hot. Although the August mess bill was due and had jumped to twenty-five dollars a month, I was still eating for less than at Theta Xi and I no longer needed to peel potatoes or make beds to pay for the rest of my living expenses. I was beginning to feel like a real live naval officer.

On the same day we arrived, UN forces retreated over the Naktong River, destroyed its last bridge and the siege of the Pusan Perimeter began. United Nations forces and remnants of the South Korean Army had been mauled since early July and had now been pushed southward into a small foothold in south-eastern Korea with Pusan its only port. From then until 15 September, the situation ashore was to remain grave and worsening.

While in Yokosuka, I went to Base Communications to pick up Officer Messenger Mail and was startled to run into a LTJG who had been in my Southeast Asia class at Cornell. The Navy had commissioned him earlier, even though he did not have an undergraduate degree. They later sent him to Cornell, as part of the 'five term' program, to complete the undergraduate degree needed for his career. We had studied for exams in his apartment while his wife kept the coffee coming. After we both graduated, they left Ithaca for the Navy's Line Officer School at Monterey, California. Instead, here he was in Japan. The Navy needed someone to find all the small mine sweepers lent to the Japanese to clear their harbors; we wanted them back. Before I could ask why, he was gone. *Ozbourn* got underway for Sasebo on 5 August before we had an opportunity to meet again.

During the early evening while passing southward along the coast of eastern Kyushu, the Chief Engineer and I stood next to the lifelines and watched high thunderheads build over the

Japanese headlands ashore. We stayed until they gradually turned into a peaceful summer sunset while we exchanged comments about the exec. LCDR Ousey was beginning to annoy everyone in the wardroom. His was the nearly impossible job of getting us ready for whatever was before us.

Early Sunday morning, 6 August, the Special Sea and Anchor Detail was called away. Sailors appeared on deck to handle lines and let go an anchor, if needed during port entry. I made my way to the bridge and relieved the JOOD for entering the harbor of Sasebo, in southern Kyushu. *Ozbourn* threaded her way in through the line of navigation buoys and then re-fueled at the fuel dock. By 1130 we had moored alongside a British cruiser. The harbor seemed packed with destroyers and cruisers. During the trip in, the commanding officer and the executive officer, serving as navigator, were both on the bridge and did most of the work but the OOD and I kept busy looking for potential problems. We watched for the lookouts, listened to the radios, checked on flags or signals going up, checked on boats crossing our path, and so forth. The harbor pilot's boat had come out and met us while we were hove to near the entrance buoy. I leaned over the bridge's splinter shield to watch our pilot, a small, older and very correct Japanese man in a dark uniform, get out of the launch. He climbed our Jacob's ladder to our main deck, marched up our own steel ladders, asked permission to come on the bridge where he then bowed to all present, and proceeded to guide us precisely in. Subsequently we learned he had been a Rear Admiral during the war and I wondered how much of what was going through my head was in his too. For me it was instant stereotypes from old war movies that rose briefly and then returned to the dead. We were really in Japan.

Liberty was called and everyone chased off the ship heading for the bar at the 'O' Club or the Enlisted Club—all except me. I needed to go ashore and send money home. In Sasebo, after you left the two officer's clubs and then passed the Army PX, nothing confronted you but a bridge over a dirty river, more muddy roads, thousands of bars, souvenir stands, and worse. I was not going to send money home from there; I needed to figure out a better way to do it and instead started an allotment to a bank in Beaver.

After a few days in Sasebo, CDR Ross Freeman, USN, the commanding officer, called me into his cabin and appointed me Assistant Communications Officer which put me in the 'O' (Operations) Division under LT Donald Abbott, USN, Operations Officer. I wasn't certain what I was supposed to be doing. Had we been in San Diego, I would have found out in a two-weeks school.

Suddenly — Korea

By 10 August, we were still in Sasebo but the rumor was that we were about to depart to escort several tankers south to Buckner Bay, Okinawa. Buckner Bay had been named for Lieutenant General Simon Bolivar Buckner, killed during the Okinawa campaign. That seemed important—we were finally doing something. During our stay in Sasebo, everyone had visited other ships at anchor or had talked to other sailors or officers somewhere ashore. An Australian sailor from the destroyer moored behind us said they had made a number of trips to Pusan, a port in the southeastern tip of Korea, escorting troops and supplies; he considered it a very safe thing to do—a milk-run. By then, Pusan was the only port open through which to send reinforcements, tanks, and supplies to the troops within the 'Pusan Perimeter'—the term didn't mean anything yet. Some of the scuttlebutt at the 'O' club was that shore bombarding was also quite safe—just don't run aground, as the charts weren't very good. Jack Worden talked to a friend from another destroyer that had located a North Korean battalion lining up for supper. They had killed all seven hundred of them with five-inch shells. How could anyone be so stupid?

Word spread quickly that we were leaving to go south to Okinawa. By now we realized that nothing was happening there and we were still missing out—nothing was happening except in Korea. We left on 11 August but instead of going to Okinawa, we escorted the refueling tanker group to the north end of the South China Sea where we met two carriers, *Valley Forge* and *Philippine Sea*, and the rest of Task Force 77. These 27,000-ton Essex-class carriers were operating squadrons flying the propeller-driven F4U or Vought Corsair, the AD-4 or Douglas Skyraider, and the F9F jet or Grumman Panther, who were providing close air support for the Perimeter defenses.

We were to protect the refueling ships from Soviet submarines. *Ozbourn*'s anti-submarine armament consisted of four K-gun depth charge gun launchers, two mounted on each side, just forward of the fantail on the main deck and to complete the depth charge patterns, tear-dropped Mark 14 depth charges could be rolled successively from the two depth charge stern racks extending over the fantail. The Sonar Officer would work with the skipper to coordinate any attacks. We had nothing to do but search for submarines that weren't there.

Most submarines running submerged on battery power probably would not operate faster than five knots, although several US submarines with new hull configurations were much faster and might reach twelve knots. Our sonar could detect submerged targets out to two thousand yards or so depending upon water conditions. The sonar was frequently being modified, tuned up or repaired by shipyards or while alongside tenders. It had also been modified to detect moored mines.

By 14 August we were back in Sasebo and the trip south had merely been a security cover. I came back even more pleased with my growing skills as a junior ship handler, the whole thing was really a terrific way to learn about ships-keeping station or position relative to the other ships, giving commands to the helm, keeping out of the way of carriers, watching jets take off and land—that was really something. It was also a war despite my eagerness to see it. When we joined up with the carriers, flags were flying at half mast in Task Force 77. The Air Group Commander, CDR R. W. Vogel, USN, had just been killed operating off *Philippine Sea*. Ashore, a major US attack to dislodge NK troops on the ridgeline at Obong-ni was not going well; they represented a significant breaching of the Naktong River line, the Perimeter's western front, and that had to be resolved. After refueling was complete, we escorted the refueling group back to Japan.

Upon our return, the ships in the harbor now ranged from a Canadian destroyer moored ahead of us to several new divisions of American destroyers nested four up behind us with more coming. The port of Sasebo itself, an important Japanese naval base in southern Kyushu during the war, was still in poor condition. Parts of the shipyard, fuel docks, and ammunition dock not damaged were now being pressed into use by the

growing UN naval forces. Life in town was still primitive and
ran to bars and whore-houses. The dock area and the shipyard
had been badly bombed during the war and many of the buildings still retained a frazzled look about them.

To overcome the primitive conditions, the British had
brought in HMS *Ladybird* as a floating headquarters for their
Admiral Andrewes, and the US Navy had officers' and enlisted
clubs nearby. Getting ashore and into the officers' club was the
best way to meet friends and former midshipmen classmates, all
of whom were somewhat stunned by the events that had overtaken us since graduation. There was an excitement that somehow we had lucked out and had gotten a jump on something for
which no one seemed very well prepared.

ENS Jack Blonsick, USN, finally completed his trip across
the Pacific and joined us in Sasebo. After high school he had
spent some time in the Marines flying as a radio operator,
attended Georgia Tech and then the University of Mississippi.
Jack's commissioning by the NROTC Unit had been delayed
until he completed his third midshipmen cruise which was first
interrupted by a hospital stay and then terminated by the start
of the war. His initial assignment had been to *Perry*, an east
coast destroyer but that was changed to *Ozbourn*. While he was
trying to find us, someone in San Francisco wanted to send him
to Alaska, apparently to find the volcano, Mt. Katmai. They had
part of it right, *Ozbourn* was then escorting the other *Mt.
Katmai* to Japan. Things back home were very confused and not
well put together. Jack finally traveled the Pacific using military
air and had priority even over senior officers—the Navy needed
all their Ensigns, and wanted them *now* in the Far East. In
trying to find us, Jack had also been fooled by our cover story
and had gone to Okinawa looking for us. What Jack really
wanted was a quick ticket to naval flight training, and the
Ozbourn was the first step.

Our division commander transferred to us on 15 August,
bringing additional personnel with him. Among others, we
inherited LTJG James 'Doc' Ketcham, the division's doctor,
several additional chiefs, and a warrant officer who later sold
me his typewriter. The doctor could be transferred by high-line
to other ships as needed and he did conduct one appendectomy
on someone else's wardroom table. The room just forward of

mine was occupied by two officers but the one aft had been vacant until taken over by Dr. Ketcham.

In the Officer's Club, I finally ran into Don Bowen, another friend from the University of Mississippi; his destroyer was obviously no longer in Rhode Island but out here also. Others from my midshipman cruise on *Boxer* showed up, including someone I described in a letter home as being stationed on cruiser 'X'—I was being 'security' conscious. The USS *Helena* had just arrived. The bar at the 'O' Club daily served as an ex-midshipmen reunion where everything got talked about and security didn't seem an issue except as reason for keeping facts from the folks in Beaver. Then somebody dragged out the 'the trip to Okinawa' story for us again and it was time to go somewhere.

PART II

THE WAR

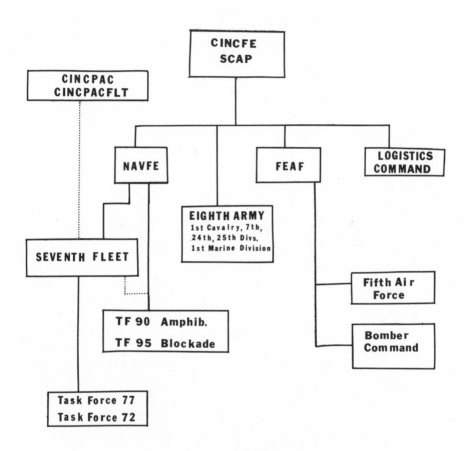

Figure 5: Far East Command, August 1950
Modified from Field (1962:4).

AUGUST 1950

On August 2, naval transports landed elements of the First Marine Division in Pusan. One transport was the *Henrico* which we had last seen off the coast of California when we had delivered that technician to her so she could limp back to the shipyard at Vallejo. She and her Marines made it just in time. They were some of the first replacement troops from the US and played a substantial role in the battles along the Pusan Perimeter. From then on would come Inchon and the Chosin Reservoir for the Marines.

Early in August, General Walker, commanding all UN forces in Korea, boarded *Wiltsie* in the harbor at Pusan to ask for all the gunfire support he could get from the Navy, "just hold them back a little longer".[1] On 13 August, the North Koreans announced the capture of Pohang-dong on the east coast forty miles north of Pusan, but they were then driven out by heavy naval bombardment. By 14 August, General Walker again desperately needed naval gunfire assistance on the eastern coast of the Perimeter in the area occupied by the ROK 3rd Division and, by 15 August, he had to evacuate the ROK Division at the village of Toksong. A heavy cruiser, *Helena*, provided gunfire support and *Valley Forge*, joined by the newly arrived *Philippine Sea*, provided air cover. The day before, a *Ozbourn* had been one of the destroyers in the anti-submarine screen protecting tankers that had refueled the carrier task force.

On the evening of August 16, *Wiltsie* escorted four LSTs ashore at the northeastern corner of the Perimeter and evacuated fifty-eight hundred ROK soldiers, twelve hundred civilians, and one hundred vehicles, which were then re-landed further south at Kuryongp'o. On one shore bombardment mission, Tregurtha saw dead South Koreans floating by with their hands tied behind them. By 18 August, the North Korean drive southward along the east coast had been halted by a combination of ROK and US Army units plus heavy shipboard gunfire support and by effective naval air bombardment.[2] We had helped by bringing up the replenishment group but it seemed very insignificant.

On 3 September, Private Howard W. Johns, son of Mr. and Mrs. Howard Johns, 377 Fourth Street, Beaver was wounded in action somewhere along the Pusan Perimeter—Beaver's first casualty. The battle of the Perimeter beginning 20 July would continue for nearly two months during which American, ROK, and NK casualties were staggering. By 15 September, the US Eighth Army alone had lost 4,599 killed, 12,377 wounded, and 1,189 missing in action.[3] By 27 September, total US ground casualties exceeded 27,500, of which 6,000 had been killed in action.[4]

Off Korea — August and Early September 1950

In early September, our commanding officer, CDR Freeman, left *Ozbourn* to become *Juneau*'s executive officer, and CDR Charles Akers, USN, left the Destroyer Squadron 11 staff to command *Ozbourn* during the remainder of the cruise. It was CDR Akers's second destroyer; he had already commanded USS *Hobby*, a Benson class destroyer, at the end of World War Two. Jerry Solomon knew CDR Akers when Akers had taught naval engineering at the Naval Academy. Was this to be another ring thumping relationship?—not once you got to know the new skipper.

Akers quickly became known for doing paperwork at his desk dressed only in his regulation white Navy underwear. It was disconcerting to enter his room with a report, see him sitting there in his boxer shorts and have him smile up at you, "Yes, Mr. Cole?" He had graduated from Annapolis, Class of

1938, and, as I began to discern differences in styles of command, he became someone that I greatly admired and respected deeply as a naval officer. During our first months off Korea, he lived every underway hour on the bridge moving only occasionally to the captain's sea cabin, a tiny room just aft of the bridge to shave, change his shirt or to use the head. It was always 'Captain' to his face but 'Charley' behind his back. As Charley Akers became more confident of his bridge officers, he finally unwrapped himself from his gray steel bridge chair and went below; it was a compliment of the highest, yet unspoken, order for him to leave you alone on the bridge. Either there was nothing that could possibly happen or you had made a favorable impression. His comment later was that while everyone else had something to do on that ship, his only task was to keep the cushion from floating off his gray bridge chair. He was the most experienced ship handler I would ever meet. He was also a gentleman to work for.

We soon had three officers that Captain Akers was willing to trust with his ship. He qualified, as his underway Officers Of the Deck (OOD): Dave Thornhill, Don Abbott, and John Hadley. Abbott and Hadley were 'mustangs' having been commissioned from the ranks without going to college, despite the fact that the Navy seemed to consider a college degree a must for a commission. Both had been in the Navy prior to Pearl Harbor and were absolutely reliable deck watch-standers. Hadley was gunnery officer, Abbott, operations officer, and Thornhill (USNA, '48), 'O' Division[5] Officer.

As the cruise continued, Don Abbott proceeded to grow a luxuriant, drooping handle-bar mustache. One morning after a long party ashore, he barely made quarters at 0800. We were lined up on the starboard main deck just aft of the midships passage when Don strode down the deck passing the Supply Department and stood before Dave Thornhill to receive the muster report, one side of his mustache absolutely gone. Thornhill suppressed giggles from the ranks with a glare, reported "all present or accounted for, sir," and saluted Abbott who then left for the midships passage to confront the exec with the news. Only then did the truth emerge. The Operations Division loved it. We never found out who was responsible.

Some said Dave was guilty, others, John Hadley. Dave Thornhill was *Ozbourn*'s 'Mr. Roberts'[6] and had a nice touch with everything. Abbott had been wounded during the Pearl Harbor attack. This attack wounded his mustache, plus a little pride. He was momentarily flustered by the executive officer's evaluation of his shaving skills and within minutes, the other hunk of this remarkable mustache was also gone. Overseas, facial hair was tolerated by some but not by Charley Akers, who was within days of speaking to the Executive officer about Abbott's mustache when miraculously it vanished.

Mustangs, like Don Abbott, John Hadley, and Armond Remmen knew both sides of the Navy and tended to look out for ensigns who needed help growing up. LT Ross Lockhart, was a mustang as well as Chief Engineer on *Wiltsie*. He watched out for Jim Tregurtha. One evening while *Wiltsie* was shore bombarding, Lockhart collapsed with a heart attack and died out on the quarterdeck despite everything their doctor could do. Lockhart's body was returned to Sasebo on the next trip in and then flown to San Diego for burial at Fort Rosecrans. Tregurtha had lost his 'sea daddy.' We each needed them and mine alternated between Don Abbott and John Hadley.

There was no drinking on ship but that was corrected whenever we came in. John Hadley set a trap for his room-mate one night by filling their room with upended chairs from the wardroom. After Abbott finally found his way into the upper bunk and collapsed, Hadley got up and put them all back except one. Abbott never figured out how that one chair had given him so much grief.

Someone else came back one night driven by an urge to "piss in the wardroom." He was in the middle of it when another officer got a two-by-four from a Damage Control locker and pole-axed him avowing that such "conduct unbecoming an officer" needed instant retribution. After being driven into the bulkhead, the 'pisser' staggered up and left. Next morning at quarters, he commented "I must have had a great time, because I feel so miserable today!"

My nickname 'Pete' transferred with me to *Ozbourn* until John Hadley temporarily replaced it with 'Cherry Tree.' The voice call sign of *Valley Forge* seemed to characterize this young soul entrusted to him. It was also a gentle put-down but it seemed fitting to a twenty-two-year-old fresh-caught ensign with red hair. The *Valley Forge* also seemed to be a 'happy ship'[7] and I was secretly pleased to be related to the 'Happy Valley.' I liked the comparison as well as the attention.

Neither my roommate, LTJG 'Pay' Jordan, the supply officer, nor the Chief Engineer, LT Armond Remmen called 'Chief,' nor LTJG Ketcham, the divisional doctor, stood watches. Their sleeping patterns were fairly normal except when interrupted by General Quarters or when they had overnight departmental problems to solve. In Doc's room, lights seemed never to be on. He had very little to do except attend daily sick call and wait asleep in his bunk for the rare medical emergency. He gradually become a near recluse easily setting our record for continuous bunk-time although he would always emerge at least for evening meal primarily to make sure he didn't miss the evening movie in the wardroom and the evening bridge game with the Commodore. On *Wiltsie*, they awarded the squadron doctor a chipping iron to scrape off his bed-sores. He was rather offended.

The rest of us stood rotating watches either on the bridge or in CIC. Had we been steaming in peacetime, the OOD would have been an experienced line officer and the JOOD either a Chief Gunner's Mate, a Torpedoman Chief or a Chief Boatswain. The CIC Officer would have either been a Chief or a First Class Petty Officer from the Gunnery or the Operations Division. During wartime conditions, two qualified line officers were needed on the bridge at all times plus an additional one in CIC. There were no Chiefs to spare as officer replacements, however qualified they might be. *Ozbourn* simply did not have enough line officers.

Jerry Solomon and I had reported for duty in June and July, respectively, and immediately replaced two Chiefs on bridge watch. Jerry had enlisted in the Navy in 1945 and then entered the Naval Academy from the fleet, which was difficult enough to do, but doubly so if you were Jewish. Jerry also wanted to go to flight school but every Ensign USN first had to become qualified as an OOD underway and this destroyer was a fine place to learn. Jack Blonsick came on board in August with the same goal, but also added another inexperienced officer to the pool composed of Jerry and me. The class of 1950, USNA and

NROTC, alike was the last class required to serve on ships before going to flight training. A year later when Jack arrived in Pensacola, the Class of 1951 was already there. Jerry arrived in Pensacola a few months after Jack.

Not until late September, would we have enough qualified watch officers to do better than a one-in-three watch. Until then, we were often on watch-on, watch-off. This meant twelve hours of watches to which would be added day work as a gunnery or communications officer and then several hours of dawn and dusk General Quarters after which another work day began. Whatever was left over was for sleeping and eating.

This became a merry-go-round of duty with little time to do anything but eat and work on the bridge. This, ultimately, exhausted people to the point of making mistakes or having memory lapses either in ship control or with radio communications within the Task Force. Flight operations required careful attention to rapidly changing formations and rapid movements anticipating oncoming ships, as well as an around-the-clock alertness to possible submarine or air attack. As time passed, submarine or air attack seemed less likely, but were supplanted with worries about floating mines.

Each commanding officer qualifies his own OODs and until he is sure of them, the skipper stays close, either by eating and sleeping in his chair on the bridge or by living and working in his sea cabin just aft of the bridge. Ultimately, such pressures might affect anyone's judgment but the only time a commanding officer could let go occurred when the ship returned to Sasebo. I have no memory of Akers ever unjustifiably chewing out someone although he dealt with several very inexperienced naval officers. Any fleet commander could anticipate incidents if he kept such under-manned vessels continuously at sea. By late September, we finally had trained enough qualified OODs and had received enough officer and enlisted reservists that the task of operating at sea for long periods was becoming easier.

As soon as we arrived off Korea in mid-August, my watch station was again changed from CIC Watch Officer to JOOD. I worked for John Hadley and learned much. He had a brusque, no-nonsense attitude that kept me buffaloed although everything ended in a smile. I also liked standing watches with Donald Abbott.

When new ensigns came on the bridge as JOODs, Hadley and Abbott were usually assigned the break-in responsibilities. In time, LTJG John Moriarty and LTJG John Bond were also qualified and soon were alternating with others, but the system of training new OODs was basically 'on-the-job.' Given normal circumstances, we would have attended schools in San Diego but they could never have provided so much training time underway as we were getting.

As JOOD, you spent most of your time giving course and speed change orders as conning officer[8] and coping with relative motion. Ship movement at sea becomes a puzzling game of relative movement, which overtakes actual movement, particularly when you are traveling with other ships. Experience on land convinces you that everything travels from point A to point B by moving in a particular direction at some rate of speed and arriving at some anticipated time. At sea, and out of touch with any land reference for long time periods, the entire world is made of water and your ship moving on it seems to be standing still. There is a feeling that the carrier one thousand yards ahead of you and off slightly to your left is also really stationary. Any moves made by your ship become relative to that fixed point and thus not real. Accordingly, course and speed changes are also relative as you fall behind in range or drift off in bearing to the carrier. You then must steer left or right or speed up to compensate. Even when seas are high and you are plowing into oncoming waves, there is more of a sense of up and down than of forward progress. Only when seas are calm and you are ordered ahead at speeds much greater than the forward speed of the Task Force does your sense of actual forward motion return. A strong wind in your face also helps forward motion return.

Movements from one spot to another are also always made in relation to the Task Force guide, usually the senior carrier, and are worked out as vector problems on paper maneuvering board diagrams. You can be on the bridge looking at the carrier beginning its right turn and know that you also need to turn to starboard and speed up to keep in position. At that moment, some inexperienced idiot of a CIC officer with the same information, after working blind off a radar and another piece of paper, calls the bridge and recommends "turning to port and slowing down." This is very disconcerting but all part of the learning process—his and yours. Although keeping the guide at a constant 350 degrees bearing and at three thousand yards is crucial, the final rule—"whatever dumb thing you do, don't hit the carrier"—exceeds all others. Even skilled skippers can make mistakes.

A new JOOD is given the 'conn' most of the time, though under close scrutiny of the OOD, as well as the captain. While conning the ship, the JOOD will be 'in charge,' ordering minor course and speed changes to keep station. Usually the OOD takes the conn back during plane guard duty close astern a carrier or when the ship is moving to a new station in the anti-submarine screen that might require experienced judgment. Until relative motion makes sense to you as JOOD, you are always 'adding turns' when you should be 'steering left.' Gradually you begin to develop a 'seaman's eye' and make the right moves.

Even when the big moves came and OOD took the conn, the JOOD was usually asked to provide recommended course, speed, and time needed to complete the maneuver before the OOD changed course and speed. It confirmed the OOD's own plans as well as gave the JOOD experience. In late August, I had the afternoon watch as Hadley's JOOD when we were ordered to take plane guard station off the quarter of *Valley Forge* during aircraft recovery. The preparatory course and speed changes had already been given on voice radio as well as by signal flags. When the carrier 'executed' by radio and simul-taneously dropped the course and speed flags, the Task Force would change speed and direction and we'd move—some-where—on a different course at a greater speed.

Every bridge has a pad of paper maneuvering boards, divid-ers, and parallel rules, and every midshipman used them for years in class. First, you plot where you are from the guide and how fast and what course both ships are on, then you plot where you want to be and when. From the resulting triangle, out comes course, speed, and time needed to get you there. It should take perhaps twenty seconds for a solution. This might be true in class but it was not always so under the real thing. I puzzled over which way the arrows went and how long the lines should be. I could not even decide whether to turn right or left and whether to increase or decrease speed and finally gave up in despair convinced I did not know how to use the board. John shook his head. When the signal came to execute the maneuver, he ordered the ship to increase speed from 'standard' to 'all ahead full' and then came left until we were at the very least aimed at the carrier's stern. Perhaps it was not the 'school' solution, but it was done on time and at least in the right direction. That lesson returns when I find myself puzzling over a problem — often I just need to come left and do something *now*. There was a precise course and speed solution to that problem which probably was better than John's but it is still waiting to be done by me on that damned maneuvering board. Virtually every former JOOD has a similar story.

LTJG Hadley quickly developed a reputation with the sailors on watch with him. You wore a frayed hat while at the helm in his bridge watch and Hadley grabbed it and threw it over the side. Wear a jumper with a hole in it and John would make it much bigger before instructing you to go below and then come back on watch in the proper uniform. For committing some minor infraction, Quartermaster Ellis was sent out to relieve the port lookout for the remainder of the watch. As Ellis departed in anger, Hadley heard him mutter, "you son-of-a-bitch," under his breath. John stalked after him and stuck his face in Ellis's: "You said what?" and back came, "I said, son-of-a-gun." Hadley smirked and again asked, "You said what?" "I said you son-of-a-gun, sir." For the last time, "You said what?" Ellis knew he was now facing a court-martial but in desperation replied "You son-of-a-bitch, sir." At that Hadley grinned at him, "I thought that's what you said," and left Ellis out in the sun to watch for mines and floating Korean corpses for the rest of the watch. That story ran around the ship. John Hadley begrudgingly had the respect of his people. They knew he knew his job and could be distressingly blunt. I admired that man.

My job as JOOD was to keep us in proper position on the screen while the entire group moved forward at fifteen knots, usually in a direction either to regain sea room for flight operations into the wind or to bring the Task Force closer to shore for recovery of aircraft. When flight operations were called, the carrier conducting operations would advise new course and speed. On signal, the entire formation would change course and

increase speed to increase air speed across the deck and en-
hance launch and recovery of jets. Although both carriers carried a mixture of aircraft types, the cross-deck speed needed to
launch jets had to be at least thirty knots. Both *Valley Forge* and
Philippine Sea carried the Panther (F9F-2), the Navy's first
combat jet, which had been operational in the fleet for at most
two years. Also on board both carriers were Corsairs (F4U) and
Skyraiders (AD), as well as helicopters.

Any major speed increase for a destroyer required adding
one or more additional boilers. Normally, we traveled with a
split plant, one boiler for each fireroom. Putting additional
boilers on line could take up to thirty minutes. The process
would often send a puff of uncombusted black oil into the
normal hazy exhaust. Somebody important on the bridge was
always yelling, "black smoke out of #2 stack," which required
the JOOD to chide the fireroom that they were indeed "making
black smoke," something they were well aware of. Usually it
would quit before the screen commander asked "Why." This
was something no one ever wanted to hear on the radio net. We
were constantly adjusting course and speed to maintain station
and had to be prepared to handle sonar contacts, radar contacts, and other emergencies. As the mine war heated up,
keeping a watchful eye for floating black things also occupied
time.

Although long deck watches left me with back aches, generally the day watches went rapidly and the summer and early
autumn weather off Korea was warm and sunny, and the seas
were calm. There was something un-warlike about all of it, at
least for those of us that were neither flying nor ashore. Watching the spectacular sunsets made all of this even more unreal.

Squinting into the bright sun looking for enemy planes that
never showed up, or looking into the sun-freckled sea for floating mines gave me a headache. You could wear the visored cap
or the garrison cap on board. The garrison cap could be folded
side to side and stuck in a pocket. It was convenient, but a fore-
and-aft garrison cap ('piss-cutter') gave no sun protection, no
matter how you moved it around. The typical naval officer's
visored or bill cap, even when you used the gold braided chin-
strap, tended to get blown overboard. Everyone had a second
visored cap on which the gold braid had turned green from salt

spray and the grommet stretching the khaki hat cover had slacked off to allow the cover to droop. I needed a salty visor cap, nicknamed 'steamer,' with its dull green braid and chipped bill, but only time would produce one out of my only cap. It was a symbol of time spent at sea, and I had not yet qualified. Meanwhile were my only cap to be blown over the side, I'd be unable to stand inspections, go on liberty and no one had told me to buy a second cap.

Then came the issue of baseball caps. Men on the other destroyers were wearing Japanese baseball caps. "Why couldn't we?" became the silent response. We felt somewhat like the kid in the neighborhood with the strictest parents. Charley Akers finally agreed that baseball caps could be worn at sea. Once they were allowed, I wrote home. Dad reasoned if a baseball cap would be fine, a long-billed fisherman's cap would be even better. It arrived late September and was promptly put to work, although it stuck out about six inches from my forehead. I was the hit of the bridge, but the cap had a short life. The second day I wore it, I turned around rapidly and stuck this damned long bill directly into Charley Aker's left eye. I hadn't realized the skipper was there. The next watch I was back wearing my only visored cap and hoping to keep it alive until we reached somewhere that I could buy a second one for emergencies or for inspections.

As more reservists arrived we were able to settle into a routine. Normal ship's activity went on with a dawn and dusk General Quarters, a four-hour watch on and two watches off except that the watch from 4:00 to 8:00 p.m. (1600 to 2000) was divided in two: the first dog (1600 to 1800) and second dog watch (1800 to 2000) allowed the watch-in-three system to rotate forward. The best part of that rotation began when you got the second dog watch, because after it you could sleep from 2000 until the 0400 to 0800 which generally coincided with dawn GQ when everyone got up anyway. This euphoric sleeping party went downhill rapidly; the day immediately following was the worst. It had the mid-watch from 0000 to 0400 and you got off duty just in time to wind down but, just as you fell asleep, it was time for dawn GQ followed immediately by day's work. When one was not on watch from 0800 to 1200 or from 1200 to 1600, there were ship's duties to be carried out. Sleeping was not one of them. You might get away with it in forward officer's country but not in any space where department heads worked; the Chiefs might, but no other enlisted man would get away with it. When not on watch, they had paint somewhere to be chipped or some other task to do. Gradually fatigue would set in around the ship. Sea routine provided us with regular beds and three hot meals but they might not offset fatigue errors made while having the conn. These errors could easily lead to collisions. Being continuously exhausted characterized those days for all of us.

In effect, we were part of a somewhat modernized version of World War Two's carrier task force, circa 1944-45. *Ozbourn* had been built to give anti-submarine and air defense. Most of our time was spent guarding carriers from submarine or air threats. We could also provide plane guard services during flight operations and carried a motor whaleboat which could be launched at sea for recovery of downed pilots as well as a captain's gig that could also be pressed into similar service if need be. Jack had a seaman assigned to the motor whaleboat as a cleaning station. Under his care, the whale boat got finer and more attractive with every passing day. A boatswain's mate realized the sailor was missing meals and never left his cleaning station. After a talk with 'Doc' Ketcham, the sailor was sent ashore for psychiatric observation and never returned.

Daylight duty on the bridge or in CIC while we were operating with carriers was always busy. Flight operations picked up before light, about 0400, with the launching of the CAP or Combat Air Patrol that kept station over or near the Task Force. Once daylight broke, regular flight operations got underway. Small or large strikes were launched, going somewhere in various forms depending on needs ashore. We were seldom privy to their armament loads or even to their destinations. Those of us living in the carrier's anti-submarine screen rarely had much of a sense as to what the daily missions were or what was going on. ADs, F4Us, and F9Fs left in smaller or larger numbers and returned several hours later, only to be followed by later departing and returning strikes. Usually what was launched while you were on watch returned when you were off so it was difficult to keep track.

Although helicopters were available for limited daytime use, most aircraft operations off carriers during 1950-51 also needed one or more destroyers from the screen to be stationed as plane guards off the carrier's quarter during launch and recovery. Hydraulic catapults and straight decks had been sufficient for and capable of launching the lighter and less heavily loaded World War Two aircraft, but, by Korea, the catapults were straining against increasing aircraft size and weight. Deck crashes and water landings during take-off and recovery became all too common. At one point, in addition to these losses, ADs were lost faster to training accidents than production at Douglas Aircraft could replace.

As aircraft weight and speed increased, the margin for error in the carrier environment decreased. The carrier landing accident rate was quite high in the early stages of the Korean War with many aircraft landing hot, breaking through the barrier, and crashing into aircraft spotted forward that were being prepared for subsequent launches.

Off Korea, during hot days with no surface wind except that caused by ship's forward motion, occasionally it was impossible for a carrier to move fast enough to launch jets using the hydraulic catapults. Steam catapults were yet to come but would be required if naval aviation was to convert to all jets by 1956 as had been predicted. Part of the weight problem centered on having to launch fully fueled aircraft. In-flight refueling did not occur until 1956.

Eighteen or more destroyers might be in the circular screen to detect enemy submarines; at other times, cruisers were inside the screen to provide anti-aircraft fire. Frequently cruisers and destroyers were ordered out of the screen for temporary assignment elsewhere such as shore bombardment assignments or back to Sasebo for repairs. Under the continuousness of the routine, days passed endlessly, but as we grew more experienced, it became easier to deal with the problems. I was becoming qualified, at least as a JOOD, and the ship and crew were performing as expected.

Every three or four days during the first month, flight operations ceased and the Task Force sailed either south to Sasebo or into the South China Sea to meet the underway replenishment group of one or more fleet oilers. Later, an ammunition ship and a provisioning ship were also involved. These visits provided mail and movie exchange and a time to transfer personnel by breeches buoy for medical reasons or for getting new officers and men who had finally caught up with the ship. Officers and men (primarily reservists) joining the *Ozbourn* during the autumn and winter had usually been in transit from the west coast traveling as transients on ships coming westward. Except for Ensigns being moved west early in the war few made the trip by air.

Initially, it had been difficult to keep carriers and destroyers replenished while they remained on or near the operating area. The group would return to Sasebo, refuel, rearm, and return. Later, as the pipeline from the States filled up and sufficient replenishment ships became available, replenishment at sea became routine. During a replenishment, you would come alongside first one vessel and then another, the first usually for fuel oil and then the second for food, mail, spare parts, and personnel. A reserve chaplain transferring to *Wiltsie*, was spun around in the boatswain's chair and then dipped into the ocean as the highline first pulled taut and then slacked owing to the rolling of the two ships; next came a LTJG holding a violin under his arm who made it safely. Crossing could be dangerous to your health if not your musical instrument.

If shore-bombarding had reduced magazine supplies of three-inch and five-inch shells, a trip alongside an ammunition ship such as *Mt. Katmai* would also occur. Replenishment at sea of bomb loads for a carrier would take a long time leaving the sailors arm and back weary after a long day of work. This pipeline of supplies, spare parts, and other items that originated in the states continuously came to us by freighter from US stores, but the pipeline first needed to be primed and filled in July and August 1950. Part of our inability to remain continuously at sea in August 1950 was related to filling up the supply lines and then having sufficient ships with the capability to resupply at sea.

Personal emergencies also arose. The mother of one of our radarmen died while we were in the Sea of Japan and his request for emergency leave had to be denied. He would have had to wait until the next replenishment even to begin the trip back and he would not have even reached Japan before the funeral. There was simply no way of getting him back in time. He and I illegally leaned against the life lines and watched water go by for awhile – little else could be done.

Several times we passed through large fleets of Japanese fishing vessels. In the darkness, you first saw a glow on the darkened horizon. The glow gradually increased and finally broke into hundreds of individual lights, each one atop a mast of a small fishing vessel. Without even turning on running lights, our entire darkened formation, traveling at fifteen knots, passed through these several hundred small fishing skiffs and larger vessels. Most were only lit with a single white range light. We never slowed down and nobody was hit.

Air raids were always a possibility. At least once a week an unidentified aircraft came close to the Task Force. Several NK craft were shot down nearby but most were simply straying US aircraft, although we did encounter one overflight by a Russian bomber. General Quarters sounded about 2300 one night which sent everyone running. This was clearly not a drill. I arrived in CIC with shoes and pants in hand. This did not please the executive officer – I saw "better dressed *and* dead" in his look.

Several night fighters were scrambled from the *Valley Forge* and one of them shot down the overflying Russian patrol plane. He was either testing us or didn't realize where he was. The pilot's body was recovered and returned to Sasebo. *Valley Forge* carried a red star on its bridge until someone with a lot of rank thought better of it. The next time the Task Force returned to Sasebo, I was in the bar at the Officer's Club and some young flier was being razzed about trying to start World War Three. I'm glad it hadn't but it pointed out the uncertainty of the times and how little we knew about who was doing what to whom and why.

The Task Force alternated between the Sea of Japan and the Yellow Sea as we operated close in to the Pusan Perimeter. Unless you checked in the chart house, you never really knew where we were, time simply went on, watch after watch. The carriers always had a daytime combat air patrol (CAP) up overhead and kept the decks spotted and ready to go according to a schedule we didn't know. Very little effort was made to keep people aware of what was going on in the war – even the officers were usually in the dark.

We maintained active sonar searching and no submarines or non-UN warships were ever detected in the vicinity of the carriers. Had any real contacts been made, all of us in the screening destroyers would have known about them because it would have been our task to sink them. Nonetheless, rumors of Russian submarines stalking the Task Force were reported in *Time Magazine* and in newspapers back home. US submarines did patrol off Vladivostok looking for any Soviet submarines likely to be moving south to visit us.[9] Any challenge by submerged Soviet submarines would have significantly changed the character of the war, to say the least.

The news elsewhere in the rest of the Far East did not look good with the continuing troubles in Indo-China. By mid-August, we were all puzzled about what was being written in the States about Korea. Anyone writing home asked, "How about sending us news clippings?" Despite the desperate times ashore, I felt I could write, "We will be up to snuff shortly as far as the Navy goes and may even begin to talk rotation." We seemed to have enough ships available, but that had been possible only by drawing upon the Atlantic fleet. At the same time, each ship in WestPac was still badly undermanned.

Endnotes:

[1] Tregurtha, personal letter to author.

[2] Hoyt (1984:194-196) for source and additional details. Cagle and Manson (157:69-70) discuss the details but are less emphatic about the crucial nature of the effort.

[3] Blair (1987:262).

[4] Blair (1987:319).

[5] The *Ozbourn*'s crew was divided into five divisions: Supply, Operations, Gunnery, Deck, and Engineering. Operations included Radiomen, Sonarmen, Mailmen, Yeomen, Personnelmen, and Radarmen. LTJG Thornhill, as 'O' Division Officer, was responsible to and acted as chief assistant to the Operations Department Head, LT Abbott. Any division

officer is responsible for training, advancement, condition of living spaces and exercises personal leadership with fifty or more enlisted men. Other assistants in the Operations Department included Custodian, Radio Officer, CIC Officer, etc. Most junior officers held multiple duty assignments in addition to these titles.

[6] *Mr. Roberts* appeared shortly after World War Two, first as a book, then as a long-running Broadway play, and finally as a movie. The titled character spends most of his Pacific war on a small supply ship defending the crew against the outrages of their tyrannical captain. Meanwhile the ship spends months traveling back and forth between two strange Pacific islands named 'Tedium' and 'Monotony.' After volunteering repeatedly for combat assignments, Roberts finally gets his transfer to action, only to be killed soon after his arrival. The book captured the monotony and the inter-personal relations of a shipboard existence, interspersed with moments of high terror – often somewhere else – that characterize much of life at sea.

[7] Even more than forty years later, former officers and enlisted men of the *Ozbourn* retain the feeling that she had, indeed, been a good ship on which to have served. Further, that feeling seemed to continue, no matter who was the captain or the executive officer. It was a 'happy' ship. Our big friend, the aircraft carrier, *Valley Forge* was similar and, thus, the sobriquet, 'Happy Valley.'

[8] Conning Officer is a term applied to the officer authorized to give steering orders to the helmsman at the wheel and speed orders to the lee helmsman at the engine order telegraph.

[9] Schrantz (1988).

INCHON

The Inchon Landing, 15 September 1950

When we returned to Sasebo in early September, plans for 'Operation Chromite,' the invasion at Inchon, were completed. Others called it 'Operation Common Knowledge.'[1] Security was poor in Japan and it was obvious something was about to happen. As soon as I saw *Ozbourn*'s copy of the Top Secret Operations Order for Chromite, I was dumbfounded to learn what was planned. Never having been confronted with anything Top Secret, how could I write home without saying something I shouldn't? On the other hand, in downtown Sasebo you had to be asleep not to sense that something was up. During this period, someone stole a copy of the Operation Order and delivered it to a spy ring in Japan, but they were unable to deliver it to the North Koreans.[2]

Mysteriously, the harbor emptied on 11 September and we were on our way to the Inchon invasion. On 13-14 September, several amphibious ships en route to the landing, were overtaken by the fringes of Typhoon Kezia. It was the second typhoon in several weeks, but *Ozbourn* missed its direct effects. The landing occurred 15 September, and the war took a different turn.

Given the state of forces available and the nature of the conflict on 28 June, or even on 28 July, an assault landing nearly one hundred fifty miles north of the Pusan Perimeter seemed impossible. Inchon, some twenty miles southwest of Seoul, was a small coastal town located on the convoluted Han River estuary. Ships used Flying Fish Channel to enter the small harbor. It had thirty-foot tides and the Channel could easily be blocked either by a single sunken ship or relatively few mines. It was also obviously far behind enemy lines.

To have sufficient assault forces for a contested landing at Inchon, the 5th Marine Regiment had to be reembarked from the Perimeter defense. It would then join up at sea with other Marines, some of whom were only just arriving from the States. There was no time for preliminary training as had happened during the Pacific war. The Inchon landing would depend on experienced naval and marine cadre.

Ozbourn again joined the destroyers screening the three Essex carriers (*Valley Forge, Philippine Sea,* and *Boxer*) which were preparing to launch air strikes. No Soviet submarines had been found in our operating area but there were plenty of them in Vladivostok, only five hundred miles north of Pusan. They posed an enormous potential threat to us as well, as well as to all ongoing resupply operations entering through Pusan for troops at the Perimeter. The UN appeared to have command of the seas except for mines. Command of the skies was less clear. Sneak air attacks on the Task Force seemed possible. As a deterrent, a combat air patrol (CAP) flew over the task force. A combat air patrol (TAR CAPs) also overflew the targets to preclude the attackers from being jumped while their attention was focused on the ingress, release, and egress.

In August USS *Boxer*, the third large carrier in the Pacific, was diverted to ferry a load of P-51 fighters needed to replace Air Force jets on close support missions. But by Inchon, all three Essex carriers then in the Pacific Fleet were available for air strikes from Task Force 77. Of the original twenty-four Essex carriers constructed for World War Two, only one additional Essex carrier, USS *Leyte*, was then in commission. It had been operating in the Atlantic and would arrive in early October. By September 1950 other Essex carriers started coming out of mothballs. Rotation of ships – carriers as well as destroyers –

needed to be planned. This was essential if ship repair and renovation, and changes in squadrons were to occur. Keeping three or four carriers continuously off Korea for several years would require additional carriers in the Pacific Fleet.

By Inchon, Task Force 77 had several cruisers for air defense. The anti-submarine screen now comprised twenty destroyers, each overlapping its sonar search pattern with those of its neighbors. The complete Task Force now traveled as a forward-moving circle, four miles or more in diameter. The destroyer screen was commanded by the senior destroyer squadron commander present who reported directly to the rear admiral in command of the Task Force. Should air defense be required, all ships would draw in close to the carriers and rely on Assistant Machine Gun Officers, like myself, for their defense.

Although Task Force 77 left Sasebo on 11 September, preliminaries had already begun on Sunday, 10 September, with air strikes made by Marine Air Groups from two smaller escort carriers, *Badoeng Strait* and *Sicily*. Their primary target was Wolmi Do, a small island attached by a causeway to downtown Inchon. A feint was also made at Kunsan well south of Inchon and much closer to the Pusan Perimeter. Kunsan had been an alternate landing site in earlier planning efforts.

On Wednesday, 13 September, a shore bombardment force of two US cruisers, two British cruisers and six US destroyers left the Yellow Sea, entered Flying Fish Channel, and proceeded toward Inchon. Nearing Inchon, they skirted a string of mines planted just outside the channel. The destroyers then anchored eight hundred yards off Wolmi Do to draw fire from hidden shore batteries. The mission was to destroy them before the actual landing occurred. Ships began firing at 1300 and immediately fire was returned from Wolmi Do. At 1306 *Collett* was hit four times causing five casualties; shortly afterwards, *Gurke* was hit twice. Finally the *Swenson* received a near miss that resulted in the death of a LTJG Swenson and the wounding of another officer. At 1400 the destroyers ceased firing, hauled up anchor and, under covering fire of the heavy cruiser *Rochester* and others, retired out the channel. On the way out, they destroyed mines. Shortly afterwards, Marine Corsairs returned to continue the aerial assault. The following day, five destroyers returned, fired for seventy-five minutes and then retired, unhit.

The assault landing on Wolmi Do began on the morning of Friday, 15 September, and was preceded by resumption of shore bombardment and air strikes. The Marine Third Battalion (Fifth Regiment) began landing at 0700 and by 0742 Wolmi Do was secured. At that point, falling tide interfered and the invasion of Inchon itself could not begin until late afternoon (1730) at next high tide. Red Beach, north of the causeway from Wolmi Do to Inchon, had a fifteen-foot seawall requiring scaling ladders. Landings at Blue Beach, south of town, required crossing extensive mud flats. Once ashore at Blue Beach, troops could block North Korean access to Inchon from the south.

Wolmi Do itself curved southward from the island end of the causeway and enclosed a small inner harbor. Because of tides, any LST beached at Red Beach to land vehicles and tanks would remain aground until it could be refloated and retract during high tide next morning. All other landing craft and small boats had to get in, unload and get out quickly or they also would be stranded overnight. There was sufficient time to land all the combat waves before tides fell, but once they were ashore nothing else could be brought ashore until the following morning.

Despite great hazards and risks, the Inchon landing was an unparalleled success and was the height of General MacArthur's popularity as a military planner. Marines landing at both Red and Blue Beaches advanced into the town before night-fall and, by Saturday, 16 September, had moved five miles toward Seoul. By that night, Kimpo Airfield outside Seoul had fallen. On the 17th, the Army's 7th Division landed unopposed and took up positions south of town before turning southward to meet UN troops soon to stream northward from the Perimeter. There were many success stories, even with luck involved, in pulling off this landing. No single event did more to restore military morale, which had been under considerable assault from 1946 onward, than Inchon and none must have felt more vindicated than the US Marines. Only a year earlier their demise had been under active review in Congress.

On 17 September, the 24th Division was repulsed attempting to break out of the Pusan Perimeter, but by 19 September, elements of NK divisions west of Masan had begun retreating. By 23 September, the NK army was in full flight northward to prevent being cut off by advancing UN troops. A US tank group, Task Force Lynch, broke out of the Perimeter and on 27 September joined the southward moving elements of the 7th Division just north of Osan. The NK Army had crumbled and was now in full retreat northward. On the same day, to the sounds of battle in the background, General MacArthur returned the city to President Syngman Rhee, timing the ceremony to coincide with the two months' anniversary of the initial NK invasion. On 28 September Marines completed the costly capture of Seoul.

The NK had used three invasion routes (east, west, and central) on their way south. These became their return routes north. The west and east routes were well blocked. The central route was not and many NK troops used it to escape north of the 38th Parallel. Of the hundred thousand NK troops invading only seventy thousand survived the Perimeter and less than thirty thousand reached North Korea. They left behind virtually all their heavy equipment and most of their arms. In sum, the North Korean Army's offensive capability had been reduced to near zero. As far as real estate owned, the Korean peninsula had been returned essentially to its divided *status quo ante bellum*.

Inchon and Ozbourn

We reached the carrier task force operating area some thirty miles west of Inchon by 14 September, and air strikes into the Inchon-Seoul area would begin at daylight. Jack Blonsick had the mid-watch in CIC and spent most of it listening to a radio exchange between members of MacArthur's staff on the amphibious force flagship, *Mount McKinley*, using the voice call 'Jehovah,' and someone in command central on the aircraft carrier, *Philippine Sea* responding as 'Onion Skin.'

Just after midnight Onion Skin was advised that General MacArthur would be expecting a gift of a naval aviator's leather flight jacket with his name and rank embossed on it at the earliest convenience. After a pause of twenty minutes, the carrier's duty officer came back, "Jehovah, this is Onion Skin—sorry, there are no embossing machines on board." Immediately came a response that someone ought to try harder on behalf of a General of the Army. Onion Skin's only answer was, "Yes sir, we have already begun." Another half hour and back came the response that the only embossing machine available was personal property. Jehovah was now getting testy and replied, "The General wants a jacket," followed by, "Jehovah, this is Onion Skin...will comply." Jehovah then said, "You will no doubt be able to emboss the General's name?" "Jehovah, this is Onion Skin, wait one...out." After some more time, "Jehovah, this is Onion Skin...yes, what should it say? We have the sailor who owns his own embossing machine present." "Onion Skin, make it say, General of the Army Douglas A. MacArthur III, General, Commanding United Nations Forces, Korea." At that point the sailor in charge of the embossing machine came up on the circuit and said "Sir, we can't get all that shit on one little leather tag." Back came, "This is Jehovah. Gen. MacArthur, USA, will be sufficient. Out." Perhaps this silliness was all planned to let those ashore know where Gen MacArthur was and what he would be wearing next day. All this transpired from 0000 to 0400 on the morning of the day before the Inchon landing while the carriers were only thirty miles off Inchon. It was still dark when flight operations commenced on the *Philippine Sea* and they dunked a pilot.

I was just being relieved on the bridge about 0355, when we were ordered to take up plane guard station behind *Philippine Sea*. As I had been relieved, it became a task for the oncoming watch and I left. The ship was darkened and I headed toward the bunk expecting nearly another hour of sleep before reveille, the ensuing Dawn Alert, and then the rest of a busy day.

As I walked through the wardroom, the 1-MC, the ship's announcing system, came alive with, "Now the Plane Guard Detail, Man Your Stations on the Double." When we trailed a carrier, we normally did not keep the boat crew at their stations. If they were needed, they would be there before the ship was in position to launch them for a rescue mission. As I pondered this, I suddenly realized that nothing ever was 'passed' on the 1-MC between taps and reveille except emergencies which probably meant a plane had already gone in the drink. While I was figuring all this out, the OOD passed an unexpectedly early

'Reveille.' A plane had gone into the sea. Not wishing to miss anything, I joined a growing crowd of volunteer onlookers out on the forecastle.

It was still pitch-black and I had lost my night vision by going through the lighted wardroom. As it returned, I could see a floating white flare bobbing in and out of sight because of a slight chop. The fantail watch on the carrier had dropped it to mark the approximate crash site. Within a minute, we also saw tracers coming from the water. The pilot was out of his plane and actively taking part in his own rescue. But the tracers were also coming from about two hundred and fifty yards away from the flare toward which we were now slowly moving. At the time of the crash, both ships had been moving forward at thirty knots but by now we had nearly stopped. We had to be careful not to run past anyone in the water. If we had to turn back on a recip- rocal course to find him, we might easily lose him in the dark- ness. Once people on the bridge saw tracers, the OOD and Captain turned on spotlights and suddenly there was the flyer with a lighted flashlight clipped on to his yellow Mae West jacket floating in a relatively flat sea.

Ozbourn backed down to a complete stop and put the motor whaleboat and crew of the plane guard detail in the water. After three tries, the engine finally started and they were underway. Within minutes they had him in the boat but as the whaleboat turned back toward the ship, its crew became blind- ed by our spotlights and nearly rammed us on their return. Just as they were about to collide, Ike Voles, the coxswain, suddenly realized they were sinking—by then the floor boards were awash. Someone had forgotten to put in the bilge drain plug before launching the whaleboat. As soon as Voles noticed it, he dropped the tiller and dove for the floor plates jamming a fist and his white hat into the drain hole. Somewhere in the bottom must be the missing drain plug which would be found later in daylight; instead the signalman in the boat crew was sitting on it. Normally, while the whaleboat was hoisted up and stored on the davits, the plug was out to allow rain and seawater to drain from the bilges. As Voles dove for the bilges, LTJG John Moriarty also dove for the tiller and swung the whaleboat away avoiding a collision. Meanwhile, sitting amidships through this demonstration of abysmal seamanship was a well-soaked ENS

left: ENS Myatt after his recovery by the USS *Ozbourn* on the morning of the Inchon landing. Myatt was flying a F4U off the USS *Philippine Sea*.

below: USS *Ozbourn* whaleboat crew returning from a fishing trip at Keelung, December 10, 1950. Engineer Atwood (*l.*) and Coxswain Ike Voles (*r.*).

Myatt minus his Corsair which was now resting on the bottom of the Yellow Sea.

Myatt had been launched as part of the night CAP that would overfly the Task Force while the dawn launches to begin the Inchon invasion were being made. Unfortunately he got a 'cold cat shot' or a reduced push from a hydraulic catapult, and it dribbled him and his Corsair off the flight deck. Instead of flying, he hit the water somewhere in front of the oncoming carrier. Even in a daylight version of the same accident, it would be hard to end up on one side or the other of the bow of the oncoming 27,000-ton carrier; in total darkness getting away from being run down was probably pure luck. By mere feet, he had first missed the bow and then the screws back aft while at the same time trying to get out of a sinking plane.

By 0800, *Ozbourn* had fed him breakfast, provided him a shower, and dried his clothes and revolver. Although tracers were not recommended as gun-loads for pilots were they captured, in this case they may well have saved his life. From him we also got our first real story of what was going on ashore. By 0805 we had sent him back by high-line to 'Carrier Baker,' as I described it in a letter home. We were still using the World War Two phonetic alphabet, *i.e.*: Able, Baker...Dog.. (now: Alpha, Bravo,...Delta). Later in Sasebo's 'O' Club, an *Ozbourn* officer could not buy his own drink if Myatt's squadron was in town.

By 20 September, we were still at sea and the long days were again getting old. In thirty-six hours on the 19-20 September, I had seventeen hours of watch standing, plus three hours of General Quarters in addition to ship's work. At least we had moved from 'watch on-watch off' into a 'watch in three' rotating forward. In CIC you could sit on a tall stool or lean on something. On the bridge 'standing a watch' meant standing at something between 'parade rest' and 'at ease' or in a semi-military lean resting against a plotting board or the splinter shield out on the open bridge. After four hours of that my feet burned and my back ached. By now, even CIC duty could be a pressure cooker with five busy radio circuits to monitor, formation changes by voice and flag signals to interpret for the bridge, and air and sea search radars to oversee. People from the staff or the CO and Exec were always popping in for ongoing situation reports.

At one point in a rejoining operation, we were two thousand yards off-station, a one nautical mile mistake. CDR Akers tended to be a lot more forgiving than CDR Freeman had been in similar screw-ups. Still no one liked to hear "Fireball, where are you?" over the voice radio. It was absolutely embarrassing if the voice was that of CAPT Roeder, our 'Commodore,' who might also be serving as Screen Commander. If the Commodore was on our bridge when that happened, he would pick up the radio hand-set and send a radio message to the skipper standing next to him, blasting us while the rest of the Task Force listened. Then Akers would use the same hand set to respond. This was the naval equivalent of being spanked in public. Shortly thereafter, the three officers on duty could expect to hear unpleasant things from Akers and deservedly so, but we did seem to be getting better.

The CIC officer and the JOOD would now change jobs sometime during their watches. I could spend two hours outside seeing what was going on or I could get in out of the sun and sit down in CIC on the stool. It was also a way of providing new Ensigns with more experience in both duty stations. Nothing Jack Blonsick and I had experienced as midshipmen during the three previous summer cruises had prepared us for duty as a JOOD or CIC Watch Officer in a war zone. One day, college ... the next, this. We were completely without training in either of these roles. It was 'on-the-job' or nothing. Night-time bridge watches under complete 'darken ship' meant reading signal instructions, operation orders, and doing maneuvering board problems while holding a red-lensed flashlight; I was easily disoriented in the dark.

When not on watch, I was still raiding the broom-closet library and had found a copy of *Raintree County* to read, as well as some short stories by William James and a novel by James Joyce. Reading concentration became wonderfully focused at sea. There are few distractions except those you couldn't control such as watches and GQ. Reading, movies, and sleeping were the best ways to 'get away' unless you got seasick. Any rough weather incapacitated my roommate, 'Pay,' who collapsed into his bunk in silent agony. He simply never got over being seasick and we received the fringes of yet another typhoon up from the South China Sea.

My writing home was interrupted by Raniag, the Filipino messman, coming down to announce early supper for oncoming watch standers. We then had a black Chief Steward's Mate, several black cooks, and three or four Filipino or Guamanian messmen to run the officers' mess, clean the officers' heads, and clean up the wardroom and our rooms. Filipinos or Guamanians could earn US citizenship by doing a hitch in the Navy, but they were never assigned anywhere but to officer messing and room clean-up duties. Newell, Gunner's Mate First Class was black and what he said went; he had been CruDesPac heavy-weight boxing champion several years before. Blonsick tried sparring with him but one of the officers thought that might be misunderstood. The Chief Steward was the highest rated black on board. There were other black petty officers but no black officers on board. I never even saw a black naval officer during my active duty years although at Cornell we had one black midshipman, 'Flash' Gourdine. He was an outstanding scholar as well as an athlete who would later compete in the 1952 Olympics at Helsinki. You had to be the best to be black *and* a naval officer then; average, like the rest of us, was not good enough.

By Saturday, 23 September, the next refueling day, we were still chasing carriers but we had also held captain's personnel inspection while underway. Everyone was out at Quarters, arranged by divisions on the main deck. The Operations Division stood on the starboard side aft of the midship's passageway, with everyone lined up with shined shoes, haircuts, and dress whites. It seemed incredible given what was going on ashore only thirty miles away or even only four thousand yards away on the carriers. There, flight quarters—launching and recovery—would be going on from before light until late in the increasing dusk. How odd we must have looked to other ships in the Task Force as we lined up—sailors in dress whites and officers in dress khakis—holding captain's inspection while planes were flying off to bomb and strafe somewhere near Seoul. We were embarrassed because other ships had seen us. It was like having to take piano lessons while everyone else was playing football in the park. "Nobody holds personnel inspections while underway in a combat zone with a Carrier Task Force," was the universal thought. This was indeed a strange war when the executive officer tried to keep up our peacetime appearances. By then we all were certain the inspections were Walter Ousey's idea alone.

Because of demands being made on the crew, the exec had started a morning rest period; now he seemed to want it rescinded. The crew wasn't working hard enough at their cleaning stations and the ship was beginning to get rusty and look bad. My ensign's assessment was that the crew was being pushed to the limit by all this stupidity. It was much more complex than that and I was not yet wise enough to become executive officer on a destroyer.

My feet and back complained from all the standing. I contracted a serious case of foot fungus that finally required soaking my foot in a bucket of potassium permanganate. I hoped a change of shoes might help and I had earlier written home asking for a set of brown loafers. Instead back came the suggestion that L.L. Bean's canoe shoes might be even better; without the Bean catalog I could only guess what they were.

I closed a letter asking dad to tell Doctor and Mrs. Partridge not to worry about their son, Pete. Doc had been my scoutmaster. Pete had just become the third member of Troop 406's Wolf Patrol to go on active duty—first Howard Johns, then me, and now him. His Marine Reserve unit had been called up in August but I was confident this would all be over before he ever got here.

The death of LTJG Swenson on the *Swenson* during the bombardment in Inchon stuck with me. First, it just seemed odd that anyone would be assigned randomly to a ship with the same name. Then as I kept thinking about it, I became somewhat obsessed by his death. Finally, someone convinced me Swenson had been killed in CIC doing exactly what I did, Machine Gun Control Officer. I never really knew what happened to him but, from then on, anytime we came under fire, I had this recurring nightmare of the same thing happening to me while, at the same time, I would be someone else standing there watching it happen. At least once it froze me like a horror-struck statue. Things are usually worse imagined than real.

Even worse, we still had not received a replacement for the burned-out bulb in the wardroom's movie projector. Given what was going on ashore, that certainly seemed trivial enough, but on board it meant we either kept the one working projector solely for use in the wardroom—and the hell with the crew—or we moved ourselves into the crew's mess to join them down there. Down we went, adding to the confusion. To top it all, the cigarette smoke was exceptionally dense. Nothing brought on smoking quite like sea stores cigarettes at seven cents a pack and nothing else to do with your money.

Lack of time to sleep continued to be a good safe topic to write about when there wasn't anything else to say; even more bitching about the poor executive officer made worse copy than the topic of sleep. My primary memory of the first three months after we were overseas was that of constantly being dead tired and never very alert.

While operating off Inchon, the Task Force routinely moved forward at fifteen knots. At those speeds you could quickly either get too far from or too close to land which required a change of course. Fifteen knots for four hours moved you sixty miles. This could be significant for returning planes, particularly if damaged. There was always the need to be positioned to provide sufficient space ahead for forward progress into the wind for launching daytime flight operations without moving the Task Force out of a useful recovery position. These moves might also require nighttime course changes by as many as twenty-five ships traveling without lights. They could also include a clockwise or counter-clockwise rotation of the screen. When that happened, the two bridge officers and the CIC officer had to keep track of who was who and where they were going by making grease pencil plots on radar scopes. The scramble resembled being in a football game played in total darkness. You made a mistake and you might either run into somebody or end up miles out of place. Even the latter wasn't a good choice. It might take hours to regain station by running as fast as possible to catch up and your absence in the screen might be the hole through which the submarine came.

Inevitably, these things happened after a long day. The captain, who had just dozed off, would have to be wakened from a nap in his bridge chair. He might even take the conn but the OOD and JOOD were still responsible for keeping things going. Those watches always went fast. When the maneuver was completed, everything would settle down to staring at the radar scope to get a range and bearing to the guide. Pandemonium would be replaced by an occasional, "add five turns and come right to course 273," from the officer with the conn as he got us back on station. Then it was boredom until the watch was over.

Down below, sonar would be pinging away but hearing nothing back—we hoped. Also down below, if it were the middle of the night, bakers would be making bread and pies for the next day; the snipes were working in the fire and engine rooms; people in Radio were copying the twenty-four-hour-a-day Fox Schedule filled with coded messages for ships and units throughout the Pacific—only rarely anything for us—while everyone else off watch was sleeping. Finally, the watch would be over with bed for an hour and then Reveille, Dawn Alert and the day began again with breakfast, Quarters and "Turn to, commence ship's work."

If you had the Midwatch (0000-0400) you would also be back on watch for the 1200 to 1600 and then the 2000 to 2400 on a one-in-three system. The 1600-2000 watch was split into two, the first and second dog watches to allow for watches to rotate forward. I hated days that started with the midwatch because I could never decide whether to try to sleep before the watch and thus miss the movie or hope I could fall asleep briefly after the movie. Inevitably, when I tried the latter, I would lie awake feeling sorry for myself not only because I couldn't force myself to sleep but also because the movie had been lousy. Suddenly, someone would come in the room waving a red-lensed flashlight into your face and whispering "Mr. Cole, time to go on watch." That was the task of the Quartermaster of the Watch—"never touch an officer while he was sleeping, just go back and yell again in his ear again and again until he gets up"—were the standing bridge orders. QMSN William Ellis enjoyed waking up officers, but somebody had to do it.

As soon as we knew when the next replenishment—oil and bombs—would occur, the word was passed announcing the time mail would 'close.' Get your letter written by then and it made the departing mail bag; miss it and the letter waited in the Supply Office until next time. With that, everyone started writing. The primary topic still seemed to be getting enough sleep but, after you tired of that, further bitching about the 'Battleship *Ozbourn*' and dumping on the executive officer was acceptable. Unlike World War Two, there was no censoring of anyone's mail but I self-censored. It took creativity to write over and over that things were O.K., the food was good, the movies were old, and still convey a sense of safety. People at home were really only interested in knowing that nothing bad had happened, at least up to time of writing, and I understood that. At least our mail was free because we were in the war zone.

Destroyer screening duty with Task Force 77 off Inchon seemed a strange mixture of peace and war. Our war centered more around the executive officer who was blamed for all the pettiness. Worse, the captain was accused of going along with him. "He was, after all, only supporting the exec," summed junior officer assessments. It seemed like the 'good cop-bad cop' routine, but even that wasn't very accurate. I wasn't as much interested in psycho-analyzing the executive officer as I was in keeping out of his way.

On 26 September, we received our first reserve officers by highline and I received letters from home postmarked 13 September or after. In the latest ones came clippings about Inchon from the Beaver or Pittsburgh papers. They moved around the wardroom table over coffee and were exchanged for clippings from San Diego and elsewhere. We read that the Russians were looking for an "easy way to back down." All were certain the Russians were behind the war.

From then on we received additional officers and/or enlisted men at nearly every replenishment. People first entered Japan by incoming ships, landing in Sasebo where they and their foot lockers or sea-bags were warehoused until time to be placed on an oiler, a refrigerated supply ship (reefer) or another ship in the replenishment force. When we joined the replenishment group, our new people were transferred by highline along with mail, movies, provisions, and spare parts. *Ozbourn* had been told to expect four or five more officers, several of whom should either be new ensigns or graduates from the V-12 Program at the end of the war who had became degree holders, ensigns and civilians nearly simultaneously. They owed somebody some ship time, but we were also picking up enlisted reservists with a lot of sea time from World War Two. These people, I assessed in a letter, had enjoyed "...a good deal and a chance to pick up some pleasure cruises in the summer and to get in on some of that free money for going to active reserve meetings once a week...."

That was a preposterous and not very charitable assessment of the Naval Reserve Program on my part. We desperately needed them and most of them had been extracted without mercy from home and families. Any complaint from a Regular to a Reservist would be met with "quit your bitching—you volunteered for this shit," or some more gentlemanly version of the same thought.

On 28 September, the Navy announced plans to call up an additional fifteen thousand reserve officers most of whom would be line officers needed for general ship duty. No doubt, some would come to us. When I first reported on board we had only three officers living in forward officers' quarters. By late September, we received our first two recalled reserve officers and bunking spaces began filling up. As more came on board we finally came close to wartime complement and then it seemed as if we had more than needed. There was a reason— underway training for people later to be transferred to ships emerging from mothballs.

We received an 'elderly' forty-two-year-old reserve mailman. During General Quarters he was to plot incoming air-raids for me on the reverse of a side-lighted plexiglass screen. If anyone in CIC wanted to see raids coming in, the mailman had to be able to write things backwards so you could read it from the front side. He just could not figure out how to write backwards. Finally he went somewhere else for GQ. Other reserve radarmen and radiomen came on board and quickly picked up from where they had been five years earlier. Equipment on *Ozbourn* was little different from that on 1945 destroyers. Even radio procedures had hardly changed, although their Morse code copying skills may have become a little rusty. We had to have help and the help had to be ready to go; we simply had neither the time nor people to train those not ready. Fortunately, they had been civilians no more than five years, they would not have been nearly as useful had the war occurred in 1955 instead of 1950. We could not have fought those ships without the influx of reservists during 1950-51.

I gradually acquired more jobs. I had been Postal Officer and recently had also become Assistant Communications or Radio Officer, which put me in charge of the radio gang. We had just received two reserve Radiomen First Class (RM1).

They were magnificent professionals. Both were superb and took over control of the radio shack watches without a hitch. One had been given only one day to sell his radio store before being ordered on active duty. Jack Blonsick, Jerry Solomon and I kept acquiring new jobs. At one point Jack had thirteen different primary duties and twenty-two collateral duties. We were certainly being integrated into the system.

We even acquired a reserve first class gunner's mate named Henry, whom I recognized from western movies. After his discharge in 1945, he had become a bit player in Hollywood 'oaters' and was usually the third guy back in the posse. LTJG Hadley, himself a former Gunner's Mate, immediately named him, 'Henry' Henry. No enlisted man escaped John's attention. Because naval tradition kept a barrier between officers and enlisted, most of the rest of us rarely knew an enlisted man's full name – not John.

GM1 Henry always volunteered for Shore Patrol and spent a lot of time lecturing kids on how to keep out of trouble. He was so dignified that had he been a senior officer planted on board to spy on illicit activity, no one would have been surprised. He once confided to John Hadley that he had an opportunity to return to Pearl and join a staff. John said, "go." Later when *Ozbourn* made a stop in Pearl, Henry didn't forget his shipmates and gunnery petty officers. The gunnery chiefs as well as senior officers, visited 'Henry' Henry in his beach front home. Well into the early 1960s, I could spot our dignified gunner's mate riding off into the sunset while I watched TV on occasional rainy Saturday afternoons.

If service to one's country required everyone to play, then the reserve call-up for the Korean War met that criterion. It represented immense personal sacrifice. Political muscle to avoid the call-up probably was exercised by some but experienced people from 'Henry' to the mailman had instead chosen to serve. I respected them for their patriotism.

President Truman had little choice but to mobilize reserve forces if he was to stem the tide in Korea and we were to keep *Ozbourn* steaming. Ninety-two National Guard and Army Organized Reserve units were called up, in addition to an additional twenty-five thousand from the Army's volunteer Reserve and inactive, involuntary Reserve. They yielded four Divisions

(28th, 40th, 43rd and 45th), two Regimental Combat Teams, twenty-two antiaircraft battalions, six engineer battalions and two artillery battalions. The entire Marine Corps Reserve of one hundred thirty-eight units and thirty-three thousand five hundred officers and enlisted men, one hundred thirty thousand from Air Force units and one hundred sixty-five thousand from Naval Reserve units were also recalled during this period.[3] During Korea, thousands of families were wrenched apart. Individuals were kept on active duty for two years before beginning to return to civilian life in 1952. By then, many reservists had six or more years of active duty, and some attempted to complete the twenty years needed for retirement. After Korea and the military was again downsizing, these were often the earliest released. Few returned to Reserve Units after that treatment.

Fankochi Point

On Wednesday, 27 September, Destroyer Division 112 (*Ozbourn, Knox, Hollister* and *McKean*), along with the light cruiser *Manchester*, Captain Lewis Parkes commanding, bombarded Fankochi Point (or Tungsan Got[4]) just northwest of Inchon. Five thousand NK troops were reported occupying the Point and our bombardment should keep them there to defend against another amphibious landing; if we killed any, so much the better. Much of what happened, I could only imagine as I stood over the radar repeater in CIC wearing a sound-powered telephone headset and listening to our bombardment described by those topside.

Ozbourn's main battery consisted of two center-line, closed, gun mounts each with two five-inch 38 caliber gun barrels (Mounts 51 and 52) located forward of the bridge, and one additional twin mount (Mount 53), aft of the deck house. We also had two 20-mm machine guns, one on each side of the 01 level below the bridge and three three-inch 50 caliber, radar-controlled mounts at near bridge level. Forward, the two three-inch single-barrel mounts (Mount 31 to starboard, Mount 32 to port) were on high boxes just abaft the bridge. Back aft, a dual-barreled mount (Mount 33) was perched on top of the after deck house and overlooked the rear-facing dual five-inch

Mount 53. I was connected by phones to the three-inch battery officers and to Jack Blonsick in charge of the 20-mm mounts. Jack could look over the splinter shield at his two machine guns or walk to either side of the open bridge and see the three-inch batteries forward in action.[5]

We had four gun or fire control Directors, which could be used to control different gun mounts. Control of the five-inch guns fell to the turret-like Mark 37 Director, equipped with range-determining optics as well as radar. It sat on top of the bridge just under the rotating radars on the tripod mast. Two Mark 63 Directors (radar-equipped and controlling Mounts 31 and 32) were adjacent to these two three-inch 50 mounts forward while the Mark 56 Director aft, was above and forward of the dual-barreled three-inch Mount 33 that it normally controlled. We could shift control between different Directors and all guns could either be fired using the Directors or locally by the gunner's mate in charge of the mount itself.

Ozbourn could provide an excellent defense against propeller-driven aircraft, but her mechanical computers and limited gun ranges were inadequate against jets. We could reach targets up to eighteen thousand yards with our five-inch mounts and provide covering gun fire for troops ashore as well as shelling targets of opportunity. We controlled our five-inch gunfire directly by telescope in the Mark 37 Director or indirectly by a trained naval gunfire spotter either ashore or in an aircraft. Destroyers had functioned as close-in artillery during and just after landings throughout the previous war and we had the capacity, if not the experience, to do the same now. We also had a variety of five-inch shells: anti-aircraft common, armor-piercing, anti-aircraft with proximity fusing, white phosphorus for smoke, and star shells for night illumination.

Although the five-inch mounts were protected from weather, the three-inch batteries were open to the elements and needed constant attention to control salt effects. A primary duty of gunner's mates (GM) and their seamen strikers was the constant care and attention of all mounts, no matter the weather. Our three-inch batteries seemed to need the most work.

Although the three-inch/50 mounts were radar-controlled and designed for use against aircraft, they could also be placed in local control, aimed like a garden hose and used against

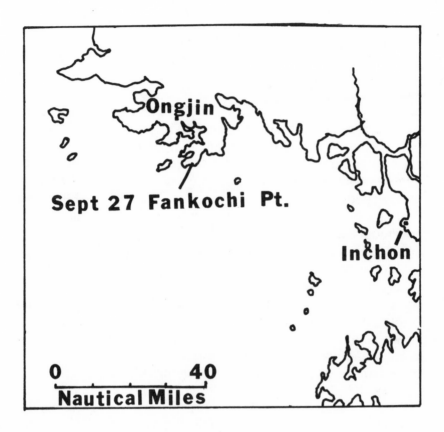

Figure 6. Fankochi Point.

shore batteries at ranges up to thirteen thousand yards. The three-inch shells were individually hand-loaded into a revolving chamber much like that of a pistol. Their rapid rate of fire (up to fifty rounds per minute per barrel) would cause a target ashore to disappear in a cloud of dust and smoke making it hard to know whether it had actually been hit. They made a lot of noise, kept everyone occupied, and were a comfort to those on board. Loaders had to watch the rotating sprockets as they grabbed at the shell; it was easy to load your hand along with a round.

Fankochi Point is about fifteen miles south of Haeju and had been bombarded earlier on 1 August. We left the Task Force at 0210 and traveled through a suspected mine field before reaching the coast and going to General Quarters at 0630. By then we had an orbiting Corsair from the *Boxer* as our spotter. When about three thousand yards offshore, we slowed to two knots and began bombarding the beach and the hill areas behind it. Unfortunately we were moving downwind. As each shell hit, it raised a dust devil which itself moved along with the wind and obscured the spotting. Those on our bridge could see people moving around in trenches and near some houses. On the first pass, we fired twenty-six rounds of five-inch in the vicinity of the houses, but we were too far away to see whether people near them had been hit. Then we fired thirty-six additional rounds at a nearby gun emplacement and the spotter reported its demise. By then it was time to turn back on a reciprocal course and firing stopped.

Beginning at 0744 we fired one hundred and forty-six more rounds at three additional possible gun emplacements. One target was a set of four caves from which artillery could be wheeled out. The other two were open emplacements. For this run we acquired a new spotter in a Corsair but, unfortunately, the pilot had no maps of the area and couldn't control our fire. At 0901 we finished shooting. Immediately, Corsairs from *Boxer* resumed the attack and reported receiving ground fire. From a distance of nearly two miles, the shoreline looked more like the San Clemente gunnery range off California. Most of us wondered if anything useful had happened but, without being provided an answer, *Ozbourn* got underway and the Division returned to the Task Force screen. After our departure, more Corsairs and Skyraiders from *Boxer* continued the attack on Fankochi Point.

While we slowly moved forward and fired Mount 53 aft, a depth charge, jarred free from our port depth charge rack, rolled off the rack and sank directly under our stern. Someone on my phone circuit could scarcely talk when he saw it happen. We all waited for an explosion of two hundred pounds of TNT under our stern. It never did. Apparently all depth charges were on safe as they were supposed to be. Had it exploded it would have had the effect of a mine. Depth charges are stored on sloping racks and kept from rolling off the ship by resting against a steel after-detente. It should keep them where they belong until someone operates the track control unit. The firing must have jiggled part of the release mechanism and we inadvertently rolled one straight down. Although embarrassing, it was not fatal. Whatever really happened, we seemed only 'sort of' at war.

After Inchon

After the recapture of Seoul on 28 September, the Marines next pursued North Korean remnants northward toward the erstwhile border while the US 7th Division swung south to reunite with armored units coming northward on the western roads, now emerging from the Pusan Perimeter. South Korean Marines chased the NK up the east coast and were the first UN unit to cross the 38th; other NK troops moved away from the Perimeter by escaping into southwestern Korea and were trapped behind lines as guerrilla forces. By 1 October, UN forces were poised along the 38th, awaiting a decision to move or not to move northward.

A very complex series of negotiations over what to do next was then underway between General MacArthur, the Joint Chiefs, the President, and the UN allies, about which we knew nothing. If winning meant total capitulation, as it had in World War Two, then the job was not finished and there was little to do but to move north. If winning meant only a return to *status quo ante bellum*, then it was already over. Thus, several alternatives existed ranging from stop at the 38th Parallel, move north to complete the reduction of the NK army with a restoration of the 38th Parallel as a guaranteed border, or a complete takeover of North Korea to bring about a forced reunification of NK and ROK into a UN-mandated single Korea. These strategic considerations were only now surfacing and were policy issues requiring UN concurrence. It was as if planning for Inchon had been limited to consideration of the military consequences, and little attention was given to political options should the war break open. Indeed, the choice was not a military but a political decision. Tell MacArthur what to do and make him do it.

We had gone from near failure to near success faster than the political system could handle. Military momentum had been restored. The US armed services, as the dominant element in the UN Command, had recovered from its 1946-50 doldrums and were poised on the mark for another unconditional victory—on to the Yalu![6] The Pacific War had been unconditional and that was the most recent experience on which to draw; the move north began.

Advice within the Washington leadership was divided; Secretary Marshall cautioned MacArthur to move northward against NK troops but *not* to announce it publicly. MacArthur chose otherwise by moving *and* announcing. By October, the Soviets had returned to the Security Council, exercising their veto. Thus, the only remaining recourse for further resolutions from the UN was through the General Assembly. The use of the General Assembly to authorize an armed invasion of a nation as a device to impose UN will and force unification through a non-free election seemed very unlikely.

MacArthur was behaving as if he misunderstood Washington's intent and the political need for caution. Further, nobody was paying much attention to very clear diplomatic signals then coming from China. Those signals advised that China considered North Korea a necessary buffer to Chinese sovereignty. No one seemed ready to infer that China, and not the Soviet Union, would be most outraged by any move northward into North Korea by UN troops.

Partitioning of Korea may have resulted from US-USSR action but the buffering played by North Korea to China was of far greater importance to China than to the USSR. Several outspoken hawkish Washington figures in the Truman Administration, such as Navy Secretary Francis P. Matthews, were replaced after making statements urging a 'preventative war,' but MacArthur was neither effectively muzzled nor prevented from moving north. The final results of this move, coupled with his continuing public pronouncements ultimately provided President Truman with sufficient grounds to justify MacArthur's removal in April 1951.[7]

Task Force 77 continued to operate in the Yellow Sea off Inchon from 14 September to early October before again returning to Sasebo. However, *Ozbourn* left early and on Sunday, 1 October, entered Inchon harbor and tied up alongside a tender. As we came up Flying Fish Channel, we entered the harbor sixteen days after the invasion and after twenty days at sea. I didn't know whether security was still an issue or whether we were allowed to write and say where we were. I finally let the family assume we were back in Japan although I wrote generally about getting off for some 'very' interesting pictures.

During the time we operated off the Inchon-Seoul battle area, people on deck continued to see floating bodies. Apparently, they were being thrown into the Han River and then washed out Flying Fish Channel into the Yellow Sea. I never saw any corpses until we went ashore in Inchon. We had a supply of 3.2 beer on board stored in a locked compartment. When we arrived, we divided the crew into two groups. First one, and then the other, went ashore on successive days for a beer party on Wolmi Do. I went along with the first group as Shore Patrol Officer. We landed around high tide across the causeway leading into the main part of town and had instructions to be back in two hours. We had to get in and get out while the tides were high.

Just as we came up the causeway, we confronted a NK corpse which had been dragged up and put on display; he was all arranged, dressed in a lumpy NK uniform, his arms akimbo with a clean shot through the forehead. Had someone sold opportunities to take pictures, they would have made a lot of money. I stared at my first violent death but could not bring myself to take his picture. Others did and there must be many sailors' scrapbooks and albums with pictures of him, whoever he was, lying on his back. One of the Marines warned us there might still be snipers in town. I couldn't tell whether they were looking merely for our reactions or whether it was true.

The town might not have been much before, but corpses or not, it was now a shambles. War at sea, out of sight of land, is very different from what it is ashore. It takes a little longer for the effects of shelling to disappear ashore. At sea, when the splashes subside, unless the ship is hit, it looks just the same—more flat water. A hundred of us semi-marched through town past the railroad station, where I took a picture of a burned-out locomotive in the Inchon railroad station. Later I would see the same shot in *Life Magazine*. We continued on past the burned and blown-out brewery at the back of Red Beach and then walked out the causeway to Wolmi Do, finally reaching the beer party site.

Someone started singing "Goodnight Irene" inside this bombed-out building. Whenever I hear that song, this strange day flashes back and I see sailors trying to get drunk on two cans of 3.2 beer while having a picnic at the bottom of this absolutely devastated hill the Marines had taken just sixteen days earlier. On our way out, we passed a Garand rifle with the bayonet jammed into the ground and a helmet on it. Someone said the owner was killed while wandering around Wolmi Do looking for souvenirs. Whether true or not, it kept us from wandering off sight-seeing on the tiny island of Wolmi Do and being killed with unexploded ordnance. It was far more effective than a 'Keep Off the Grass' sign. All too soon we returned to the ship. The next day the others did the same thing. I never again went ashore in Korea during the remaining six months we operated there as much of our remaining time was spent out of sight of land.

Jack Blonsick had more luck. He was ashore on a task that turned into a walking tour on the day MacArthur visited town. Jack watched in amazement as an exhausted ROK Marine was summoned out of a passing throng and the General presented him with the Bronze Star. Jack and I would have done nearly anything brave or stupid for the same honor.

Inchon then had a field hospital staging wounded Marines in from near Seoul on out to a hospital ship in the harbor. Jack wandered into a dressing station and saw the other side of glory—maggots in wounds of captured North Koreans as well as American amputations.

In stark contrast, our Inchon experiences included twenty days at sea with the carriers, interspersed with one day of shore bombarding. It seemed unreal and more like peacetime cruising than being at war. Only when we returned to Sasebo on 6 October, did I write that we had been in Inchon for four days and most of it was spent having radios and other minor items repaired. We missed all the excitement of the actual landings, the contested bombardments by destroyers, and even the cruisers or later, *Missouri*'s bombardment of the approaches to Seoul. Inchon became the second UN port in Korea and, although it had a far smaller capacity for handling shipping than Pusan, it was closest to Seoul and, thus, to the fighting along the 38th parallel. While we were there, the wounded continued to flow from the fighting around Seoul out to the hospital ship in the harbor, but the big guns of the cruisers and *Missouri* were silent. The fighting had progressed beyond their range.

While we were in, we were tied up, four destroyers abreast. That meant no more underway CIC or JOOD mid-watches and you could sleep all night unless you had the duty. Sea time was over when they turned on the overhead lights in CIC and secured the main engines. When they secured 'The Special Sea and Anchor Detail' and turned on the overhead lights in CIC, it always reminded me of having the lights go on in a fun house at a carnival—all its warts and bumps were there to see. All its mystery disappeared in a wink.

Outboard along our port side were two little wooden-hulled mine sweepers, USS *Partridge* (AMS-31) and USS *Osprey*. Sweeping mines had to be the most dangerous job in the fleet.

Later, I wrote while in that "unknown port" to let them know I was OK and that, suddenly after the recapture of Seoul, the war looked like it would end quickly. I mentioned we had been parked in the shadow of "that island" and talked about press releases concerning the wounded on board the destroyers hit off Wolmi Do. Privately, I wondered what it must be like reading about it in the newspapers and wondering when or if a telegram would come. Someone with family in San Diego received a letter including a clipping on *Wiltsie*'s exploits in July—nothing on ours, we hadn't any.

During the Inchon period, we received three new officers on board, ENS Charles Jarrett, and two LTJGs—Ray Eades and Robert Whitten. That was enough to put us on a watch in four. LTJG Robert Whitten, USNR, had graduated from King's Point Maritime Academy in 1947 and served a year on an oiler before being released. He was on training duty on a destroyer escort when the war started and volunteered for recall. He arrived by highline on 26 September. ENS Jarrett also volunteered. LTJG Ray Eades was recalled while working in South America.

By 2 October, at least four Class of '50 NROTC Cornellians were in Inchon. Ian Johnson was in harbor on *Southerland*; Don Darnell on *El Dorado* and Jim and I on two destroyers. There was not even an officer's club in which to hold a class reunion. Even Herb Nehring on *Manchester* was close by serving as an assistant in the gunnery department. That was nearly all of our class.

We got underway and on Saturday afternoon, 6 October, reentered Sasebo after nearly a month's absence. The PX at the Army Encampment in Sasebo was now doing a land office business. They were out of film. I had hoarded ten color shots and now wished I had used them all in Inchon. The best bargain was still ice cream at twenty-five cents a pint; they listed fifteen flavors but only had chocolate. Make your choice. This time in, the Chief Engineer and his new Assistant, Bob Whitten, came up forward looking into the possibility of adding a third bunk in one of the forward rooms. We were beginning to get crowded.

Endnotes:

[1] Acheson (1969:447).

[2] *Ibid.*

[3] Blair (1987:126-7). These figures give a sense of the magnitude of the upheaval in peoples' lives from July through September 1950.

[4] Fields (1960:218) provides this description of the bombardment on 27 September by *Manchester* and four destroyers, assisted by planes from *Boxer*.

[5] Refer to Figure 3 on page 17.

[6] The Yalu River forms the boundary between North Korea and Manchuria.

[7] Alexander (1986:228-248); Whelan (1990).

WONSAN

The October Landing at Wonsan

The decision as to what to do next seemed made by default, if not by reason. Movement north of the 38th Parallel began. There appeared to be little war left—only the rounding up of strays. It had to be nearly over. Shortly afterwards, on 9 October we got underway with the light cruiser, *Manchester*, and two carriers, *Philippine Sea* and *Leyte*, and twelve destroyers. The *Leyte* had just arrived from the Atlantic Fleet. This time the carriers went back to work supporting an amphibious assault landing on the east coast at Wonsan some one hundred and twenty miles north of the 38th Parallel.

Although the war seemed over and all organized NK units were now north of the 38th Parallel, how to end the war had everyone from the UN Security Council, the President, the Joint Chiefs, down to the local commander in a quandary. On 29 September, MacArthur advised Washington that he intended to invade the north between 15 and 30 October. On 3 October, K. M. Pannikar, India's ambassador to China, passed on to his home government that he had been told by China's Foreign Minister Chou En-lai that China would intervene if the UN forces crossed the 38th Parallel.[1] This diplomatic signal of Chinese intention was disregarded by US-UN planners as untrustworthy. By 9 October, the ROK Marines were now well north of the 38th parallel and were proceeding along the coastal route toward MacArthur's next amphibious assault site, Wonsan. It was the largest and best harbor on the North Korean east coast.

MacArthur's decision to sweep far north into North Korea inevitably changed the nature of the war. World War Two logic said: "You hadn't won a war until you owned the other side's capital and all their land." That meant on to the Yalu River and right up to the Manchurian and Russian borders. October became a rush northward with an excess of *ad hoc* activity. Because most of us involved assumed that capturing the other side's capital and all its land was the only way by which wars were won, it seemed reasonable to keep on going.

Whether or not we won should have been decided by whether aggression was contained and which side ended up in control of South Korea. This definition of 'win' would have been far less costly in terms of lives—both American and Chinese—had it made sense earlier. Too many of us took the opposite definition and continued to come up with the operative word 'lost' when we were asked later about the war.

Two Sumner class destroyers, *Brush* and *Mansfield*, hit mines on 27 and 30 September, while operating off North Korea. *Brush* had her forward hull opened, thirteen killed and thirty-four wounded; *Mansfield* had her bow blown off and twenty-eight wounded.[2] Neither ship was sunk but both were extensively damaged with plenty of casualties. *Mansfield* returned to the US for repairs. *Brush* limped back to Japan, was placed in a dry-dock in Sasebo where, later, several of us visited her. Resting on blocks was *Brush* with her starboard side exposing the extensive damage from running into a contact mine. She had a hole beginning at the waterline and just forward of Mount #51, large enough so one might drive a jeep in one side and out the other. Had she been *Ozbourn*, Pay, I, and our room would have been obliterated in the blast. Between having fiberglass in my bunk every time *Ozbourn* fired her forward batteries and seeing what damage hitting a mine would do, I became quite convinced I wanted to move to After Officers' Quarters. I little considered that a mine could hit anywhere else.

Seventy-three US vessels became casualties during the war, most due to hits by shoreside artillery, but five were sunk by mines. Three additional destroyers were to be mined, including *Barton* which hit a floating mine ninety miles off the coast while screening Task Force 77. The ability of mines to keep a fleet off-shore was one of the naval lessons from Korea.

Four American mine-sweeps were sunk. The last was *Partridge* which had tied up alongside us in Inchon and with whom we had exchanged movies, given their crew ice-cream, and made visits to respective wardrooms. You could walk along our main deck and look down to see this tiny thing way down there. Something is really small when it is "way down" from the deck of a destroyer. I had the midwatch in CIC on 2 February 1951 when the message about her sinking came in; a pall descended for the rest of that watch. We came to know her officers and men as people. Mines were a serious concern and I was scared of them.

Wonsan — The First Time

By Thursday, 12 October, we were in the Sea of Japan with the carriers awaiting the landing at Wonsan. We had just recovered from another air raid alert that turned out to be friendly. The amphibious assault at the port of Wonsan would again use X Corps (1st Marine Division and 7th Army Division). When ashore this time, their mission would be to cross the peninsula east to west and then block all northward flow of NK troops, finally capturing the North Korean capital, Pyong-yang. In addition to throwing a line across the peninsula, the capture and possession of Wonsan would provide another excellent port facility.

As late as 2 October, Marines were still heavily engaged just north of Seoul but, by 15 October, they were being combat-loaded out of Inchon, first to be ferried south out of the Yellow Sea, and then around the southern tip and northward in the Sea of Japan to Wonsan. Several other east ports also existed in North Korea that might be suitable as alternative landing sites. The port of Hungnam, fifty miles further north, or the beach at Iwon, seventy-five miles north, had both been proposed as alternate landing sites; only Hungnam was reported to be heavily mined.

One plan split forces, putting the 1st Marine Division ashore at Hungnam further north and the Army's 7th Division at Wonsan. Unfortunately, only enough landing craft existed to support one assault landing. In the other plan, the First Marine Division would land at Wonsan and the 7th Division at or near Chinnampo on the west coast, the sea port serving the North Korean capital of Pyong-yang. The North Koreans were falling back faster than orderly plans could be laid to create an assault landing behind them. This fiasco has been described as "X Corps...all dressed up..with no rational place to go."[3]

To make matters worse, all three ports (Chinnampo, Wonsan, and Hungnam) were found heavily mined and the Navy could not remove them fast enough. In addition to using all available steel and wooden hulled mine sweeps such as *Partridge*, UDT swimmers also found and destroyed mines. Even PBMs flew missions dropping bombs to trigger sympathetic explosions of planted mines. Most of these techniques could not substitute for the standard mine-sweeping practiced during World War Two.

The Navy forgot about mine warfare following World War Two. In 1947 MinePac was dissolved because of a financial retrenchment and, by 1950, only three senior officers with mine warfare experience remained with CincPacFlt. During World War Two, mine warfare required up to 550 ships in the Pacific Theater. In June 1950, one steel-hulled sweep and six wooden sweeps were in commission in the Far East. A second steel-hulled sweep was in standby condition in Japan. Four high-speed minesweepers (*Doyle, Carmick, Endicott,* and *Thompson*) arrived in WestPac by October, but these still were not enough to sweep three major invasion sites. In addition to needing more ships, the Navy had few trained people. Nearly all officers and men in mine warfare during the Second War had been reservists and by 1950, they were long gone. Mine-sweeping had nearly become a lost art. The Navy was not prepared to handle mines in Korea and mine warfare was dangerous work.[4] Nonetheless, on 2 October, Joint Task Force 7 was formed for the assault on Wonsan and the landing was scheduled to occur on 20 October, after mine clearance had been completed.

The sweepers had a daunting task facing them. The field at Wonsan alone was later estimated to contain from two thousand to four thousand mines and included contact, magnetic, and pressure mines. It was a very sophisticated field and its clearance would take far longer than expected. Early during the Wonsan clearance, USS *Pirate* and USS *Pledge*, the two 180-foot steel-hulled sweeps, were sunk by mines. Despite every sweeping effort, the planned D-Day of 20 October could not be met. By the time the US Marines were able to land, the ROK Marines had already moved north along the east coast and captured the city by land. Even Bob Hope was able to land at the Wonsan airport before the Marines could get ashore. Two ROK mine-sweepers were also destroyed before Wonsan was declared open.[5] The Wonsan field has been described as the largest, most dense field ever set. It would have been foolhardy to bring in troop transports and attempt a landing until paths were cleared.

A meeting between General MacArthur and President Truman occurred on Wake Island on 15 October. At that meeting, MacArthur was awarded his fifth Distinguished Service Medal for his success at Inchon. MacArthur expressed his belief to the President that NK resistance would be over by Thanksgiving and that the Eighth Army could begin to withdraw to Japan no later than Christmas.[6] He also advised Truman that since the Chinese had not come to the aid of the NK forces during the Perimeter period they would not come to their aid now. Furthermore, although any response from Soviet air might be substantial, he considered the Russian ground capability to be quite limited. Apparently, nobody mentioned Russian submarine capability and what they might do to the UN supply routes extending to the Korean peninsula.

MacArthur's assessment concurred with that then held by most Washington analysts, including the CIA. Although their meeting ended cordially, both men continued to dislike and distrust each other and it would not get better. On the same day, 15 October, elements of the Chinese Fourth Field Army crossed the Yalu River into northwestern North Korea, beginning the buildup that would reach thirty divisions and as many as three hundred thousand troops.[7]

At home, on 17 October, the *Beaver Valley Times* announced that one hundred and four men would be inducted from the County in October and that the Beaver Board's quota was thirty. By 24 October, however, the editor was writing,

"Now that the war in Korea is rapidly moving into its final stages, the United Nations should lose no time in taking quick and decisive steps to bring an end to...fighting...in Indo-China." There was much more left to Korea than he realized and he was a little premature about Indo-China, or Vietnam as we would come to know it.

Wonsan was finally sufficiently cleared on 25 October to allow the First Marines to make an administrative landing, this meant no one was shooting back. Wonsan had already fallen to the South Koreans. By then Pyong-yang had also been captured and so, instead of moving west, the Marines moved north and northwestward toward the Manchurian border. This would set the stage for the Chosin Reservoir and the Hungnam Withdrawal, among other upcoming December events.

During all this, *Ozbourn* had little to do except screen the carriers. We also now had enough officers and men to go into a four-section watch. Doc Ketcham had taken over the unofficial task of listening to whatever news came over the wardroom radio. Unfortunately we lost our 'news listener' when he was temporarily transferred to one of the other destroyers which was awaiting arrival of a Hospitalman Chief. Hospitalmen or Corpsmen were in short supply because they were also assigned to Marines as field medics. On board we had one Chief Hospitalman and a petty officer, plus the doctor. A ship without a Chief needed Doc more than we did. He could always return in case we had an emergency requiring an operation. When we were underway, we could always transfer a patient to a cruiser or carrier by Stokes stretcher or breeches' buoy if someone needed surgery or hospitalization.

Our income taxes went up. Some wondered why we should have to pay taxes for a war as well as fight it. There was scuttlebutt that servicemen would be getting a fifteen-hundred-dollar exemption plus an additional one hundred dollars per month while in a combat zone. Dr. Howard Evans, my old laboratory instructor, was now teaching at the Cornell Veterinary School and wrote that there were *no* Marine reservists left in the Ithaca area. However, most Navy, Army, and Air Force veterans in the region had not yet been recalled. He and other junior faculty, graduate students or teaching assistants, as well as World War Two veterans, were still there.

Dad wondered whether going up Flying Fish Channel into Inchon was as described in the *Saturday Evening Post*. No. By the time we did it, it was as tranquil as a trip on the Ohio River. Everything looked better; even my foot fungus improved. On 17 October, we were still going around in circles in the Sea of Japan and I was in a rush to write something before we met the 'mail buoy,' which arrived one day earlier than planned. Unfortunately, when I used my typewriter on our desk, the carriage was athwartships rather than fore-and-aft. All ship's property typewriters on board are mounted fore and aft so the rolling doesn't affect them. When I did it my way, the carriage spring worked either with or against the roll of the ship. When the ship rolled in the direction opposite to the carriage's forward motion, it just stopped and printed one letter on top of the previous; in the other direction the carriage raced across creating blank spots on the page. My typewritten letters looked awful, but years of piano lessons paid off in typing speed, if not accuracy.

I could see oncoming winter weather as the days were now overcast with cooler air and water temperatures. Some of us came down with 'sea colds' and the never-ending quest for more sleep went on unabated. Also, the *Stars and Stripes* informed us about more trouble in Indo-China. The ship received several copies of the Armed Forces newspaper with the incoming mail on replenishment days. Usually one vanished to the Division staff and the other into the wardroom. How did the crew get theirs? Bob Hope had visited the *Missouri* while she was off Wonsan. We could see his helicopter off in the distance going from somewhere to someplace else. *Ozbourn* was too small to have a helicopter land him on board.

Rumors were that we should be back in San Diego by 14-15 February followed by time in the shipyard. During this time, we would receive a thirty-day leave period which would be split so that each half of the crew could have fifteen days. That meant Christmas overseas. Where could we find Christmas presents even if we got back to Sasebo? Grandmother Cole wanted Japanese flower seeds for Christmas—impossible. Some of the sailors had found souvenirs the last time in, so there had to be something besides bars and whore houses. We were paid in occupation money—paper from ten cents to ten dollars which was legal ashore at $1 = 360 Yen; the black market rate ashore for real dollars was much different. I was gradually overcoming culture shock and no longer expected a Sears in downtown Sasebo; only the PX approached that.

On Sunday 22 October, we were still in the Sea of Japan. The Marines had obviously missed their scheduled D-Day because of the mine sweeping problems inshore. Rumors were building about breaking up Task Force 77; our work seemed nearly finished. The events in Wonsan harbor with mines and then the two destroyers mined late in September also required some explanation at home. Some of these details made it into the *New York Times*, but to a far lesser degree into the *Beaver Valley Times*. All I knew was that we still couldn't get the Marines in.

We operated in deep water, free from any chance of running into moored mines. On the other hand, floating mines, either deliberately launched from small boats or mines that had broken free from their moorings and not equipped with automatic destruct mechanisms were a problem anywhere. Some three hundred mines were sighted floating free during this period and were a definite menace to any ship, combatant or neutral, day or night. In reply to questions from mother about "being in action," I went back over the Fankochi Point shoot and, except for also shooting aircraft belly tanks to sink them when we found them, we really had done nothing at all. In response, came a box of books and magazines—even a cake was en route.

Movies of the past several days included *Twelve O'Clock High* and *Come to the Stable*. We even had a matinee performance because it was Sunday. In addition to not knowing how mail ever got to us, I never understood about the distribution of movies. There seemed to be an endless string of different ones in the pipeline. We would send three or four over to the oiler during replenishment and, suddenly, back would come the same three or four we had returned the last time; from then on, we couldn't get rid of them. Whenever we went alongside a ship underway we requested an exchange, but it was not considered good form to ask what you were getting. Half the time we didn't want the other guy to know what he was getting either. It was like a game of Old Maid played at sea. If something was good it might get held over for a few days but, really, how many times do you want to see *Twelve O'Clock High?*

When we refueled, took on provisions from 'reefers,' or rearmed from ammunition ships twice a week, we were always in the same general area. Mail and other things easily found us. It was much tougher being on the minesweepers and other little ships that move around on a twenty four-hour notice. Someone in a 'movements of ships' office figured out where they would be next, but by the time their mail arrived, they had moved elsewhere. There were worse reasons for being on minesweepers, but that one sounded good in a letter home. Bitching about the mail had finally pulled ahead of bitching about the executive officer in letters home; sleep seemed to be dead last.

On 25 October, the day the Marines finally landed at Wonsan, we were still running around in circles in the same place chasing aircraft carriers. From all I could tell from the intelligence reports, our troops were within fifty miles of the Manchurian border. I had this mental image of a single line of soldiers and Marines holding hands from the Yellow Sea to the Sea of Japan across Korea and moving northward at so many miles per day. Once you get away from land and out to sea, it all tended to become something drawn in green or yellow ink, like a map in an atlas. In actuality, units were all over the place mopping up, moving forward, or standing by. It was a confused time ashore, and so were we. Although carriers continued to launch strikes, they were on a reduced schedule because the situation ashore was so confused. It would be too easy to bomb advancing UN units by mistake. There didn't seem to be anything to shoot at or a clear target to bomb.

We finally got Doc Ketcham back. He resumed his duties of listening to the radio and almost immediately reported that Al Jolsen had died in San Francisco. I was lucky with the mail and service now took only seven to ten days. It took our two reserve radiomen nearly two months to cross the Pacific and find us. We had a mail bag full for them by the time they arrived. The rumor mill remained hard at work. The latest was that when TF 77 was broken up, all the carriers and individual destroyers would be moved into various Japanese ports for periods of liberty and ship upkeep. There they would remain awaiting conditions to become complicated again.

The next rumor was that *Ozbourn* and the rest of the Division would be moving south to Formosa. By now the weather up north was getting quite cool and the foul weather gear issued in San Francisco was necessary on the bridge. A trip south would be nice—back to warmth. We had already had some snow.

Word from home listed a long line of friends being drafted. I had once wondered whether being in the Navy and splitting undergraduate from graduate school would hurt. That no longer mattered. The draft meant that anyone who had gone directly to graduate school would probably be drafted out of it or would be called up right after graduation. Then I wondered whether others might not ever go and, thus, forever be two years up on me and my career. Somehow that didn't seem fair. Although I had a nice bed and three warm meals each day, I still had not been convinced to make the Navy my life's work.

After chasing my life's goals around the room one more time, it was now time for supper and a movie called *Molly X.* We had reached the bottom of the barrel and would never get rid of that dog; some oiler would keep sending it back again and again to us. The book, *Kon Tiki,* plus some paperbacks, had just arrived from home and they would make the rounds of the ship in time to come. My librarian aunt, Elizabeth, was hard at work for *Ozbourn* and together we would gradually overwhelm the broom-closet library.

We had just heard that the President would probably sign the new income tax remission bill for servicemen in the 'fighting zone.' Everything up to two hundred dollars earned per month would be tax free. I was now running out of cliches and finally wrote, "I find it hard to believe it's almost November. Where has the summer gone?" It had indeed been a very busy four months.

We returned to Sasebo Monday, 29 October, for another limited tender availability period alongside the destroyer tender, *Hamul.* This time we had the boiler tubes cleaned and ship's company did some topside chipping and painting. I had always thought topside painting was just Navy make-work designed to keep sailors busy until they were all needed at General Quarters. Actually, a ship that has been underway continuously and exposed to the elements in the Sea of Japan for a month looks pretty rusty.

Force 77 now had four Essex class carriers: *Valley Forge, Boxer, Leyte,* and *Philippine Sea,* plus several cruisers. In mid-July we had only *Valley Forge.* By August *Philippine Sea* had arrived, next came *Boxer,* and finally *Leyte,* in time for Wonsan. There were two jeep carriers, USS *Badoeng Strait* and USS *Sicily,* with Marine Corsair squadrons on board that flew close ground support for the Marines. We had never worked with them but from the newspaper clippings we received, everyone back home knew all about them. Shipboard attitude could be summed up as "It looks as if this show is over...."

The rumor was correct. DesDiv 112 was going south to join Task Force 72, the Formosa Patrol. Mail service from Formosa would be lousy. All we had heard from other destroyers that had been there was, "If you think Sasebo is awful, wait until you see Keelung." I was going to miss life's simple pleasures like ice cream at the Army PX. There was so much Navy now in Sasebo that the Army had begun to ration things; when the Navy came in, we really cleaned their shelves.

When we came in, I ran into Jim Tregurtha in the Officer's Club. He was bemoaning the burden put on a destroyer when you have the Squadron staff on board. The same Navy Captain was both ComDesRon 11 and ComDesDiv 111 and he was senior to ComDesDiv 112. I visited *Wiltsie* and they were really overloaded with staff officers. ComDesRon 11 had been screen commander during much of the last time out and the communications, CIC, and cryptographic duties were very tiring. Jim's complaints about overwork and being crowded all sounded very familiar but it made time speed along even though people became short tempered. By now we had enough officers on board to go to a one-in-six watch which meant only one four-hour watch per day. You could almost forget what you were supposed to do at that rate. That was a drastic change from the twelve hours, or worse, of watches per day before Inchon.

I received a big box from home just in time for Halloween; everything got through fine except the cookies were broken and the cake squashed. Whatever came—pepperoni, cheese, etc., would go up to a midwatch party in CIC some boring night when the Commodore was not likely to intrude. To keep busy, I enrolled in a German reading course from the University of Chicago which required translating passages and then mailing

Korea Remembered

the results to some poor soul in Chicago who would correct them and return them with a grade. I was anticipating boredom in the Straits of Formosa since we would be operating either in a two-ship extended search pattern or alone, either of which would be quite easy after the carriers.

Charles Jarrett was the new ensign from Pittsburgh. At six-foot-three and two hundred twenty pounds, he had been on the Williams College football squad. John Hadley immediately began calling him 'Tiny.' Tiny graduated early from high school, joined the Navy at the age of 17, saw the end of the Okinawa campaign, and then spent time in occupied Japan before going to college. He completed his Bachelor of Science in slightly over three years, received a reserve commission, volunteered, and arrived in time for Inchon. There were others from western Pennsylvania and vicinity. A Radioman First Class came from New Castle, several sailors were from Parkersburg, West Virginia as well as a Radarman Third Class from Indiana, Pennsylvania.

Everyone expected that once this tour in the Straits was over we would be sent back to the States around the first of January. At home, Pete Partridge was doing his final stateside training. Were he to get over here, all he would do would be occupation duties because things were just about over in Korea. I remembered how I had felt when the Pacific war had ended and I had missed it. I hadn't seen anything here but I was now certain I hadn't missed a thing. Perhaps Pete would feel the same.

By 1 November we were in Sasebo wondering when the war would be over. I had been shopping at the Sasebo stores and found enough to send home three boxes of Christmas presents. Either they had been there all along or had just come to flower along with the arrival of the fleet. I suspect the later.

Our war record to date included four sleeves shot up by my starboard three-inch battery, three belly tanks found floating with gas in them that the Navy didn't want adrift, one large glass ball net float that someone thought was a mine, one rescued pilot, one pillbox, two trenches, three wooden shacks, and a latrine. That didn't seem like much.

Endnotes:

[1] Cagle and Manson (1957:117).

[2] Field (1960:217).

[3] Blair (1987:347).

[4] Cagle and Manson (1957:107-164). See pages 125-6 for details on the retrenchment of 1945-50. Blair (1987:343-345), for further details on Mac-Arthur's strategy and the Navy's ability to respond. See Lott (1959), for details of mine sweeping operations around Japan and in Korea before and during the Korean War.

[5] During the later days of the Vietnam War, the port of Haiphong was closed following the planting of no more than forty mines by US naval aircraft. It is the potential presence of mines, often more than their shear numbers, that controls the decision not to move ships through a field.

[6] McCullough (1992:796-7; 800-808). At the meeting, General Mac-Arthur also privately apologized to the President for his embarrassing public comments made in August to the Veterans of Foreign Wars.

[7] For a much more detailed review of the political activity within Washington, consult Whelan (1990), and McCullough (1992). Much of what was going on to redirect the purpose for the war was obviously unknown to those fighting it in Korea.

THE FORMOSA PATROL

On Friday, 3 November, *Ozbourn* and *Knox* sailed from Sasebo for Keelung, Formosa to begin a tour with the Formosa Patrol. The Patrol, Task Force 72, came into being shortly after Truman's 27 June proclamation and was now headquartered on the light cruiser, *Manchester,* in Keelung harbor. Various cruisers, replenishment ships, and several destroyers had come and gone; it was our turn.

A patrol squadron of PBM seaplanes, a support ship based in the Pescadores Islands southwest of Formosa, and a second squadron of P2Vs, land-based patrol bombers, based in northern Philippines were also part of the Patrol. There had also been several very secret submarine patrols gathering military intelligence in the Straits unbeknownst to either Chinese government.[1]

The Patrol's mission was to prevent hostile traffic moving from mainland China to Formosa or from Formosa going back to the mainland, either of which might retrigger the civil war. Any invasion of Formosa from the mainland would inevitably use a large number of motorized junks. If the Chinese Navy or any fleet of junks went to sea the Patrol had to learn about it.

Once US intervention in Korea had occurred, the US simultaneously needed to signal that it would also militarily oppose any Formosan invasion attempt. Likewise, Chiang's Kuomintang Army had to understand that the US did not want the war used as an opportunity to return to the mainland. To send these messages during the first six months of the Korean War would stretch available US forces to the limit. The need to keep a strategic reserve in the Atlantic to oppose expected Russian aggression in Europe, meant, among everything else, that the Formosa Patrol would have few ships with which to patrol a lot of water. If an invasion began, the several US ships and patrol bombers then on patrol could only serve as a trip wire to detect Chinese activity.

PBMs and P2Vs conducted daily patrol runs up the Straits looking for changes in Chinese fleet dispositions or for large collections of junks while US destroyers steamed up and down the Straits on routine patrols as well as responding to visual sightings from the aircraft. The Nationalist Chinese forces on Formosa were still raiding Red Chinese-held coastal islands off the mainland as well as conducting resupply missions to the Nationalist-held islands close to the mainland such as Quemoy and Matsu. Nationalist lighters and small trawlers convoying these troops and supplies to the islands departed from the pier just forward of US destroyers docked in Keelung. I had no idea what those Nationalists were doing or where they were going. These forays would later lead to more serious tensions during the Eisenhower administration. An invasion from the mainland seemed very likely.

We arrived in Keelung early 6 November; the trip south had been somewhat rough with off-and-on rain squalls. We practiced depth charge firings—my first experience with depth charges that exploded—while on *Ozbourn*. Before leaving Sasebo, the officers had been told to expect social activities and that the Chinese Nationalists would provide dances and trips to keep the crew occupied. I was looking forward to something beyond the monotony of days with carriers; by then, even the evening movies had paled. I was also pleased to be away from the tension of working with the carriers. Even when you weren't being personally responsible for the safety of everybody on board, someone else was and it was not easy to get away from the pressure. We all felt the tension after coming off watch while working with the carriers. Sometimes it took hours to get to sleep after coming off the 'high' of a night watch either on the bridge or in CIC. Jerry Solomon complained that he awoke hearing ranges and bearings to the guide in his head after a busy night watch and wondering whether he still had *Ozbourn* on station. It was difficult to let go.

I wrote Dad that we had qualified for the China Service Ribbon because of our patrol status, but we were being tossed around by little understood forces that only a future historian could unravel. We could make little sense of what was going on by reading snatches of confidential and secret dispatches; you wondered who was doing what to whom. This conflict was being controlled by rules of war far different from those governing the total war of 1941-45. I subjected Dad to questions to which there may have been no answers. Why were we here? Who were we helping? Who wore the white hats? And, finally, back again to why were we here? It was an endless circle. If everything went as planned, we would be back in Japan about Christmas, in time to be rotated out of WestPac and returned to the West Coast where I knew the rules.

Intelligence reports from Korea intercepted for the Commodore were disturbing. At one view, the war was running down and, at the same time, other troubling signals were in the air. The US was involved with Japan, China, Korea, and Formosa. I wondered whether we knew much about what we were doing with these foreign cultures. Were we trying to make them look like us? Were we expecting them to play by our rules or what? The USS *Ozbourn* was in the middle of a cultural-cum-communism issue that would still be going on forty years later. In our effort to roll back naked aggression in Korea, we needed to be very careful not to get plastered onto a Chinese tar-baby with which, no matter what you did, things got worse. Finally, nothing you did made any difference. At the time, the shooting war seemed far easier to solve than these questions but in time, it, too, would be just as difficult.

I barely made the mail going back to Sasebo on board the destroyer we had just relieved. She was due to get underway in half an hour and we were due for quarters in eight minutes. Many questions and not much time. All we knew was that the pattern had been to patrol the Straits of Formosa for three days and then return to Keelung to spend four days in port.

Across the lifelines came word—liberty in Keelung wasn't bad—just don't eat the food or drink the water because of dysentery. Keelung was warm and muggy; the monsoon season had just begun and we could expect a soaking every day. The day before they had a three-hour downpour which brought even the dockside basketball game to a halt. I hated basketball but it was to become our standard form of exercise; on top of everything else, nobody had sneakers and we played in leather shoes. Formosa was going to be an experience.

A Typhoon in the Straits

We hadn't been in Keelung a day when a PBM seaplane crashed in the Straits of Formosa and we made an emergency trip out to look for the crew. We left Keelung at 1720 6 November and, with *Manchester, Hollister,* and *McKean,* formed a search line. *Knox* had already departed to occupy the southern patrolling station. There had been some earlier attacks by Red Chinese P-51s on PBMs. This PBM had not been attacked but, if the aircrew had survived the crash in the Straits, finding them would be like looking for a needle in the haystack and, further, the weather was turning bad.

By noon 8 November we were close to the southwestern tip of Formosa in the vicinity of the crash site and had begun to move northeasterly through the straits. However, we were also feeling the effects of Typhoon 'Clara' as it approached the east coast of Formosa. Finally, as seas built and northeast winds increased, we had to slow and choose a more 'comfortable' course. By 1635 the seas were so bad the search was discontinued. Then, at 1803, we lost powered steering control when a load of seawater crashed into the after-steering compartment and shorted out the electrical steering motor. After that, it was steering by hand. Normally, when the helmsman on the bridge turned the wheel he actually activated an electric motor that turned the twin rudders left or right. Without power assistance in after-steering, two sailors had to move them by hand; in a typhoon that is hard work. Meanwhile, as the seas became progressively worse, we slowed to three-and-a-half knots, which was little more than steerageway. At least, that would reduce incessant pounding as the bow rose clear of the water and then slammed down into the trough; it would also be enough to keep us heading safely into the seas. Life in forward officer's became a series of crashes in a free-falling elevator mixed with blanket tosses by giants; it was impossible to sleep and stay in the bunk.

This typhoon, as hurricanes in the South China Sea are known, had developed somewhere in the southeast Pacific, moved west and then northwestward, along a clockwise path akin to that followed by hurricanes in the Atlantic. Typically, typhoons curve northward out of the South China Sea and then northeastward towards Japan. Our only information on storm location came by radio from Fleet Weather advisories. They originated from other ships at sea in the affected area or from the patrol aircraft also searching for survivors. As with hurricanes, typhoon pathways are always unpredictable. Meanwhile, waves were building to twenty-five to thirty feet from trough to crest with typhoon level winds and it was now impossible to return to Keelung. Finally the task force commander on *Manchester* ordered all ships to steam independently and evade the storm by reversing course, moving south, and seeking refuge in Hong Kong.

Standard heavy storm procedure normally is to head into the waves and wind of a storm jogging ahead at a slow speed just sufficient to keep the ship heading into the waves. If at any time, the ship lost power in a storm, the chance was very high of 'having the ship's head fall off' and the ship ending up beam-to or 'in the irons' in monstrous wave troughs. The same effect could occur in a turn. When beam-to in a trough in a typhoon, massive waves crash green water over the ship's side rather than over the bow. Waves and wind combine to cause a heavy list. With these two forces in combination, the opportunity to flood engine spaces and short out ship's electrical power becomes very great. Once power was lost, below-decks flooding could not be controlled by pumping, and ultimately, tons of water would destabilize the ship causing it to capsize. However, in order to jog ahead, a ship needed sufficient sea room to allow moving slowly ahead for as much as three or four days. Even running for a day at three and a half knots a ship moves forward eighty-four miles and sea room disappears in a hurry.

The Straits of Formosa are very shallow and scarcely more than a hundred miles wide. Waves forming in such a shallow sea quickly become steep and treacherous. In addition, the operating area outside Mainland China's territorial waters was even more limited. We did not want to become an international incident by being caught trying to turn around within Communist Chinese territorial waters, nor did we want to run aground or founder in her waters. As the storm worsened, we were running out of time, space, and options.

Turning a 390-foot ship onto a reciprocal course in a storm is a good way to sink but there may be no other choice. Even if successful in completing the turn, when your stern is exposed to oncoming waves and wind, your ship begins wallowing badly and that makes it difficult for the helmsman to maintain a general heading. It is a Herculean effort without electric power to the rudders. All the while, the possibility continues for the ship's head to fall off and the ship then returns to life in the trough. This is similar to being overtaken and then wiped out on a surf board. Many things can go wrong while maneuvering in a major storm.

Despite the problems, we were better off at sea than tied up in port and being pounded against a pier or swept up onto a piling with structural damage, flooding water, and waves. Anchoring was also not a solution, in port or elsewhere. A grounding was nearly inevitable. Few options were left but to stay well ballasted, keep at sea, and head into the waves as slowly as necessary. Admiral Halsey's loss of three destroyers during a typhoon off the Philippines in 1944 was still in the mind of every senior officer.

Halsey had lost two Farragut-class and one Fletcher-class destroyers during a typhoon in 1944. They were preparing to refuel and nearly empty fuel tanks reduced their stability.[2] Furthermore, as they rolled, they took tons of water down main-deck air intakes into the boiler rooms where it quenched boiler fires and shorted electrical systems. This sloshing water then changed their righting ability as they rolled without power in the trough and ultimately capsized. On the newer Sumner and Gearing class destroyers, the air intakes to firerooms had been moved or were protected, but the new three-inch mounts had increased topside weight which could offset this advantage.

Initially, we ran for the center of the Straits moving into the storm while the eye of Typhoon Clara passed over Keelung. Finally, as we ran out of sea room, the captain had no choice but to reverse course if we were to avoid the shallow Chinese territorial waters. For us to make a turn as promptly as possible, the captain put all four boilers on line, and then backed full astern on the port screw and full ahead on the starboard in order to swing the bow as rapidly to port as possible. Once the swing began, high winds against the superstructure assisted until we were broadside. Going the rest of the way meant climbing out of the trough and bringing our stern into the wind; that was a problem.

We started the turn and the word was put out—"hang on." By now, every dish likely to break, chair to fall over, or thing to break loose already had. First our head fell off rapidly as we swung into the trough and the wind pushed us into a roll well beyond thirty degrees, from which we barely righted before the next battering wave. Finally, I could feel the props taking us through the trough. We had survived the full 180-degree turn and now were taking green water and crashing waves over the stern as we tried to maintain steerage with the following sea crabbing against our stern. From the exhausted sailors in after steering to the black gang[3] in the firerooms, a now experienced crew made Charley Akers' outstanding seamanship possible. In order to outrun the waves, the skipper next increased speed to twenty knots. We had no place to go but to Hong Kong and there we proceeded.

We had been in the typhoon's full effects only two days but it was a lonely two days. During most of it, winds exceeded one hundred knots. After the anemometer blew away, there was no way of telling how much beyond. At that level, visibility forward of the ship often disappeared completely and radar turned into complete clutter. The wind drove wave tops into a horizontal hail-like, hard-driven spume; you couldn't stand up in it. While moving into the sea, green water waves routinely broke over the two forward gun mounts smashing onto the open bridge and against the glass portholes to the wheel-house. Several portholes were equipped with windshield wipers but each swipe only revealed more on-driving water. Only occasionally could someone even sense the exploding sea surface. When you could see waves marching by, they were monstrous and you felt water was everywhere. The entire bridge watch huddled and hung on in the pilot house, always tensed for the next battering. When steaming into the storm, the ship seemed to stop as if deciding whether to go on or quit, after which it then pounded hard into the next wave front. When traveling stern to the waves, *Ozbourn* would yaw twenty degrees or more off course before the helmsman and those poor souls in after steering could bring it back.

There was no point in having lookouts out on the wings of the bridge. Most of the time they couldn't see anything. Even when they could, they could not stand up in the wind. Had they tried, they would probably have been pushed or thrown overboard by the battering winds and water. As the ship dropped into a trough, you and your feet left the deck and the wind literally propelled you backwards into a bulkhead or overboard. Anyone out on a weather deck would probably be swept overboard by green water. If swept overboard, there would be no chance of rescue given the sea state and the difficulty, if not danger, of trying to reverse course. An attempt to lower the whaleboat would result in the senseless loss of an entire boat crew. Wind noises were continuous and overpowering. Aerials, signal lanyards, and everything else either hummed ferociously or snapped back and forth with whip-like cracks. It was a wild music permitting no conversation below a shout. Needless to say, the crew of the bomber had disappeared from our concern. Even if we found them it would have been impossible to lay alongside and make a rescue. We could only go south, and that meant Hong Kong.

The only place 'outside' anyone went was the midship's passageway when coming from after officer's to the wardroom and bridge or from after crew's to the mess decks and watches forward. Anything topside that could break loose was a potential projectile and dangerous—boats, depth charges, torpedoes, and their tubes, electronics, even the spud locker. Everything topside was being battered by solid waves and water driven at one hundred knots and could itself break free and then take off to hit someone or something else. It was a dangerous time. No food except sandwiches could be prepared. Everything and everybody was either damp or soaked with seawater. If you were not on watch, there was little to do but wedge yourself in your bunk and hope for no surprises. At least the ship's blower noises drowned out the sound of the wind when you were in the bunk.

Suddenly we had come around and were wallowing on our way to Hong Kong. Once he got *Ozbourn* around, Akers probably could have been elected God—at least for a few minutes. In the middle of all this, I took on another task.

Becoming Custodian During a Typhoon

Just before leaving Sasebo, Captain Akers decided that ENS Jack Worden should become our Anti-Submarine Warfare (ASW), or Sonar, Officer. This meant Jack needed to be relieved as Custodian of Registered Publications. Registered Publications generally meant all encoding and decoding materials held by the ship, plus Operation Orders and similar documents.

One of the few perks with this position was a bunk in After Officer's Quarters, and I moved from where I thought mines hit destroyers. In after officer's quarters, no more of those pile-driving stops, elevator descents ending in a shudder, and bouncing and crashing. Life should become tolerable. My new roommates were Jack Blonsick and Ray Eades.

This room was bigger and had several chairs which, when not lashed to something, would take off and sail across the room. I got the bottom bunk and soon found that getting hit by our wandering and sometimes flying steel chairs was far worse than glass slivers from the overhead had ever been. My one set of civilian clothes and spare uniforms hung on a thwartships clothes-rod and waved back and forth against themselves gradually wearing holes in the sleeves. We shared the room with a floor-to-ceiling safe welded to the deck, the sole property of the Custodian of Registered Publications.

Jack Worden and I inventoried all the ship's Registered Publications and transferred them, and the job, to me in the middle of the typhoon. The safe's heavy steel door slammed back and forth and secret things moved back and forth to the rhythm of the storm until we finished. When satisfied, I signed the inventory and was now responsible for keeping up the ships's ability to decode and encode radio traffic and for maintaining current aircraft recognition signals on the bridge. Lost documents, improper records of burning of out-of-date items and so forth might have serious consequences for national security. Using the system incorrectly or even the right system on the wrong day could make it susceptible to foreign decoding. The rules were complex, required close attention to detail and often mandated daily changes. Other publications on the bridge contained recognition signals to use with overflying aircraft. I liked details and it was a perfect job for a detail person, but it contained all the chances needed for someone to do something wrong at least once a month. A mistake could lead to serious problems.

Sending incorrect responses to challenges from aircraft usually meant a high-speed flyover at low level but it might also result in someone shooting first and then asking why you made the mistake later. I made one once and got yanked to the bridge by Charley Akers just in time to watch a disgruntled patrol bomber disappearing into the distance.

Needed coding materials were kept in the locked coding shack off Radio, access to which was controlled by a lock with a single key held by whomever had the twenty-four hour coding duty. Changes were made on a varying schedule but the coding shack always included what you needed to break incoming messages. Traffic came in from Pearl Harbor on a continuous broadcast called the Fox Schedule being copied on every fleet ship by radiomen listening to CW. Thus a radioman on a four-hour watch would spend much of it listening to and then typing out a complete file of all plain word messages as well as coded messages being sent to the Pacific Fleet. It meant nearly continuous typing during a watch in the radio shack although the task of copying the Fox Schedule could be passed around if there were enough qualified operators. Some traffic was encoded and some was in the clear, but little of it had anything to do with us. It just kept coming hour after hour and being copied and typed by hand on ship after ship throughout the fleet. Only when you came in and went alongside a tender could you get the Fox Schedule copied for you. This gave your own people some respite from this hour after hour drudgery.

All manner of incoming coded material existed and you could intercept and break anything from or to anybody as long as you held the keys to the system then being used. The Commodore liked to snoop through the Fox Schedule and then 'peek' at the business of others. The radiomen knew to awaken the officer with the coding duty when something hot came in. It might be snooping into someone else's business but, at least, you could make translation or typing mistakes while decoding Situation Reports and not get into trouble. Mistakes made while encoding your own outgoing messages might compromise a particular cryptographic system in use by the entire armed forces.

Several months before, the exec had assigned Pay and me, as detail persons, to take on round-the-clock code-decode duties. As Supply Officer, Pay was responsible for keeping supplies on board, ordering ahead of replenishment, running pay-day as well as being in charge of the cooks, bakers, laundrymen and the list went on. He was not pleased to have additional duties in the coding shack. Gradually, Pay and I became deeply involved in breaking messages for the divisional commander, Commodore Roeder, we three knew how many ox-carts had been claimed on what Air Force strafing raid and which hill was now theirs or ours, etc. Later it sounded like the same thing appearing in the daily action report in the *New York Times* after I returned to the States. However, there are only so many hours per day available for such luxuries and too often these assignments were followed by a need to send a coded message out, go on watch, update publications, stand General Quarters, and so forth. Pay and I finally earned our first naval 'black-eye' by making an error while encoding an outgoing message. Fortunately, it was not serious enough to qualify as a significant compromise of the system then in use.

Gradually, the typhoon moved on up the Straits and into the South China Sea. As we moved south toward Hong Kong, the seas settled and life returned to normal.

A Stop in Hong Kong

Knox joined us during the early morning of 11 November and the four destroyers formed a screen for *Manchester* We then formed a column and began entering port, trying not to look like five drowned rats. Our first greetings came from a brace of RAF Spitfires that buzzed us no more than forty feet from the water. We came along portside to *Manchester* for refueling and then moored at Buoy #2. Later, *Hollister* moored to our starboard side.

Everywhere I had ever been, 11 November was Armistice Day, but not in Hong Kong. Great Britain and her colonies had chosen 12 November as Remembrance Day to commemorate the end of World War One and we were just in time. Tying up to a buoy reduced the need for anchor watches, gone was the worry about 'dragging' anchor in Keelung harbor and everyone was ready for a proper liberty. We were also taken over by 'Bumboat Annies,' garbage scows, suit salesmen, and anyone else who could get on or near the ship. The entire ship was painted by Chinese willing to paint in return for our garbage. We supplied the paint, brushes, and supervision to ensure nothing vanished over the side. We would leave looking a lot nicer than when we came in but they refused to chip, and much of the rust was just painted over. Still, we looked good.

Any naval ship entering a foreign harbor becomes the guest of the host nation and must observe their rules. Thus, the commodore and captain had to make formal calls upon the British admiral and upon our consulate before liberty could commence. Such calls were made in any foreign port in which there was not a continuous US naval presence. These visits were more than naval etiquette; they provided an opportunity to exchange ground-rules for behavior ashore, warnings about problems with the Chinese communists beyond the New Territories and other sensitive issues.

When they returned, liberty was called. Jack Worden and I changed into civilian clothes and went ashore for the first time in civvies since 21 July in San Francisco. We first did a quick reconnaissance of the shopping district and were overwhelmed with ivory, English linens, woolens; everything I had hoped to find for Christmas presents in Sasebo and hadn't.

As the 11th ended, Doc Ketcham, Bob Rogers, Jack Worden, and I reassembled at the Hong Kong Hotel. We then had dinner at the Parisian Grill or 'P.G.,' reputed to be the best in town, and finished the evening touring places like the American Club, Cock and Pullet, and the Club Lido. We were back on board about midnight coming out on a wallawalla or water taxi that operated all night and cost four Hong Kong dollars: the official exchange rate was then about five and a half Hong Kong dollars for one US dollar.

Not everyone got back on board the same way. During one midwatch, a Royal Navy motor launch approached out of the darkness and stood off as the bow hook went through the fancy boat hook drill. It then approached the lighted area at the base of the *Ozbourn*'s gangway leading to the quarterdeck. On closer inspection, the Officer of the Deck on watch could see a nearly naked body stretched out on the bottom. Pinned to the underwear shorts, all that remained of the uniform, was a note saying,

"He says he's your skipper, if so, please take him on board."
Upon inspection and a stout, "he's not ours," off went the British to the next buoy. It was not Charley.

Hong Kong is a very small British colony stuck onto the
coast of a very large communist-dominated land mass. Because
both the US and British were technically "at war" with some
communists, anyone going ashore needed to be alert. In early
November 1950, although the Red Chinese had not yet officially entered the Korean War, Americans ashore needed to think
what they were doing. The Chinese Civil War had just ended
and our support of the Nationalists, though limited, had been
real.

Canton was only thirty miles upstream on the river flowing
into Hong Kong harbor and its takeover had been one of the
final events of the Civil War. What the Chinese position towards Hong Kong might become was not clear and an armed
takeover was considered possible. We were advised to be very
careful in the New Territories, the mainland additions to the
island of Hong Kong itself. Kowloon in the New Territories,
had a fascination of its own and soon attracted sailors. Two
officers picked up two White Russian women, took a taxi in the
New Territories and went through somebody's road-block into
Red China before realizing where they were and turning
around. If captured, how, or if, you were to be released was not
something I wanted to learn. Besides, Hong Kong was enough
to keep anyone busy for four days.

After liberty commenced, Charley Akers and the Commodore returned ashore to attend a British Admiral's cocktail
party. When the cocktail party was over, they returned to
announce to the wardroom that we were having guests for
Sunday supper, a girl and her escort. That changed the wardroom atmosphere. On Sunday, everyone dressed in their best
khakis and waited patiently for guests who never came. We had
been stood-up. After finally eating in silence, the Captain gave
ENS Jarrett the girl's telephone number with instructions to go
ashore and find out what happened. She was quite embarrassed
to find the offer had been for real. Jarrett then turned her
apology into a Monday luncheon on board for her and two of
her friends.

That meal went swimmingly. When lunch was over, the
Captain asked Jarrett and me to escort them back to town,

giving us permission to go on liberty but with orders to come back 'sometime.' We carefully followed his instructions and turned the afternoon into a three-girl guided tour of Hong Kong ending up in a hotel bar overlooking a park with its inevitable cricket match. The rules to cricket take a long time to explain and that inevitably required us to escort one of them, Jillian Arnold, home to her house on top of the mountain overlooking Hong Kong where we then stayed for tea. Jill worked as a stenographer in a tobacco import house in Hong Kong. Her father, who worked for Butterfield and Squire, was off somewhere in China with their export-import business. Jill's sister came home from work in time to join us for tea.

Finally it was apparent even to us that Jarrett and I were overstaying our welcome and we left. By now both of us were about ready to jump ship; I was remembering that there were other things in the world besides destroyers and seawater. We hung around the tram station for about an hour and then called back asking Jill and her sister out for dinner the next evening at the 'P.G.'—we didn't know anywhere else—and then dancing at the Ritz. Jarrett was a good person to stick to and was obviously better at this than I. We had a beautiful time next night talking about British politics about which neither he nor I knew anything, hearing what had been going on in the world of which we were a very minor part, literature, stage productions, etc. Just being with someone who didn't wear a white hat was a return to humanity as it is supposed to be practiced. Jack Blonsick, on the other hand, had a date with a long-legged English strider who walked him into the ground. Jarrett and I returned late that evening to the envy and admiration of the entire wardroom; no one else had been so successful.

We got underway early on 16 November for the return to Keelung. When I see pictures of the Hong Kong harbor taken from the top of the tram, I wonder what ever happened to Jill. Thanks for the wonderful time, wherever you are.

Back to the Pits

The crew enjoyed themselves ashore in Hong Kong. First, it was the deck gang in a fight with the operations sailors. Next night, it was *Ozbourn* sailors against those from the *McKean*. *Ozbourn* sailors kept on winning until they mixed it up with an

Australian Artillery unit. Next morning after Quarters, 'Doggy' MacLawhorn, a little worse than usual from that one, advised Jack Blonsick that there would be no more beer brawls. Our warriors had reverted to lovers. The Aussies had truly cleaned our clocks. Later John Hadley and I spent several hours trying to locate a Chief who had gotten drunk, fallen in love, and subsequently vanished. By the last morning everyone was alive, made Quarters one way or the other, and *Ozbourn* left for the return to Formosa.

By late Saturday afternoon, 18 November, we were back in Keelung. Mail from home caught up with us, and John McLaughlin, my friend since third grade, had just been drafted. I knew most of the other names on the long draft list. On the up side, food from home and magazines poured in.

After one day in Keelung, we went on patrol. Upon our return, we anchored in the outer harbor because there was no space alongside the pier. It had been raining steadily for the past twenty hours. Anchoring is a nuisance because failure to secure a solid grip on the bottom inevitably results in dragging anchor with a change in wind, tide, or currents. Whenever anchored, the ship needs to be ready at all times to get underway. That means a full engineering plant and black gang on duty and an officer of the deck and others on the bridge alert for large changes in bearings. Being anchored is not nearly as relaxing as being tied up.

The rain gradually turned into a real storm and we rolled as much as thirty-five degrees; it would have been more pleasant underway. Sometime in the middle of the night, we began to drag, at which the OOD called away the Special Sea and Anchor Detail and replanted the anchor. The breakwaters protecting Keelung's outer harbor could not provide sufficient breakage to the waves and our rolling had broken our hold on the bottom. The bunks in after-officer's quarters were not easy to stay in when the ship rolled. They had no metal hoops that could be inserted to keep you in.

As Custodian, I also became Recognition Officer and was responsible for a trunk full of ship models made of lead and glass photographic slides of aircraft. They were more appropriate to the last war than this, being mostly Japanese battleships and Zeros. The trunk was stored next door in Jarrett's and Thornhill's room and it weighed a ton. It had been lashed down but broke loose during the night and crashed around their room like a drunken elephant before they could contain it. During the typhoon, they threatened to throw it overboard.

This time while we were out, you could pick up snatches of instructions for Task Force 77 over the tactical radios in CIC even though the ships were over six hundred miles away. They were very busy. Much had happened and, again, we again were not a part. On the night of 13 November, while we had been enjoying liberty in Hong Kong, Jim Tregurtha saw CDR Memel who was sitting in the Officer's Club in Sasebo. Memel had just been transferred from the Cornell NROTC Unit and was now assigned to the Air Group on *Leyte*. About 2100 as they were talking, all officers were told to return to their ships immediately. China was upon us. *Wiltsie* sortied later that night and immediately ran into our friend, Typhoon Clara, now passing northward, having left us in the Straits of Formosa several days before. As *Wiltsie* passed through Straits of Tsushima, the bouncing in their forward officer's quarters was so bad that Jim had to wedge himself into a space on the deck between his bunk and an ammunition hoist in order to sleep. He awoke in a foot of sea water that had come down the forward ventilator intakes. He then crawled to the ladder to get to the wardroom all the while the pounding kept throwing his knees into his face. More than any other experience, that night convinced him to get off destroyers and into submarines. This time out, *Wiltsie* remained at sea sixty-five days.[4]

On Monday, 27 November, we were still in Keelung. Rumor now had it that we would be relieved by mid-December but, before leaving, we would sail around Formosa on a flag-showing tour, probably after our next patrol. Further, Bob Rogers received word from the San Diego *Ozbourn* Officers' Wives' Grapevine that the destroyer division slated as our relief was leaving San Diego sometime toward the end of December. They would reach WestPac about 10 January, relieve us, and we would be back in California by February.

These rumors had just enough substance to raise hope. Reality returned to bring hope back down, usually while I was lying in the bunk trying to get to sleep. We now had a full complement of people on board due to the influx of reserve officers and enlisted men. Most of them had home commitments from which this was taking them. One night at a bar,

Charley Akers was heard to observe, "reservists saved my ass." Here or back in California, it didn't make a lot of difference to a twenty-two-year-old, unmarried ensign. All this had become much more exciting than I had anticipated.

Thanksgiving and Worse

On Thursday, 30 November, three destroyers and *Manchester* celebrated Thanksgiving in Keelung. *McKean* and the fleet oiler, *Ashtabula*, were on liberty in Hong Kong. After the holiday, *Ashtabula* departed directly for Japan. We four were in Keelung, having been kept from patrol by bad weather in the Straits. Each crew had the works—turkey, ham, cranberry sauce, pickles and olives, mashed potatoes, and vegetables— even a free cigar and a pack of cigarettes. It was Holiday Routine meaning sleep as you wish and movies in the afternoon in the crew's messing compartment as well as one in the wardroom. In the midst of our consuming all this food, *Manchester* received orders pulling it off the Patrol to return north to the war where the action was becoming very tough.

That ended Holiday Routine and converted Thanksgiving into a day spent racing around helping Commodore Roeder assume two jobs from the skipper of the *Manchester*. First, he would become Senior Officer Present Afloat (SOPA) and second, become Commander Task Force 72 (CTF 72). As SOPA, he determined when liberty started and what to do with mail. As CTF 72, he arranged patrols, coordinated communications, and had duties that were secret enough not to be generally known around the wardroom. The Commodore became Commander Task Force 72. *Ozbourn, Hollister, McKean, Knox,* and an oiler to arrive later became Task Force 72, along with the patrol bomber squadrons.

By 1700 *Manchester* was on its way north taking outgoing mail. Shortly after Thanksgiving, USS *Guadalope* was scheduled to arrive in Keelung as duty oiler. At that point, our mail first went to the US Embassy in Taipei and then out on a Northwest Orient flight. The Formosa Patrol was getting a little thin.

Communications requirements suddenly became very important. Once again, our radio gang seemed stretched beyond limit. Our radio people were quickly standing watch-in-three and we weren't even underway. No liberty for anyone would get old quickly. I was also Radio Officer and had to sort out all the personality problems as well as take over nearly all of the coding activity. Meanwhile, the Commodore's need to know everything kept everyone on edge and upset with each other. Then the Commodore's Staff Lieutenant began bypassing me and assigning tasks to my Radio Gang. This caused problems that took several hours to resolve. To top it all, the Custodian had not been to the Registered Publications Mobile Issuing Office (RPMIO) on a destroyer tender since late October. As the new Custodian, it was my task to worry when our crypto-graphic communication supplies would become dated. To prevent that catastrophe, the captain needed to schedule a visit from Japan of an officer courier flying down with enough material to keep us current. I hoped it could wait until we returned to Sasebo but no one knew when that was to be.

Meanwhile, Captain Akers and the Commodore increased their social commitments ashore. One night at Kaoshiung, both were summoned to a bridge game involving several admirals of the Nationalist Navy as well as Generalissimo and Madame Chiang kai-Shek. The Commodore and the Captain were very embarrassed to discover they were trouncing both admirals in a highly undiplomatic fashion. Throughout the debacle, the Generalissimo spoke no English so most of the discussions were with Madame. Later, when the Generalissimo left the room, Madame expressed in her fluent English how much she had missed American celery, which she could not find on Formosa. Ever gallant, Commodore Roeder assured her that *Ozbourn* would be delighted to provide her with a crate. Next morning Jack Blonsick loaded our last box of celery into a borrowed jeep and delivered it to Madame Chiang. Ensigns did just about every task imaginable, even becoming the world's only commissioned green grocer.

Yuans were the only money used officially ashore and the then current rate of exchange was 10.25 yuan for an American dollar. Doc Ketcham and I spent some on a Sunday bus ride to Taipei. It was my first time off the pier and the trip to Taipei took about thirty minutes. It was a relief to see the weather change; raining and dull in Keelung along the coast; in Taipei, broken clouds and sunny. We wandered around looking at food stalls and finally found the National Museum. The only things I could recognize were the Latin scientific names on some cobras preserved in jars, everything else was in Chinese. I finally found some flower seeds for my grandmother. The picture on the package looked something like sweet peas and they went in the next letter home. Others found more excitement near the ship. A woman was shot to death by a Chinese security guard. Her stinking, bloated corpse was left on the pier near the landing for over a week. After the Commodore complained bitterly for several days, someone came and moved it. One evening, Coxswain Ike Voles, his crew, and whaleboat failed to return on time from a routine harbor trip. Three hours overdue they finally returned. They had inadvertently run over a corpse and his clothes became twisted around the screw and shaft. Removing the body had taken a great deal of time. Life seemed to be rather unimportant.

On Sunday evening, I made a collect call home from Keelung and talked to everyone but my sister Susan. There were about twenty of us on the pier trying to do the same thing. I started trying to call at 1900 (0600 in Beaver) with the help of three Formosa Foreign Persons Police. Calls then went by cable either to Hong Kong or Manila, from there by radio-phone to San Francisco and then by landline in the States. Although only about a third of us got through, my call was short but 'loud and clear.' The big news back home was that I had missed the 'big snow of 1950.' Ohio and Pennsylvania were paralyzed with nearly three feet of the stuff. For years afterwards, I had to remind family I really had missed the 'big snow' – and why.

While we had been in Keelung, someone on board discovered that the Chinese would barter almost anything for cigarettes. Our sea stores suddenly became vulnerable. At the same time, the number of mail bags leaving the ship went up remarkably. They were full of cigarettes leaving the ship. I never knew of this while it was happening or ever learned who ran the scam but the mail clerk in our Division must have been involved along with someone in the Supply Department. It all came out when Ships' Store inexplicably ran out of Commodore Roeder's brand of cigarettes.

On Tuesday, 5 December, *Knox* and *Hollister* got underway for patrol duty while *Ozbourn* and *McKean*, having returned from Hong Kong, had sole possession of the dock. We had been in Formosa for five weeks and were still expecting to leave before Christmas, go to Yokosuka for some anti-submarine training and then home. But, by now, the situation up north looked very dark and it was apparent that a new war had taken over. The troops ashore and the fleet serving them had highest priorities on supplies. Common sense suggested that the four destroyers and *Guadalope* would remain alone in Keelung through the Christmas season. At least it was raining equally on both sides of the Straits and the weather conditions at sea would remain very poor, thereby preventing any invasion for at least the next four months. By then, we would be out of there. We expected to spend the next four months going to sea occasionally and the rest of the time tied up to the pier with the crew ashore on liberty finding trouble in Keelung. Perhaps we might get back to Hong Kong or even to Manila on a port call; I would have preferred Hong Kong.

On Thursday evening, 7 December, *Ozbourn* and *McKean* received emergency orders to sortie from Keelung and intercept a huge flotilla of junks moving eastward from the Chinese coast toward Formosa. They had been first spotted and then illuminated and counted by a low flying PBM from VP-46 operating out of the Pescadores.[5] The patrol bomber making the report had flown low over two groups, one of five hundred, and the other of two-hundred-fifty motorized junks. We sortied so fast that we left some crew behind on the beach.[6]

When the captain set the detail for getting underway, I reported to CIC which had again become my Special Sea and Anchor Detail station and was amazed to find one of our steadiest radarmen scared silly when he realized what we were being asked to do. He had become convinced that we were being asked to sacrifice ourselves trying to stop an oncoming horde of hundreds of thousands of Chinese communists. Fear became very infectious and the atmosphere in CIC quickly changed from one of, "who screwed up liberty?" to one of near-panicked terror. Momentarily he had us all convinced that, by the end of the night, we would be consumed by hordes of motorized junks. 'Doggy' MacLawhorn, radarman and former infantryman, brought us all back to sanity with one of his World War Two infantry jokes. 'Doggy' was the only sailor I ever met with the

Combat Infantryman's Badge, which he had earned in the European Campaign. The executive officer made him take it off for captain's inspection—it was not a Navy award.

We spent the remainder of the night searching for and finally locating a large fleet which, by then, was already on a course back to mainland China. With that, we turned around and returned to Keelung. Whether or not this had been the beginning of the landing which was aborted or just a very large fishing expedition remains a mystery.

It was just as well by us. Intelligence reports were then showing that it was nearly impossible to sink a junk—let alone seven hundred and fifty of them—with either three-inch or five-inch shell-fire or anything else. We had tried it once with three-inch shells and we knew they didn't work. Most of our shells were either designed for air bursts or to pierce ship's armor and then explode. The latter would pass completely through the wooden hulls of junks before exploding. Shot-up junks tended to float forever even though they might look like a colander after such treatment. It would have been impossible to do more than shadow the fleet or harass them. If they had been equipped with machine guns, mortars, recoilless rifles, or bazookas, even that might have been a very dangerous undertaking. Any efforts to board at night would have been foolhardy and how do you board seven hundred and fifty armed junks? We returned to Keelung the next day without incident and picked up those of the crew who had missed the excitement. It seemed silly after it was over, but a shadowy story remains that this indeed was the invasion fleet, which was under orders to turn back if detected. So, perhaps we really did save Formosa that night—two destroyers stopping Mao Tse-Tung? It is difficult to imagine.

Ozbourn sortied from Keelung on Monday, 11 December, en route to the Pescadores Islands off the southern side of Formosa. We were on our show-the-flag tour. That obscure collection of islands seemed scarcely important to anyone and was still devastated from the US bombings of Japanese naval facilities in 1944 and 1945. Even the power plant had not been repaired although the port was now the center of the Nationalist Navy.

We arrived on 12 December. Immediately, the Captain and Commodore made their courtesy calls on the headquarters of the Nationalist Navy. Afterwards we were treated to a very plush luncheon. I was invited as part of the officers' contingent and quickly became a social embarrassment to the US Navy. I was then a teetotaler. The Chinese admiral started 'gombei' toasts that continued throughout the meal. Nothing I knew about good manners prepared me for this. I finally raised my water glass with each toast. Because I couldn't speak Chinese, I couldn't even apologize for my rudeness to the Chinese on either side of me. 'Gombeis' went on without my full participation and I continued to damage Sino-American relations. Back on board and depressed, I lay down at 1900 to rest and awoke at 0600, just in time to dress and be ready to get underway at 0700 for the next stop at Takao.

Jack also had problems at the same meal. He thought the first course was the only course and overate the lobster soup in the ten-course luncheon. He spent the next nine courses in quiet agony before drifting into oblivion with incessant gombeis. In late afternoon, he and the others returned to *Ozbourn*, whereupon Jack immediately threw up and then collapsed in bed. Scarcely an hour later, he was shaken awake by John Hadley for required attendance at the evening banquet. At least I had been spared that.

By Wednesday night, we were moored fore and aft to buoys in Takao harbor. More parties were planned for the next day, but at 0700 15 December, we were ordered to make an emergency sortie to find a refugee ship. Unfortunately the seas had again built up because of gale winds. We could only make thirteen knots, instead of the twenty-six knots needed to reach the site. We then returned to Keelung early 16 December and refueled from *Guadalope*. Commodore Roeder was a good Catholic and to help overcome ship's boredom, he requested the Squadron's Chaplain come down from the Sea of Japan for the upcoming holidays. We did not expect even the best of Chaplains to improve a wet, dreary, rainy Christmas time.

Endnotes:

[1] Field (1960:67). *Catfish* began patrols on 18 July and *Pickerel* the next. See earlier comments on *Perch* patrol in Straits of Formosa.

[2] Reilly (1983:134-138) discusses the recurring problem of declining stability as the result of adding topside armament, radars, etc., and failure to ballast fuel tanks before heavy weather.

[3] A watch spent with boilers in destroyer firerooms was very unpleasant. Temperatures routinely exceeded one hundred degrees, and by the end of a watch those on watch were grimy, dirty, and exhausted. The *Ozbourn*'s boilers were oil-fired, but as late as World War One, boilers were coal-fired. Hence, the watch emerging from those firerooms was black from coal-dust. The name 'black gang' lasted after coal was replaced and was routinely applied to those working the ship's engineering spaces.

[4] Tregurtha, private letter to author.

[5] Cagle and Manson (1957:383-4) for details of the sighting. I made no mention of this incident in letters home but remember it well.

[6] Field (1960:308) describes a fleet of twenty ships being reported as having sortied from Shanghai on 8 December en route to North Korea. By the time they had been investigated they turned out to be fishing vessels. I believe these are the same incidents. The *Ozbourn*'s War Diary for 7-8 December inexplicably says, "moored as before."

BACK NORTH – QUICKLY

Suddenly, on 18 December, the Formosa Patrol became the sole property of the patrol bombers. *Hollister* and *Ozbourn* received orders to go north and departed late that afternoon. We were first visited by a Chinese general from the Generalissimo's staff and then by the US Embassy's naval attaché. Whatever passed back and forth during those visits was not the business of ensigns. The trip north on the 18th and 19th was uneventful and remained so until the beginning of the midwatch on 20 December, when *Hollister* had a minor engineering casualty. Despite it, by late the same day, both ships were in Van Dieman Straits off southern Kyushu waiting for our old friend 'Cherry Tree' to emerge. We would screen her on the trip northward. *Valley Forge* was to join the other carriers now operating off Hungnam where the withdrawal was still in progress. We assumed *Valley Forge* had been in Sasebo for downtime and were shocked to learn that she had returned to San Diego in November after nearly a year in the Far East only to be recalled for the 'new problem.' For the crew of the 'Happy Valley,' their Christmas at home consisted of about two days in the States before getting underway for the trip back. Christmas 1950, for us at least, meant being reunited with others in the Task Force, our Navy family. It was strangely comforting to be back with others in the same boat and to be joining a Task

Force that now had four or five carriers with a lot of protection no matter what was happening ashore. If nothing else, at least the mail ought to become regularized again.

As naval forces in Formosa were drawn down and sent north it was more difficult to be refueled and reprovisioned in the south. The potato locker was beginning to get bare and our celery was all gone but mail delivery was really bad. To make matters worse, when we moved north, much of our Christmas mail had already been sent south toward Formosa and was now stuck somewhere. Also, some idiot had left three thousand pounds of our mail on the runway in Okinawa. When that message reached the ship, the Commodore gave someone so much hell that they sent a cargo plane to return it to Japan. Maybe, it would catch up with Santa Claus somewhere in Japan and then make the next replenishment run. In our last mail, I had received a package from Aunt Izzy which included a hand-knit green wool sweater. A watch on the bridge out in the cold biting wind required lots of warm layers and it became one of many. Her fruit cake was saved for a midnight Christmas party in CIC if all else failed. From the last mail call, all of us in After Officer's had enough cheese, crackers, and hard salami for a party. We could have scheduled a Christmas open house except you couldn't go across the street and invite the neighbors in for the festivities.

The evacuation of the Tenth Corps from the port of Hungnam had been underway since December 11.[1] The Tenth (X) Corps included the First Marine Division returning from the Chosin Reservoir area and soldiers of the 3rd and 7th Divisions. Within two weeks 105,000 troops and 98,000 Korean civilians, plus massive amounts of cargo and vehicles, had been removed.[2]

Fire on Board

Early on 21 December *Hollister* and *Ozbourn* were routinely screening *Valley Forge* off the west coast of Kyushu moving north to the carrier operating area off Hungnam. Our peaceful trip was interrupted at 0835 when we had a fire. Outside the wardroom door was an oval man-hole or scuttle with a vertical ladder that led down to the forward fireroom. I was seated at the juniors' end of the wardroom table when someone from the galley burst in through the wardroom across the table from me. All I could see behind him were flames and smoke filling the passageway. Just as suddenly they were gone, but were followed by a rapidly ringing General Alarm and the word, "Fire, Fire." One of the nozzles injecting hot oil into the boiler had burst, flashing burning oil back into the fireroom and I had seen the ball of smoke and flame that shot up the trunk. We were not buttoned up as we would have been at General Quarters. It could easily have been much worse. Jack Blonsick came forward in the passageway just in time to see Bob Whitten resolutely donning a rebreather. Bob then entered the choking, charcoal gray smoke which was pouring out of the fireroom space before anyone else. Bravery comes in doing things right. Bob was on his way down into the fireroom to look for casualties and shut off the oil. He came back covered with the black oily corklike material off BX cables that had been seared by the fire. Despite the black gang's efforts to limit damage, we had lost a fireroom as well as a boiler. This made us a possible liability in any forward area. We needed time alongside a tender.

Surprisingly no one was even injured. We could easily have had people killed from burns. A fire on board ship is something everyone fears; normally you expect them as the result of battle damage or from a plane crash on a carrier. By 0925 we were back up to 20 knots and by 2000 we entered the northern end of the East China Sea en route to the Straits of Tsushima and northward to Hungnam with our old friend.

When we got *Valley Forge* on station, *Ozbourn*'s very minor contribution to the Hungnam Withdrawal was over. We were in close enough to see the USS *Begor* with UDT personnel on board, beached LSTs, and the general uproar of the beachhead. We moved mail and passengers until 1630 on 22 December when we and the destroyer *John A. Boles* were released to return to Sasebo. By then, the redeployment was virtually completed. There is now a veterans' organization called 'The Chosin Few' made up of those who served 'in, above, or around the Chosin Reservoir' during November or December 1950. We had barely qualified.

Ozbourn arrived in Sasebo 1100, 23 December, went to the fuel docks and by 1335 we were alongside *Hector*, a repair ship.

It took several days to repair the fire damage, plus a few other things on a long shopping list that had grown while on the Formosa Patrol. At least we would be in port over Christmas. It had been also nearly two months since the former Custodian had visited the cryptographic office (RPMIO) on the tender. As the ship's new Custodian, an armed guard and I, visited the RPMIO and brought back enough new instructions to enable us to decode messages for several more months. Now to celebrate Christmas in Japan.

Christmas 1950

I went ashore briefly but when I couldn't get near a tele-phone, somewhat unwisely, I sent a telegram wishing everyone Merry Christmas. Sending a telegram was much easier but not a very acceptable substitute. Too many of them getting back to the States those days were beginning, "The Navy Department regrets...," and not, "Alive and well in Sasebo." What a stupid way to spoil Christmas in Beaver.

Even before tying up to *Hector*, we launched the motor whaleboat and sent the mailman and some seamen off to the base post office. Within an hour they were back with forty bags of mail. Whoever left our three thousand pounds in Okinawa had corrected that, plus whatever else was adrift and it all came in like a delivery from Santa Claus. Even when we ferried mail around the Task Force, we never had that much on board. My packages from home arrived twenty hours before Christmas and so did everyone else's—a real visit from Saint Nick. We had only a few days alongside the tender and we were not there for fun and liberty. Christmas Morning 1950, we were awakened with some version of "Reveille, Reveille, The Smoking Lamp is lit in all authorized berthing spaces. All Hands Heave out and Trice Up," followed immediately by, "Sweepers, Sweepers, man your brooms. Give her a clean sweep-down fore and aft, sweep down all lower decks, ladder wells, and passageways. Now sweepers...." Then someone else hit the 1-MC with a more unusual, "Happy Ship, Happy Crew, Merry Christmas, TURN TO." Christmas 1950 in Sasebo, Japan.

It was the first time away from family at Christmas for many of us. On Christmas Eve, Jack Blonsick, John Moriarty,

Armond Remmen, and I sat on bunks or chairs in my room and opened presents, ate Remmen's cheese from Wisconsin and feasted on crumbled cookies and fruit cake from various parts of the US. Instead of the typical Christmas wrappings spread all over a living room, our room had become awash in cut twine, brown wrapping paper, stamps, and lost tags from presents. As usual, I never kept track of who sent what. I ended up with three more fruit cakes, adding them to the store-house of 'food for the future' now being saved in the Ships' Confidential Files, another accouterment in our room.

I also received a pair of loafers that fit just fine. Salt air, and sea water, and trying to cram feet into shoes needing to be tied while the General Quarters gong was going off said loafers made sense. Further, even though you might get shoes resoled or reheeled on board one of the destroyer tenders, you never were alongside long enough to count on getting your stuff back. Also, your shoes might end up returning to San Diego if *Dixie* or *Hamul* were ordered back before you picked them up. A similar thing was true about getting medical or dental appointments on the tender—your appointment came up in five days and you were in Sasebo for four.

Dave Thornhill was itching to get off. He had been on board since graduating from the Academy in 1948. To get off he had applied for everything he could think of. The yeomen in the ship's office reminded him monthly that, again, it was time for him to turn in his request for reassignment to something else. He had volunteered for Underwater Demolition Teams, transfer to the Civil Engineering Corps, or anything else just to move on. He had been sending in his monthly request to the Bureau of Naval Personnel asking for reassignment and, lacking that, even for a chance to resign and get out. Since June, the latter had not been the sporting thing to do.

Finally he got his wish and, during the Christmas break, was ordered to the *Tingey*, a destroyer coming out of mothballs and being reactivated in Long Beach, California. We also lost five or six petty officers to similar projects at the same time. The only thing Dave hadn't tried was for flight training. However, Jack Blonsick, Jerry Solomon, and I decided to go over and take a pre-flight physical on *Leyte*, the first step in applying for flight school. I went over but chickened out after I got there—not so

Jack and Jerry. Flying had always interested me intellectually and I liked to watch the Corsairs land but anyone applying for flight school was required to stay longer in the Navy. The same was true for sub school. Dave Thornhill had told me about a master's degree program in oceanography at Scripps Institution of Oceanography which interested me, but it also required three years active service before you could apply. Then one year of additional active duty was required for each six month's of school. This sounded like the start of a career and no naval officer appeared to need an advanced degree. I was getting pretty good at being an Ensign on a destroyer. I was even growing to like it when we looked smart in the Task Force, but I still had not changed my mind about getting out and returning to graduate school.

We all missed Dave. The crew liked him, he was a great division officer and always carried off things like Abbott's mustache with a certain elan. He managed to keep people from becoming too serious while personally doing a superb job as an officer. I thought he represented the best of the post-war breed from the Naval Academy that I had met and I was sorry to see him go. In 1954, Dave was killed in a catapult explosion and fire on the *Bennington*, a renovated Essex class carrier. He had been a great friend.

While we were in Sasebo a number of destroyers came in from the Hungnam evacuation operations up north; many had been underway for fifty-two days without a port break for repairs, shut-downs or anything else. Another coming in from shore bombardment duty was reputed to have been at sea for one hundred days. It came in, refueled, had some tender time and went back north next morning; I don't think the crew even got off ship.

These extended stays would not have been possible had not the replenishment pipeline been filled with food, fuel, ammunition, spare parts, and the people to use them; very few of the ships were more than six years old which also helped. In contrast, the longest we had yet been out was about thirty days in October. We felt like pikers.

While we had missed much of the events of late November through mid-December, it was quite clear that a different war had taken over. Any plans to begin to return destroyer divisions or squadrons back to the East or West Coast went on hold until the 'new war' made sense. We now knew we would not be in San Diego in January.

There was renewed concern about Russian submarines and the damage they could do to ships in the Sasebo harbor. We got underway 27 December to act as an anti-submarine screen for Sasebo, came back in briefly and then returned to the Sea of Japan for duty in the carrier screen. We refueled on Sunday 31 December and celebrated New Year's Day and the beginning of 1951 at sea.

John Bond was officer of the deck from 0000 to 0400 on 1 January. Naval tradition required him to write the ship's log for this midwatch using some form of poetry. John attempted the task but humor was hard to come by. It was going to be a long hard winter here and we all knew it would be much more so on the beach. On New Year's Eve, the next Chinese offensive began.[3]

Endnotes:

[1] Cagle and Manson (1959), Chapter 6 describes in detail the Hungnam redeployment. Task Force 77 was then operating off-shore but providing daily ground support to the withdrawal. Ships in the immediate vicinity of Hungnam became part of Task Force 90 and provided gunfire support and on-loading capability. Other outloading took place at Wonsan on the east coast and at Inchon on the west coast.

[2] See Alexander (1986:367) for source of figures. Those in Field (1960) differ slightly but the 'redeployment' itself was nearly miraculous and took place in an atmosphere of uncertainty about Soviet intentions.

[3] Blair (1987:592) *et seq.* for details ashore of the Third Chinese Offensive. Cagle and Manson 1957:165-192 for the Hungnam Deployment. The author's details are from letters written home during the same period.

KOREAN OPERATIONS –

JANUARY 1951

On December 23, the destroyer *Sperry* was hit three times by shore batteries at Songjin, a major North Korean port on the Sea of Japan. Shortly afterwards, she returned to Sasebo for repairs and tied up next to *Wiltsie*. Jim Tregurtha saw a shredded mattress on *Sperry*'s quarterdeck and asked their JOOD what had happened. An officer had slept through the general alarm only to be awakened when a round passed through the ship's skin, entered his bed, went into his mattress and out the other side before exploding.

We were now chasing the only four Essex carriers (*Philippine Sea, Valley Forge, Leyte,* and *Princeton*) in WestPac. *Princeton,* recommissioned in August, arrived in the Sea of Japan on 30 November with Air Group 19 and a crew composed largely of reservists.[1] *Boxer* left for the States on October 29 to undergo an overhaul. *Valley Forge* had departed in late November and we had escorted her back with *Boxer*'s air group on board.[2]

I returned to the bridge as JOOD, this time with John Moriarty. He was always quiet and easy to work with. The weather up north was awful, but different, from the high seas, rain storms and 55-degree water off Formosa. Up north, it was bitterly cold when we operated at twenty-five knots. This meant the wind speed across the deck could be fifty knots. At 15 degrees F. That is a wind chill of -31 degrees F. It was difficult to stay out on the wing of the bridge and keep looking forward for things like mines floating in the water. It was also not very good form for the JOOD to come out of a nice, warm pilot house, give the lookouts hell for standing with their backs to the wind, and then retreat back into the pilot house. A four-hour watch out in that wind was impossible; we had to alternate people on lookout.

After nearly six months on board I could guess within a knot or so how fast the ship was going. Normally 'standard speed' meant fifteen knots, 'full,' twenty, and 'flank,' twenty-five or more as far as the engine order telegraph is concerned. The bridge commands to the engine room were made using the pillbox-like brass engine order telegraph with the paired handles, one for each propeller shaft. Minor changes in propeller revolutions needed for station keeping were made by a set of knobs connected to bell cables. "All ahead flank, make turns for twenty-five knots," was the command from the officer with the conn to the Lee Helmsman at the Telegraph. He repeated the order adding, "...Aye," back to the officer. If not corrected or countermanded, the Lee Helmsman grabbed the Engine Order Telegraph handles and rocked them into place. The engine room then responded by moving the arrows on the face of the Telegraph and changed the revolutions for the new speed as appropriate. If they had been warned it was coming, the needed boilers would already be on line. As the speed came up, the ship shuddered and took off.

We could make twenty-seven knots with two boilers on line and we used one in each fireroom. Steaming with 'split-plant' allowed us to have an emergency in one fireroom and continue steaming with steam from the other fireroom. It had helped during the fire and was necessary under combat conditions. For speeds greater than twenty-seven knots, all four boilers were needed on line. It might require thirty minutes to heat cold boilers up to the white-hot temperatures needed to produce superheated steam. How much faster than thirty knots *Ozbourn* could travel would depend on sea state, a clean bottom, and the condition of the boilers themselves. Speeds greater than thirty knots used too much fuel and were rarely necessary.

Frequently a command to change course, "Right standard rudder, come to course 270," would come concurrently with a

speed change and the helmsman at the wheel repeated it before
beginning to swing the wheel. No matter where you were on
board, when the ship heeled or the revolutions changed, with
experience you knew we were doing something different. It was
good to be back on the bridge. If you are ever to qualify as
OOD Underway, that is where you needed to be. It was part of
what ensigns do if they are to grow up to be lieutenants junior
grade.

It was now very cold in the Sea of Japan, even though the
weather might be bright, clear and sunny, and the ocean relatively calm. It took about ten minutes to put on enough layers of
clothing to keep alive and alert for four hours out on the open
bridge. The uniform of the day was whatever was "warm
enough to last" and, more than ever, I appreciated Aunt Izzy's
green wool sweater—anything to keep warm. Even when we
were only doing fifteen knots between flight operations, it was
so bitter that eyes watered incessantly making it difficult to scan
the sea surface for mines. The cold binoculars even made your
sinuses and eyeballs hurt. When the formation cranked up to
nearly thirty knots and then turned into a fifteen knot breeze
for flight operations, you couldn't keep your eyes open facing
into the oncoming forty-five knot blast. I had always enjoyed
winter weather but I just couldn't stay outside in that weather
for the full four hours. Fortunately, as JOOD, I didn't have to;
not so for the lookouts. They were always looking aft or moving
into some kind of shelter. I didn't blame them—but what about
the mines?

Under these clear arctic conditions, every evening watch
would be blessed with a spectacular sunset with deep reds dif-
fusing over the western skies but unless you had the right watch,
you never went outside to see it. During twilight after flight
operations had ceased, there was nothing to do but listen to the
bow cutting calm water, making a hissing sound as you slid
forward. Then finally it would be so dark the horizon disappeared. Yet, when you carefully scanned with binoculars, you
could still find the darkened carriers in the center of the formation. When you looked directly at them, they vanished but when
you looked just off your point of focus, they would dimly reap-
pear. To preserve night vision, red-lensed flash lights were used
on the bridge and red night-lights dimly lighting passage-ways

and compartments were everywhere. At 'lights out,' the enlisted spaces had their overhead lights turned off and replaced by red lights.

Every ship traveled darkened and the only inter-ship communication, except for voice radio, would be occasional infra-red signaling using mast-head lights. Any administrative signal traffic between ships was held until morning when it was done by flashing light. Night-time course and speed changes were made by voice radio. Changes were usually made only to regain sea room, for night flight operations, launching night intruders, or for a pre-dawn CAP (Combat Air Patrol).

It was intriguing to go out on the open bridge at night, look off towards the horizon, see nothing and then come into the pilot house, look at a radar repeater and realize there were twenty or more ships steaming in formation and each right on assigned station. Everyone was getting good but the nicest thrill occurred at night following a simultaneous course and speed change. You completed the maneuver placing the ship within one hundred yards of station and then a look at the bridge radar tells you that everyone has been just as accurate. It had a ballet quality.

We had gotten away from Dawn Alerts because they kept arriving during breakfast but we were having unannounced fire drills. That real ship's fire got everyone's attention; whether you have a fire drill or General Quarters, almost everyone goes to their General Quarters stations anyway, although my job during a fire was to worry about classified documents in the burning compartment. When we had Abandon Ship Drills, I also had to be prepared to get all the classified decoding stuff gathered up, loaded in a lead-weighted bag and ready for deep-sixing over the side.

I hated mid-watches. One particular night I had expected to see the movie *On the Town* at 2000 in the wardroom but instead Jack Blonsick offered to exchange my mid-watch on the bridge for his 2000-2400 in CIC. Getting out of a bridge mid-watch meant I could go to bed just after midnight, sleep until 0715, make breakfast, get to quarters and still not have another watch until 1200. On top of everything else, it was nice and warm in CIC and they had coffee to boot. I took Jack's offer and missed the movie.

By mid-January, I had received more books from my librarian Aunt Elizabeth. I also had accumulated three fruit cakes, miscellaneous cheese, crackers, and a stick or so of pepperoni. All were stored nicely in the locked Ship's Confidential Files. We would have failed an on-site security inspection because of having personal items stored with confidential documents.

By now John McLaughlin, my best friend from Beaver, had been drafted and was somewhere stateside going through basic training. John's parents sent me a Christmas present that arrived while we were in Sasebo. Boxes then being sent overseas usually were made of sturdy cardboard and well wrapped with brown paper and held together with string and scotch tape. Instead of plain scotch tape, this package came all wrapped with special scotch tape with 'Fischer's Hardware' emblazoned on it and repeated over and over. It had been wrapped and sent from Fischer's Hardware Store in Beaver. I immediately recognized the tape from thirty feet away as that cardboard box sat on top of a big pile brought to the wardroom by the mailman. The tape, who sent it, and where it had come from were more important than the box and its contents. I was glad to know that somewhere there was still a Fischer's Hardware Store. John and I later were to be each other's Best Man, but not until he had completed a two-year tour in the Army dealing with Korean War frost-bites in Fitzsimmons General Army Hospital near Denver. There he saw after-effects of a first winter in Korea that I never experienced. Frost-bite resulted in loss of toes, fingers, and even feet among many who otherwise survived the first winter ashore in Korea.

Given all the food and supplies received from home, I was now ready for a long winter. My comments home included: "The days go by and we do the same stuff over and over again and it gets to be a nice calm routine that everyone fits into," and, "It all counted on thirty." Thirty years was the usual number spent on active duty by those making a lifetime of the Navy.[3] It had been a challenging experience so far and, six months into my naval career, I was beginning to feel useful and able to enjoy much of what I did.

I had visited the RPMIO in Sasebo and by now had entered all those changes and revisions to the ship's coding material. I had also finished my end-of-the quarter report and submitted it to the Ship's Office on time. The Navy ran on a quarter system and, at our level, in addition to reports such as mine, the fiscal system allocated funds quarterly. Unlike a child's allowance, you could not save it to spend on something in the future. We often had tons of toilet paper and enough paint to last forever while running out of light bulbs. Any excess you temporarily had could always be traded to another ship with a different shortage. The Chinese word, 'Cum-shaw,' from Asiatic Squadron days was used to describe this process. Although I didn't have any quarterly money to worry about, the First Lieutenant (Deck Department) and others whose departments used consumable supplies were affected. I just had to be sure that I kept communications in order and the Commodore happy.

By Sunday, 7 January, we were in the Sea of Japan just north of the 38th parallel. Weather had again changed and the seas were rough. Just when you became used to the roll and the rhythm of a course, a nearby carrier would carry out flight operations. Their course and speed change requirements inevitably put us into the trough of the waves or banging head first into them. My typewriter's advancing spring could not cope with the rolling. In addition to bothering my typing, bad weather also hampered flight operations, making it difficult to deliver on the beach the ordnance needed to slow down or stop the Chinese advance. Sometime on that Sunday one of the screen destroyers got a sonar contact, but it was finally identified as 'non-submarine.' Most likely it was some poor whale or a school of fish. There was usually a sonar contact once a week, but the identification was always 'non-submarine' in the end.

After being up, ready, and willing to stay all winter, I was now down reflecting on the discouraging scuttlebutt about rotations and when we might be out of there. It now looked as if we were fourth on a list of destroyer divisions due to be rotated back to the States, if and when, that ever commenced. I had the midwatch the previous night and slept from 0415 until lunch at 1100, which gave me just enough time to get ready for the next watch. On went the tedium of flight operations, launches and recoveries, and death and destruction ashore while at sea we went around in circles.

Usually, we didn't hold Quarters at 0800 on Sunday but routinely held them every other day and always out on the weather deck, unless it was unsafe to be there. Rather than a military organization, we looked more like a sleepy chorus from a performance of *The Pirates of Penzance*. Uniforms underway were wash khakis for officers and chiefs, dungarees for enlisted, and white pants and aprons for cooks and bakers in Supply; you wore foul weather gear as needed. The Supply Department mustered starboard side just forward of the midship's passage; Operations Department, aft on the same side. I never saw the other Departments at muster, but First (Deck) Division was on the forecastle and Engineering on the fantail; the rest were spread on the maindeck beginning just aft of the foredeck. After completing muster, each department head received a verbal muster report from the division officer and then presented it to the executive officer in the midship's passage. A few minutes later, the department head returned to the department or division with "the word" from the XO, (executive officer or exec), including items not published on the 'Plan of the Day,' and made whatever comments he wished before dismissing the troops. Immediately afterwards began 'ship's work'–chipping, painting, working on guns, and on it went.

When weather was bad, we might go to foul-weather parade in the passageways or just hold muster 'on station' which meant counting everyone at work or asleep to see whether anyone had fallen overboard. Sunday's 'muster on station' meant counting people asleep in bunks but, one way or the other, everybody was accounted for each day at 0800.

If they needed you and you hadn't fallen overboard, you could always be found on a 390-foot ship. The 1-MC could be split so that not every announcement would be heard in chiefs' or officers' country. Crew were always paged, "Smith, Bosun's Mate Third–lay up to the forward peak tank–on the double," and Smith took off–or had better. When the 1-MC was used to call a chief or an officer, the ship was probably sinking. We also had a telephone system on board with a hand-set in 'After Officers.' Usually the bridge just send out a messenger.

Pete Link's family sent pepperoni. Pepperoni, cheese, and crackers did just fine on the midwatch in CIC. We could also get 'mid-rats' or midwatch rations of pie, sandwiches, and so forth for those on the midwatch, but the 'CIC pepperoni parties' also helped pass time. After several weeks at sea, the routine again became old. We did anything to break the monotony. The most different thing I could think of was to borrow a pup tent and camp out in the woods near home, falling asleep to whippoorwills and waking up to crows. The sound of "reveille, reveille, all hands heave out and trice up," could easily be replaced by crows. Even though I had a feeling of accomplishment, of being able to do what we had been sent here to do, at the same time there was also a sense that there were other places just as nice or better. Were we really doing any good? Further, unless the ship sank, we were living in near opulence compared to life on the beach. It embarrassed me but I couldn't change it.

I would not have put camping overnight in a woods near home at the top of any personal list until I could not do it. I was also not walking the four or five miles daily that I would have done routinely at school and I had eaten too much of Link's pepperoni. I also wondered whether dad had seen any ducks this winter at a swamp he passed on his way to work? Suddenly, I'd be asleep and too soon it would start all over again when the quartermaster and his red flashlight showed up.

More Christmas cards arrived. One, from my scoutmaster and his wife, brought back memories. Royal Suttkus, 'Sut', a friend from Cornell, had also written. He had just completed his PhD and was now beginning to teach at Tulane. He had been a second lieutenant in the field artillery in Europe. So far he had not been called back; once was enough. Sut, Ralph Yerger, an ex-something from the war, and I had collected fish specimens for Suttkus's dissertation the previous Christmas holidays. How much had happened since. Ralph had just taken a job at Florida State College (now University) at Tallahassee. Ralph and Sut were starting two outstanding graduate programs and each remained at those institutions until retirement. They had used the GI Bill to complete their doctoral degrees. Sut, Ralph, and Howard Evans at Cornell, were my role models.

It was now Saturday, 13 January. We were still at sea, but Task Force 77 had moved considerably south as the front line moved south. We were also getting out of bad weather further north and were operating about seventy-five miles west of Sasebo somewhere in the Straits of Tsushima. The weather up north had been cloudy for days making for poor flying conditions. The rough seas made it difficult for aircraft to take off and land on the carriers. Ashore, the troops were still 'shortening their supply lines,' a euphemism for being pushed back toward Pusan. The Third Chinese Offensive was in full swing.

On Christmas Day, while *Ozbourn* had been in Sasebo for repairs, Commodore Roeder transferred himself and his staff onto *McKean*. It was nice having him off the ship because his presence increased the pomp and formality and heightened our communications problems. He and all his people and papers rejoined us later.

We were now occasionally refueled from a carrier in the Task Force. Destroyers were so 'short-legged'[4] that they needed servicing more frequently than anyone else. Topping off our fuel tanks kept the Task Force intact and allowed for more continuous flight operations. The carrier did become another barrier between us and our mail and passengers and we might not receive them until we or the carrier visited the replenishment group. Occasionally, a destroyer would also be assigned to serve as mailman and move mail, supplies and people around the Task Force.

On 9 January, we refueled from *Leyte*. The seas were so rough the ships surged apart, breaking the oil hose on the carrier's deck. Before the pumps could be shut down, they had painted an inside passage with some three hundred gallons of Navy black oil. It went everywhere and really stunk. Later we did the same thing to *Valley Forge*. Jarrett said the broken line on their side looked like a Spindletop geyser before they could shut it off.

When refueling began, the destroyer would begin to overtake the underway tanker from astern. Once alongside, the destroyer would gradually move in until the distance had closed to fifty yards. A line-throwing gun fired from the pumping ship would begin the process of getting heavier lines, sound-powered telephone lines, marker lines, and, finally, the span wire rig and six-inch hose. Once the six-inch hose arrived from the carrier, our deck gang placed it into a forward fueling trunk with an opening about garbage can size. Before pumping began, we lashed it in, but the real problem was to keep a nearly fixed distance between the two moving ships so the hose didn't snap. Because both ships were independently under way, keeping the distance between the two was nearly impossible. Although the hose hung in loops from trolley blocks riding on a fixed wire, it could be stretched if the ships separated. If the hose broke on our side or pulled out of our fueling trunk, the disaster happened to us. Wherever it occurred, everyone in the area received an oil bath. Further, the snapping of rigid hoses and the breaking of manila haul-in lines can easily maim or kill deck hands. Even if nothing happened and delivery went normally, a faint aroma of Navy black lingered in the living spaces around the forward fueling position.

When the hose was full of oil under pressure, it became as hard as steel. One hose broke free from a fueling trunk on a destroyer with us and flailed around taking off the top of a seaman's head, from the eyes up. The next day on board the same ship, the distance between ships suddenly closed and before the excess hose could be taken up by the outboard saddle, the hard hose swung aft along the destroyer's main deck and mashed three seamen to death. On one refueling Charley Akers decided to wear his brand-new visor cap, scrambled eggs and all. One look over the splinter shield at the water heaving and rushing past as we closed, a surprise wind gust, and in went his cap—a thirty-eight dollar mistake. We used a lot of oil, or 'Navy black.' In three successive refuelings in January 1951, approximately three days apart, we took on 51,000, 36,115, and 102,710 gallons.

The typical highline transfer of personnel could also result in a dunking or even breaking of lines if they got too tight. The whole process of maneuvering a destroyer alongside an oiler, reefer, or ammunition ship, and keeping it there at a fixed distance, is a most demanding and skill-requiring, ship-handling task. It is usually done by the captain. We once managed to touch an ammunition ship very gently while underway and taking on five-inch ammunition. Nothing happened but it was nonetheless very scary.

After Ray Eades left our room, Jack and I tried to convince the Chief Engineer to remove the third bunk and match up the two reading lights with two bunks. That would also lift my bunk from being so close to the deck. We both left things out when seas were relatively calm, but with course or weather changes, *Ozbourn* would begin to roll and things began to fly. Jack once left a heavy manual on our desk. On a roll it launched itself off the desk and flew across the room bouncing off my pillow. I would have been cold-cocked, had it hit my head.

Our two steel chairs had the same potential unless lashed down. When the chairs began to slide sideways they'd first hit a riveted seam half way across the room, causing them to fall over on their sides and slide into the side of my bunk rather than jumping in bed with me. I wondered who thought of that when they designed that riveted seam in this ship? You could really get hurt. What a nice way to get wounded at sea—impaled by the leg of a flying chair. Destroyer people got beaten up rolling around in the troughs of waves while carriers remained as calm as if anchored in an Iowa cornfield. Being back aft was still better than being up forward. Back aft we did not experience the elevator drop-like crashes that drove you deep into the bunk and then the next instant launched you upwards towards the overhead. Still, you did need to think about flying chairs.

We were still in the Sea of Japan on Tuesday, 16 January, and it looked as if this trip out might be our longest yet. The seas had again become almost as calm as they had been in August and September and the carriers went back to launching a full suite of daily strikes. Mail remained feast or famine; the last mail was a bonanza with another pile of books from Aunt Elizabeth, all my pictures from Inchon, Hong Kong, and Kee-lung arrived plus many letters that had missed us here and there. My camera light meter finally died, probably because of salt spray. I hoped to pick up a new one at the Army PX next time in Sasebo even though the Army had imposed informal rationing on us. The meter returned to Beaver by mail for repairs. Too bad you couldn't mail yourself home the same way.

We were still getting excellent food on board. LTJG 'Pay' Jordan spent the Wardroom's mess money well every time we came in. We also bought basic supplies from the crew's mess but added shrimp and other exotic things when available in the markets in Sasebo.

On 17 January, the Commodore and his staff came back on board by highline transfer from the *McKean*. In their absence, we had cleaned up our food supplies in the Confidential Files and had consumed fruit cake the last two nights running in CIC. The piles of Christmas 'rations' became smaller while we were all getting larger. The Commodore often dropped in to CIC early in the mid-watch and might misunderstand our 'picnics.'

On Friday morning 19 January, we were still with the carriers but now I was able to write during the 'morning rest period' that ran from 0930 to 1100—a new twist. The exec became convinced that people needed more time in the rack. We had also been having 'dusk alerts' instead of 'dawn alerts' because it isn't light until 0730. This would put 'dawn alert' into the middle of the crew's breakfast. You would scarcely hold off a real General Quarters until breakfast was over but the crew would not appreciate a practice GQ while they were eating. We were not having daily air raids nor were we in trench warfare with troops raiding us at dawn, so why inconvenience ourselves? Since dusk occurred just after the early meal in the wardroom, as well as after the crew had been fed, the ship shifted to dusk alert.

At 'alerts,' I was still the Machine Gun Control Officer. After each mount manned their telephone and reported, "Mount 'X' manned and ready." I then reported, "All manned and ready," to the bridge. Then, staring at an empty air search radar repeater and hoping never to see any incoming aircraft, I made up drills to 'exercise' the three-inch batteries. I would announce an incoming raid, "270 True, 6 miles, and closing." Outside, the guns would train, elevate, and pretend to track my pretend aircraft. Finally, the bridge would see all these waving muzzles and determine that we indeed were ready. At that point, the Captain would then pass "secure from GQ" over the 1-MC and everyone would pack it in. Then back we went to the rest of the events on 'The Plan of the Day.' Off Korea, it was difficult to make it seem real. Even though MIG-15s could be only minutes away, we never saw any.

Before returning to *Ozbourn*, the Commodore, his Flag Lieutenant ('Flag'), their records, and their enlisted men had spent the last ten days in Sasebo with the other three ships in the Division. Two divisions of destroyers rotated back to the States while they were in Sasebo. The staff had scarcely been back on board when a rumor began floating around that we would soon be going into Sasebo for ten days of tender availability, plus some 'R and R' time. Our few days there at Christmas had been limited to repairing fire damage in the forward fireroom and there had been precious little time off the ship spent by anyone. I needed to make another crypto-publications trip to the RPMIO (Registered Publications Mobile Issuing Office) on board the destroyer tender, USS *Dixie*.

Jack Blonsick needled me some about my continuous typing but we got along better than I did with Pay. Everyone's warts show during this close confinement but it must be much worse in the crew's quarters. There was really no place to get away from people you didn't like, or from bullies, except by climbing in the bunk and facing the green bulkhead or staring at the canvas bottom of the bunk overhead. Even then you are aware that someone is in it because his butt is pushing down toward you. Getting into the rack is the ultimate form of escape time for people who don't like the constant hassle of others around them all the time. Tensions between officers were remarkably few. The wardroom generally was an amiable place, or was until someone wrote his wife in San Diego naming officers he suspected of visiting Japanese whore houses. The details quickly traveled through the *Ozbourn*'s Wives' San Diego Grapevine. We didn't need any wives upset with that unsubstantiated rumor.

In addition to learning about war, the cruise presented an opportunity to learn about other things and not everything was easy to understand. We had a homosexual incident during the cruise which finally came out in the open during the *Ozbourn*'s next trip to Korea. Someone who had been transferred was beaten up on his next ship because of his sexual aggressiveness. During the course of an investigation, he also revealed his partner on *Ozbourn*. All was handled on a 'need to know' basis between the captain and the executive officer. It was then Navy policy to put investigators on board, often as petty officers, to observe. Once participants had been identified, another group of investigators came on board with authority to transfer them off and the participants were off the ship within the half hour. Life was too close during extended sea time for one to make the 'consenting adults' argument. There wasn't time or space to be any more tolerant of sodomy than one might be of the crime of harassing, fighting, or any other antisocial behavior. The code of sexual misbehavior didn't cover heterosexual activity ashore unless you happened to get the clap.

In moving further south, we profited a little from a different set of oceanographic conditions. A narrow slice of the Japanese

Current turns northward into the Straits of Tsushima and keeps the western waters of the Straits somewhat warmer than the remaining very cold waters in the Sea of Japan. I made an ignorant comment about the weather in a letter home "I guess the Marines coming back from the Yalu River really had bad weather." I meant the Chosin Reservoir but it sounded more like they'd had a picnic rained out. It obviously had been no picnic, but where we were, we were unaware of what miraculous events the Chosin Reservoir campaign and Hungnam withdrawal had actually been.

On 19 January, *Ozbourn* and *Duncan* were detached to escort *Valley Forge* back to Sasebo. When we arrived on 20 January, we had been out twenty-two days. We moored port side to *Sperry* who was alongside *Dixie*. On this trip in, we learned more about our December trip north escorting *Valley Forge* to the Hungnam withdrawal. 'Happy Valley' had finally gone home after having had her normal tour in WestPac extended from July. She left in November when the war seemed nearly over and had only just arrived in San Diego when the Chinese problem started. She then embarked *Boxer*'s Air Group only seventy-two hours after arriving and sailed in such hurry that they left sailors ashore on leave and liberty. Only a few deliberately missed movement; the rest knew they were needed.

'Happy Valley' had not seen much more of the Hungnam redeployment than we had. She spent several days in the south training new flight crews and requalifying the old ones. Then she met *Ozbourn* and *Hollister* and returned to duty on 22 December. Despite our fire, we escorted her back to Task Force 77, but only two days before the last troops came off the beach on 24 December.

We had been off Hungnam for no more than a few hours transferring people, picking up mail, and tending to other matters before being ignominiously sent back to the tender in Sasebo. We were close enough that Jack Blonsick saw the USS *Begor*, a high-speed transport, which was carrying the Underwater Demolition Team personnel responsible for blowing up the main dock at Hungnam. I saw little going on as we moved back and forth but remember that Hungnam looked raw, damp, and overcast. We could see the snow-covered mountains behind Hungnam but we had little chance to be of much assistance.

Mother and Dad found more Beaver residents serving in the Navy somewhere in WestPac. Later, during our stay in Sasebo, I just missed a friend, 'Sonny' McClurg from Beaver, who was on *Leyte*. The *Leyte* had been ordered back to the Atlantic Fleet and was being escorted by one of the departing East Coast destroyer divisions. On 18 February, Seaman Albert McClurg, Jr., on leave from the *Leyte*, married Mary Ellen Patton in the United Presbyterian Church in Beaver according to the *Beaver Valley Times*. On 26 February 1951, Ensign Jack Schlosser, USNR from Beaver, completed instrument training and returned to Fighter Squadron 721, US Pacific Fleet. VF-721 was equipped with Panthers and would serve on *Boxer* from 27 March to 3 October 1951.

Meanwhile, the Beaver Draft Board continued to pick up most of my high school class-mates whether they had gone to college or into the steel mills. I may have been the only one in my high school class to have gone through an ROTC program and then been commissioned. But, despite being off Korea, I was luckier than the draftees headed for the infantry. *Ozbourn* was doing the job we had been asked to do, which was the same being asked of infantry ashore.

Every few days, someone in the screen acquired a sonar contact but, inevitably, it was evaluated as 'non-submarine' which meant fish, whales, or a ship's wake. At this point, mines, bad weather, and boredom were our primary foes. Over the horizon on the mountains in the snow and cold, things were very different. What we were doing offshore seemed rather insignificant.

We returned 20 January for our longest stay in Sasebo and moored alongside a tender. Shortly after our arrival someone heard Seoul City Sue on the North Korean radio. He was dumbfounded to hear her not only welcome the *Ozbourn* to Buoy #3 but then to continue to describe an explosion that would overtake us later that evening. How she got the first part right, no one knew. Fortunately, the second part didn't happen.

Time spent in any month in the war zone now took $200 off your taxable income; we might even get into the war zone again for a day or so in February before returning home. Time operating with the carriers counted, but Formosa Patrol time did not. In 1950 I earned $1,686.21 from the Navy and $91.88

working for Dr. Raney at Cornell. As a result of four months in the zone, my taxable wages were $978.09. Dad sent the necessary tax forms to start the filing process; income tax forms were almost non-existent in WestPac. People on the beach worried about saving some part of the peninsula and staying alive while doing it; I worried about taxes.

This time in, I painted the coding shack. Only certain officers and two of the radio chiefs were authorized to enter the room. I couldn't bring myself to ask chiefs to do it—it seemed beneath their dignity—so I did it. Smirking sailors kept coming by the open door either to see some stupid ensign in dungarees painting or to satisfy their curiosity about what this otherwise always locked-up space really looked like. I liked to paint and since nobody considered it beneath my dignity, I got away with it. Now we had a sparkling green coding shack for upcoming operations.

On Saturday afternoon, 27 January, Jack Worden and I went on liberty to take pictures in downtown Sasebo. It was difficult to stop taking pictures of Japanese children. They were lovely, with exquisite black hair and big eyes. Everyone was bundled up as it had been cold and raw, but then a thin sun came out and the streets became packed with people going everywhere. By now the supply of things to sell had gone up markedly, in contrast to when we were there during October. In desperation, I had then finally bought Mother a rather undistinguished cloisonne vase for Christmas; now the stores were flooded with some very beautiful ones. You could even buy bags of Japanese tangerines. In the midst of all this I glanced up a hilly road and saw an Underwater Demolition Team platoon running along the streets of Sasebo with wire-stock sub-machine guns. What were they doing here?

By Sunday night, 28 January, we had been back long enough for my typewriter to have made a refurbishing trip to the tender and be returned. The Chief Engineer always placed my personal typewriter on his tender repair list because he borrowed it daily to write engineering reports in his room. He and the executive officer occupied the two senior officer's rooms just forward of the two junior officer bunkrooms in After Officers'. Chief was now sharing his with Jerry Aachus, Flag Lieutenant. Their room, just off the port-side passage, shared a common bulkhead along with our tiny Ships's Store. The executive officer's room was on the starboard side and Walter Ousey was its sole occupant.

Having the Navy in Sasebo really helped the economy of this part of Japan. Everything looked much better now than when we had first arrived. There was a real sense of friendship building between US sailors and people in town. This new friendship was the first step in removing the hatred left over, on both sides, from the war. A number of Japanese war brides, as well as thousands of 'R & R' arrangements went a long way toward removing either the anguish of Korea or simply the loneliness of being away from home and at sea.

Sasebo had more than its share of whore-houses and some resulting problems. A seaman from the deck division returning from a social night ashore stopped at the fleet landing pro-station. The Hospitalman in charge of dispensing drugs to prevent gonorrhea told him to insert the salve from a small tube. In went the salve and back to the ship he came. Three days later he was in so much pain that Jack Blonsick, his assistant division officer, sent him to sick-bay. There Doc Ketcham surgically removed the cap from the tube that had also vanished up his urethra. Venereal disease was a serious problem in Japan, but so was stupidity.

My parents continually asked about my nickname 'Cherry Tree.' I may have convinced them it had something to do with my then red hair. After I had been on board five months, John Hadley gradually modified it into 'Bush,' 'Cherry Bush,' 'Cherry Stump,' and so forth. I finally became part of the wardroom when my nickname simply went back to being 'Pete.' It had taken some time to feel like an officer.

We were now in port along with our old friend, *Valley Forge*. Task Force 77 now had enough carriers in WestPac to be able to send one carrier in for repairs and upkeep along with a chance for flight crews to break off their heavy deck and flying schedules – R & R, I & I, or A & A as appropriate.[5]

Whenever we went ashore, there were always aviators at the bars. *Valley Forge* expected to return to the operating area with the next replenishment group. We considered ourselves to be a big production since there were up to five Essex-class carriers operating in WestPac. By comparison with the Pacific War, we were still small potatoes. At one time in 1944, Task Force 58 had fifteen carriers, although some of them were the smaller jeep carriers.

Dad began to complain about a news black-out. It was almost as though the war was not as interesting as it had been. It was moved off the local front pages and then finally out of the local papers to be replaced with something more newsworthy. By the time I saw the *Beaver Valley Times* in May 1951, there were days when I couldn't find anything at all about Korea. The war was becoming forgotten even while it was on.

On the other hand, we found that when the Commodore's secret Situation Report was cleaned up and rewritten, with only a few items deleted, it was being used as a daily press release. The only paper I ever saw that carried the daily release in the entirety was the *New York Times*—"all the news that's fit to print." Dad received the Sunday Times for years and finally took daily *New York Times* as well so that he and Mother could figure out what was going on. Meanwhile, I asked that they turn off the flood of airmail stamps. While we had been in Formosa, and thus out of the War Zone, we paid for our own outgoing mail. Accordingly, the ship's post office bought seven hundred dollars worth of airmail stamps to meet the demand. No sooner had they arrived than we returned to the War Zone where mail was free. Meanwhile, everyone had also written home for airmail stamps. By mid-January, we had so many airmail stamps on board we were afraid we might have cornered the US market.

On 31 January, shortly after breakfast, we got underway, met *Valley Forge* and escorted her back to Task Force 77. By 1 February, TF 77 was smaller and consisted of only two carriers, *Princeton* and *Valley Forge*, plus the cruiser, *Juneau*, and twelve destroyers. We now operated in the Sea of Japan, just north of the 38N line but well behind enemy lines. On 2 February, we went inshore again on an uneventful Bird Dog Station, acting as a potential rescue ship for planes unable to make it back. Fortunately, we had nothing to do.

By now we were becoming the lost sheep of Division 112. When we are out, the other three destroyers were in, and vice versa. This time the others had gone on in to Yokosuka for a week of R & R. From there you could easily get in to Tokyo. No matter how nice Sasebo had become, it was not Tokyo, and we never went into Sasebo except to work while tied up alongside a destroyer tender.

Both the Ship's Laundry and the Ship's Office had doors that opened onto Midship's Passage but the yeomen in the Ship's Office were tight with any information and their door was always closed. On the other hand, perhaps because of the heat from steam presses, the laundrymen always had an open door policy. As a result, anyone knowing anything or needing to know something, used the laundrymen instead to spread the unofficial scuttlebutt. By the end of January, the nearly official word at the laundry was that we were due to depart from WestPac on 8 March and arrive in the States on 26 March. It was a forty-eight hundred mile trip from Japan to San Francisco, which required a stop in Pearl Harbor unless we escorted something like a carrier from which we could be refueled. Supposedly we could do it at fifteen knots without refueling but we'd never do that long trip without a break. At fifteen knots or three hundred and sixty miles a day, the trip would be thirteen days. A stop at Pearl Harbor added several more. We might make it back to San Diego in sixteen days.

By late January things ashore seemed better. The retreat south had not only stabilized but a roll-back had begun. When the Chinese advanced too far out of Manchuria, they either outran, or we cut off, their supplies and back they retreated. We were seeing one of Mao's rules of war that governed their movements back and forth through summer 1951. By the end of summer 1951, the front line became stabilized and the war turned into one of very costly, bloody mountains, trenches, patrols, and raids.

We had been advised that our new executive officer was on his way, and we were waiting for Lieutenant Commander H. Barr Palmer, USNR, to complete his trip from the States. He had been recalled from his farm in Oregon, and no one knew where he was or when he would catch up with us. We seemed to be getting 'short' enough that he might get to WestPac in time to find us already on our way back. If I had been making that trip across the Pacific, I would have hoped for at least a few days in the operating area before going back home; you'd feel like a fool otherwise. If he was coming in as a passenger on an aircraft carrier or cruiser coming to WestPac, it could be a fast, direct trip; if he was being shunted around on supply ships, it could easily take a month to six weeks and he might be bounced off a couple of times and then lie around southern Japan for another week or two waiting to get on the right replenishment ship. It was also not unusual to hear we had mail and passengers somewhere within the replenishment force but we would be unable to get them transferred. Instead they would be returned to Sasebo to try for the next rendezvous. When LCDR Palmer would show up was anyone's guess.

On Wednesday morning, 7 February, we were still in the Sea of Japan. One of the oilers had twelve bags of mail, some freight (spare parts, most likely), and a passenger for us; we expected to be alongside them next day. We now had more people transferred off, having already lost a RD2 (radarman) to a Ground Control Approach School and several more sailors were transferred to new commissionings. I hoped something like that would not happen to me. At least on *Ozbourn*, I knew where everything was and who all the people—good and bad—were. I was adapting to the, "it could be worse elsewhere," philosophy of coping. Further, there was something homelike about this ship, an assured 'three hots and a flop.' For some, it may have been the first real home they had ever had. On top of it, I could see myself coming on board a new ship and having its captain ask what I did on *Ozbourn* and finding myself someone else's Custodian. I missed the point that officers go through 'experience stations' and that being a punk ensign and Custodian was only one of many required, but probably not repeated, steps in a thirty-year career. There was a lot of learning that went on in the first year while one was an ensign. Ship handling and taking care of the troops was much of it. I gave myself a grade of C+ for figuring out what was up and how the system really worked.

Some of the un-mothballed destroyers were now joining the Task Force. There is a breaking-in period for new crew and ship that takes several months, even in the middle of the action. It is not that *Ozbourn* was so good, but we had been at it awhile and the others were still green. Even I was beginning to be more of a value than an hindrance; perhaps nobody else said so but, at least I felt so.

We had been getting Korean snow on board ship the past few days; it usually did not stay on deck long. What didn't melt became snowballs that fueled snowball fights. A sailor in the Supply Department devised a plan to use the ship's freezer to store Korean snowballs that he would sell as souvenirs back in San Diego. A Supply Chief changed his mind for him.

Bridge duty was still very chilly but we were now rotating our lookouts on the open bridge every hour. Everyone else on bridge watch spent most of it inside the pilot house. Someone in the signal gang also had to be out near the flagbag and blinker, but generally they could get out of the wind by hiding behind the pilot house at the base of the tripod mast. We were fortunate in having a urinal back there which helped; however, getting through five layers of clothes to find your plumbing could be a problem.

Aft of the bridge was the signal bridge where two signalmen on duty watched every ship in the formation for signal flags flying and for incoming messages sent by flashing light. They concentrated their attention on the Task Force Commander to catch maneuvering signal flags. As midshipmen, we learned the flags and pennants by using flash-cards in a class but identifying them as they flipped out of a flag bag on a carrier at three miles distance was different. On the Task Force Commander's ship, flags went to 'the dip' or, only part way to the top of the mast. We then put up the same flags showing on the carrier and our flags also went to 'the dip.' A good signal gang had our flags in the air almost simultaneously with the gang on the carrier. We would 'two-block' our flags, or raise them to the top of the mast when we understood the message. When the carrier 'hauled down' her signal, it was time to execute and every ship involved executed at the same time. Most signals were obvious course and speed changes but no sensible OOD or JOOD ever trusted his memory of the Signals Book. The book was too big, so check everything in the air, confirm the flags up on the carrier, those out of our flag bag, and then tell the OOD what the signal means. Another detail job for the JOOD.

The signal gang also kept lookout for blinker traffic which could come from any ship in the formation, although most often from the Task Force Commander. The JOOD also watched for the same thing. While he might not be able to read Morse

Code, he liked to yell back, "flashing light on the *Leyte,*" perhaps taking perverse pleasure in catching some Signalman First Class doping off. Done correctly it was just a way of making the ship look smart. Done the wrong way, an enterprising signalman would figure out some way to get even. The guy who invented "don't get mad, get even" was enlisted and worked for a smart-ass ensign.

As you looked forward over the bridge's splinter shield or aft along the shield leading to the flag bag, you could always see a few people out on the weather deck. There were almost always a few white hats at work on the three-inch guns, others were going in and out of a forward five-inch turret or carrying trash and garbage to the fantail; otherwise, everyone else was inside. Only during time of refueling, rearming, or transferring people, mail, movies, and 'stuff' by highline did the deck fill up with firemen or seamen handling lines. Though the ocean was near freezing temperature, the ship radiated heat from the fire-rooms and engine room, but unless watertight doors were dogged shut, heated air seeping out was replaced by damp, cold, clammy sea air. Inside, as you walked past the galley, or by the uptakes from the firerooms, heat poured out, but if your bunk was close to the ship's skin, you felt the chill. Back in After Officer's or 'Boys' Town,' we were over the engine room and heat radiated upward from the steel deck plating. In summer it might almost be uncomfortable walking on it in bare feet but during the winter it felt snug and nice. The ship was designed to circulate low pressure exhaust steam to jackets in the air ducts which can really warm things up inside in the compartments. As soon as some snipe (engineer) came through opening those valves, someone else came right after him turning them off; next watch, the snipe comes through and does it again only to be...and so forth. Somebody is always fiddling with the thermostat no matter where you live.

Being at sea was a relatively healthy experience. Hay fever, allergies, and sneezing went to zero, and sinus headaches disappeared. Too bad there was no way to bring that weather back to the Midwest.

Endnotes:

[1] Field (1960:266).

[2] Field (1960:253), for details of carrier movements and the decline in movement of ships and personnel to WestPac during the lull.

[3] Letter from author to his family, 1/2/51.

[4] Destroyers were considered 'short-legged,' a term describing the limited fuel capacity of a destroyer compared with that of cruisers and aircraft carriers. A destroyer with 650 tons of fuel might have sufficient fuel for twelve days at no more than fifteen knots, but needed refueling every third or fourth day because of Task Force operations at speeds often in excess of twenty-seven knots. Failure to refuel routinely might endanger a ship forced to travel light in progressively worsening weather.

[5] Alexander (1986:396-98), describes R & R as it applied to soldiers and Marines coming back for five-day periods and called by its other initials: 'I & I,' or 'A & A,' for 'Intercourse and Intoxication,' or 'Ass and Alcohol,' Such periods were not unknown for sailors as well. More often, time in port just meant lots of sleep. R & R arrangements for *Ozbourn* did not begin until late in the cruise.

BLOCKADE DUTY

On 8 February, we departed Task Force 77 to become part of Task Group 95.2. By 12 February, we were still in the Sea of Japan but I no longer was adding the phrase "still with the carriers" to my letters home. We weren't and I didn't want to say why. We had not operated with the other three destroyers in our division for a month and our 'lost sheep' status was probably the reason for moving us out of the carrier screen. Destroyers in the screen generally stayed together by divisions and we had been disposed of by transferring us to Task Force 95, the Blockading Group.

I was still writing home that we didn't expect to be out more than ten or twelve more days, the weather was cold and so forth, all vacuous statements. I also thought it would be nice to get another income-tax free month by earning a few days in March as well, although I knew you could earn it the hard way with Task Force 95. We were probably not leaving any time soon because we were still expecting eight more transferees, seven bags of mail, and some freight at the next refueling on the thirteenth. They hadn't yet turned off the pipeline coming west to us and where was our new executive officer? When he arrived, Jack Blonsick and I would need to be on our most mature behavior because he would room with us and use Ray's old bunk. After a few days though he would relieve Walter Ousey who would go off by highline to do other things somewhere else.

In the midst of all this, I remembered that by mid-February in Beaver, red-wing blackbirds, song sparrows, and robins would be starting to sing. No birds were singing out here nor were pussy willows budding, but the days were getting longer and spring was inevitably coming. At which point it could get worse again out here and the war was already in bad enough shape ashore.

Nonetheless, I had finally seen a confidential message planning our return to the States. We were to depart on 8 March going via Midway Island and stopping at Pearl Harbor with an arrival in San Diego on 26 March. The people in the ships' laundry had been right–having the laundry across from the ship's office did some good. They put too much starch in shirts but they outdid the local drinking fountain as a place to get news. A Navy drinking fountain had been a scuttlebutt before the name was also applied to rumors. We still had time in WestPac before us; our table was not yet cleared and there were other things to do.

Task Force 95 had grown out of the initial 'coastal response' group that started to work 30 June 1950. That group initially was composed of the cruiser *Juneau* and a few destroyers. It remained loosely coordinated until 12 September when it became Task Force 95 under the command of Rear Admiral Allen E. Smith, USN. Just before the Inchon landing, Task Force 95 was divided into Task Group 95.1 on the Yellow Sea side of Korea under Rear Admiral Andrewes, RN, and Task Group 95.2 on the Sea of Japan side under the command of whichever senior US officer happened to be present. That officer was usually a US Navy Captain commanding a Cruiser or a Destroyer Division (4 DDs) or Squadron (8 DDs).

Admiral Smith commanded TF 95 from September 1950 until January 1951 when Rear Admiral Andrewes was promoted to Vice Admiral and took command until relieved in April 1951.[1] During *Ozbourn's* period of attachment, she served under Admiral Andrewes. The primary mission of TF 95 was to enforce the US blockade of the Korean coast. The blockade had been instituted by President Truman in accordance with the UN Resolution asking for "support to the Republic of Korea in repelling the North Korean invaders...."[2] The British concurred with the blockade and also assigned their vessels as needed. Concurrent with the blockading mission was the task of conducting shore bombardment of targets of opportunity along the enemy coast. The blockade was to become a major element in confining the war to the Korean Peninsula and in keeping the Communist supply lines limited to land.

Four factors made the blockade particularly difficult.[3] First, the North Korean coastline was five hundred miles long and, on the western side, particularly cut up by innumerable shallow bays, islands, and inlets served by tides of up to thirty feet in amplitude. This made small boat traffic difficult to intercept and mine laying operations particularly easy to conduct. Second, neither China nor the USSR recognized the blockade although, fortunately, neither country ever challenged it. Third, the blockade was supported by supply sources in the US and often required destroyers or other ships to operate alone, close to shore, and in a position as to be very vulnerable to mining, shore battery attacks, or even to low flying jets. Finally, for a blockade to be recognized legally by the international community, every portion of the blockaded coast had to be under ship surveillance each twenty-four hours. Patrol by aircraft could not be substituted and considered a form of 'effective' surveillance.

Without an 'effective' UN blockade,[4] the North Korean ports of Wonsan, Chongjin, and Songjin on the east coast, as well as Chinnampo on the west coast, would have remained open to non-belligerent shipping without regard to cargo contents. Most sailors considered the Soviet Union or Red China to be 'belligerents' but they probably were not under international law. Without an effective blockade, we could not have prevented Soviet freighters from entering North Korean waters. Also, without an effective blockade, ships from any third nation could not have been prevented from entering. It had to be 'effective' if it was to work.

President Truman instituted the blockade in response to the Security Council's Resolutions and declared it to be in effect as of 4 July 1950, under the terms of the 1909 London Conference on Naval Warfare. It remained in effect for the following thirty-six months, becoming the longest legal blockade in the history of warfare. By keeping it functioning throughout the Korean War, the flow southward of men and materiel was limited to the overland supply routes within the peninsula. No neutral ships, nor ships of the Soviet Union, or China, ever challenged the system. Although North Korea had used coastal shipping in the initial invasion, once the blockade was imposed, even that option was effectively sealed off by the action of the Blockading Force.

Truman's decision to blockade was in marked contrast to the US position developed later during the Vietnam War. As a result, the port of Haiphong was usually filled with non-belligerent vessels delivering armaments from Eastern Bloc nations and only when Haiphong was mined in 1970 was that seaward flow of contraband controlled. Although the internal Korean Peninsula routes for men and supplies were very effectively used by the Chinese, they were apparently not sufficient to keep their forces fully supplied once their supply lines had to be extended far south of the 38th parallel.

As our first assignment, on 8 February, we relieved *Chandler* on a gunfire support station at the eastern end of the main line of resistance just north of the 36th parallel. We lay hove to or steamed at five knots near Yongdok for three days awaiting call for gunfire support for the ROK divisions holding the line ashore. This period has been called the Fourth Chinese Offensive and was bitterly contested further west along the line from Seoul to north of Wonju, but the extreme eastern end of the line where we were was inactive. No calls ever came and at 0905 on 10 February, *Ozbourn* was released, meeting first with the American destroyer, *English*, to exchange intelligence information and then proceed to join *Manchester* as her anti-submarine screen. At 1120 on 11 February, while screening ahead of *Manchester*, we sighted a North Korean power boat, at which we fired forty-seven rounds of 5"/38–effect unknown. At 1240, the Australian destroyer, HMAS *Warramunga*, joined us to increase the *Manchester*'s screening destroyers by one.

At 0414 on 12 February, while still steaming north on blockade duty, we picked up an unidentified radar contact, fired one round of illumination from the ready mount, and then went to General Quarters, during which we expended thirty-nine rounds of five-inch common and twenty-seven rounds of illumination while trying to sink the craft. Later that morning, we again entered Kiachie Wan harbor to attack targets of opportunity and fired eighty-seven rounds of five-inch at shore targets. At 1322, we sighted two Russian Mark 26 mines drifting

Ozbourn Radio Gang while lying to in Wonsan, February 16, 1950.
l. to r.: Cuthbert, RMN1; Jones, ET2; Hinzpeter, RMN1; and Kish, RMN1.

free and sunk them with 270 rounds of 20-mm. At 1733, we rejoined the *Manchester* and *Warramunga*.

On 13 February we rejoined the replenishment group and LCDR Barr Palmer, USNR, our new executive officer, joined us by high-line from oiler *Passumpsic*. We also sent over all our empty brass to an ammunition ship and took on board one hundred rounds of fixed three-inch and one hundred eighty-seven rounds of five-inch, plus the flashless powder used for nighttime firing. Later, LTJG T. C. Kang, ROK Navy, reported on board as our interpreter. By noon on 14 February we were just northeast of Hungnam and steaming northward on independent blockade duty.

At 0215 on 15 February we fired illumination rounds at a village at 41-02N and then fired five rounds of five-inch at a large building. At 0658 we sighted three fishing junks under sail. After we had fired five rounds, they stopped and *Ozbourn* came alongside. Crew members told LTJG Kang that North Koreans required them to fish in order to pay their taxes. Kang replied that the next time they were found out on the water they would be sunk—not a nice option. At 1025 we sunk another drifting mine with 20-mm fire and at 1110 we used our Condition Three mount to take Ryuchi Byocki under fire.

Beginning the Wonsan Blockade and Bombardment

Very early 16 February, we met the destroyer *Lind* and her captain came on board for a conference. Both destroyers had orders to enter Wonsan harbor and provide gunfire support to the mine-sweepers already at work clearing the harbor and to provide interdiction fire against the transportation system. At Wonsan, many internal supply routes approached the sea and were vulnerable to naval gunfire.

Ozbourn and *Lind* entered Wonsan at 1253 Friday, 16 February, all buttoned up with Condition ABLE set throughout

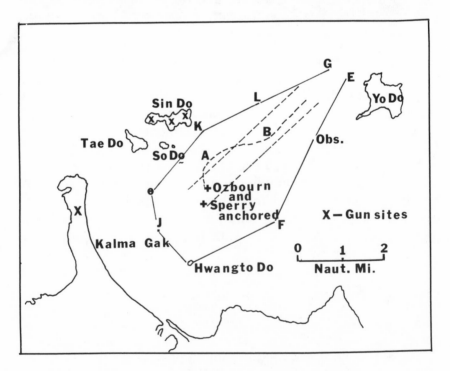

Figure 6: Interdiction in Wonsan, February 18, 1951, from *Ozbourn* Action Report.

the ship to minimize any damage from a mine explosion. At 1428 *Ozbourn* anchored in some seventy feet of water within the area already swept. We provided cover for mine-sweepers but also to began what became known as the siege of Wonsan. After all the carrier chasing out of sight of land we had done, it was exciting to be on your own and close enough to see land. Here we were finally helping. At 1757, *Lind* began firing on known shore targets and at 1804 *Ozbourn* commenced firing. We both left later that evening. The next day *Ozbourn*, with *Sperry* replacing *Lind*, returned to continue the assignment. On the morning of 17 February, *Ozbourn* was again anchored and at 0852 resumed firing on shore targets until 1020. We resumed firing at 1646 at a known shore battery site and at 1735 we departed the inner harbor and the swept area.

By 0800 on Sunday, 18 February, we were again off the mouth of the entrance channel awaiting sufficient light to navigate back into the swept area which was still quite small and confining. At 0922 we reentered and by 1110 had anchored in sixty-six feet with forty-five fathoms to the port anchor. *Sperry* and assorted mine-sweepers were also present.

Sunday morning I began a letter for Monday's replenishment. We had planned to leave the limited sweep area Friday evening, go back to sea and then refuel Saturday, but those plans had been changed to Monday. Not wishing to alarm anyone at home about our new and obviously more dangerous assignment, I repeated all the nonsense about the weather and the latest scuttlebutt about when we were going to leave. Nothing was said about what we were really doing. In the week since being assigned to Task Force 95, we had been all over the east coast of North Korea helping meet effective blockade requirements, namely, see everything every twenty-four hours. During time working inshore, we also served as a recovery ship for ditched pilots. Fortunately we had none to rescue; expected survival time in that icy water was very short.

We entered the swept zone mindful that this harbor was more than one hundred twenty miles deep in enemy-held territory north of the eastern end of the front lines. In addition to interdicting this important transportation hub and protecting the sweeps, our presence should suggest another amphibious assault like Inchon, which ought to draw troops from the front to shore up the defense of the port. Similar landing feints and bombardments were being made elsewhere northward along the coast as they had been during Inchon. Our 27 September bombardment at Fankochi Point just north of Inchon was an example.

In October, Wonsan harbor and its notorious minefields had already cost the US Navy two steel-hulled mine sweeps, USS *Pirate* and USS *Pledge*. The ROK Navy had also lost several wooden-hulled sweeps during the sweeping preceding the delayed landing of the First Marines 25-31 October. Once the Marines had completed their December redeployment through the port of Hungnam, forty miles north of Wonsan, the North Koreans and Chinese had then swept south reoccupying the harbor on their way down the Peninsula.

On 24 January, the eastern end of the front line was anchored at Samchok only about one hundred twenty miles north of Pusan, but it began moving slowly northward. By 12 February, it was anchored at Kangnung twenty miles north of Samchok. We were still deep in enemy territory and very vulnerable. Life was suddenly a lot more sticky than it had been with Task Force 77. Our new executive officer arrived just in time for the excitement.

Wonsan also represented good sheltered water into which US pilots might ditch damaged planes if they were unable to complete their return to the carriers or to bases in the south. Air Force and Marine aircraft from shore bases and naval aircraft from Task Force 77 were being subjected to increasing ground fire and Wonsan made a good ditching site. Here they could expect to be rescued.

A number of offshore islands exist in the Bay of Wonsan and the inner harbor is separated from the outer bay by a dominant peninsula, Kalma Pando, with its tip called Kalma Gak. This peninsula sticks northward like a long curled finger from the south shore. When we arrived on 16 February, the swept bombardment zone and the swept entrance channel were still quite small and somewhat club-shaped, allowing ships to come within three nautical miles (six thousand yards) of Kalma Pando. The swept channel to the firing zone was considerably more narrow and passed within two thousand yards of several islands. Anchoring would ensure more accurate fire and would prevent us from drifting into the nonswept area. However, being anchored might cost valuable time while trying to get away from a counter-battery shelling. Here, anchoring required the ship to keep the engineering plant on line in case you began to drag or had to leave in a hurry.

Not only were we fully ready to get underway but the bridge and all other spaces were manned, in addition to manning one five-inch mount. Under normal circumstances heaving in the anchor might consume five or more minutes and only when the anchor had broken contact with the bottom would the ship normally begin to move. In an emergency, any paid-out anchor chain can be parted by using a sledge hammer on the forelock pin in a detachable Kentner shackle. When the shackle breaks, the freed section of chain and the anchor fall to the bottom. Nobody sacrifices a valuable anchor without a very good reason; being shot at and hit qualifies.

Mine Squadron 3 had already begun clearing a bombardment channel on 12 February.[5] On Friday afternoon, just after our arrival, a helicopter flew low over Sin Do, one of the largest of the islands, and the pilot determined that all the revetments and emplacements on the island were heavily damaged and the island appeared to be uninhabited. We then anchored about two thousand and five hundred yards south of Sin Do in the swept bombardment channel.

After supper on Saturday, I went back up on the bridge with four or five officers to look over the extent of the bay. Off to the west four miles in the distance you could see the darkening peninsula, Kalma Pando, stretching out from the south shore and running north. Far back behind it and behind Wonsan forming the horizon were the eastern mountains over which the sun was setting. Just before we got underway at 1735, I saw a light ashore 'wink' on once in the dark on Kalma Pando. I walked over and took its bearing much as you might on a navigational light ashore. I expected it to happen again. When I tried to point it out, nobody else had seen it. While talking and looking on the same bearing, I then saw a wispy plume of water rising about one thousand yards away; naturally nobody saw that either. Someone had fired a ranging shot at us from Kalma Pando. Kalma Pando was lined with revetments and caves from which artillery could be rolled out, fired, and then returned to hiding and safety. The harbor also had a number of moored poles that probably served as aiming and distance stakes.

Just before we left, *Lind* fired six gun salvos onto the beach in a spectacular night shoot. They must have emptied their magazines of every piece of three-inch and five-inch ammunition on board. It went on for a half hour, blanketing road networks then being used at night to move men and supplies south. This display looked like the climax to some evil Fourth of July—very dark, no moon, and hundreds of shells going somewhere. *Lind*, due to visit the supply and ammunition ships offshore the following day, apparently decided to go out empty. I never knew their target. Later we also were assigned coordinates of road junctions that were to receive random harassing fire.

We left Saturday night to meet the replenishment group on Sunday morning and then someone decided to defer us until Monday. We returned to the harbor about 1100 Sunday (18 February) and anchored in the swept zone, again about two thousand five hundred yards south of Sin Do. After we secured from the Special Sea and Anchor Detail, I went on watch as JOOD. We recommenced our assigned fire missions using the Condition III duty mount. I helped informally with some of the spotting and, at the change of watch, left the bridge just before noon and went directly to the wardroom to wait for lunch. We had a full wardroom with ten of us waiting to eat. The captain was then in CIC plotting fire missions for the afternoon and the Commodore was in his room. Had it been the earlier junior officers' lunch, I probably would have gone first to my room to drop off my foul weather gear. Fortunately I didn't.

I remember this meal above all others. By 1206 I had only eaten two fork-loads of cole slaw when I heard two giant metallic 'thungs,' like we had been hit twice with a giant sledgehammer. Almost instantaneously, off went the General Alarm, at which everyone bolted to their GQ stations. Mine was just out the wardroom door and up at the top of a ladder and through the door into CIC. People ran from everywhere and we were manned and ready to do something in less than a minute. The question was what to do.

The executive officer's battle station was in CIC along with about twenty of us and both the old and new Execs were present. I was absolutely petrified. Our new XO was short, redheaded, and looked like he could do the job. He stood right next to me and you soon saw exactly what sort of a person he was. Palmer glared up at me when he realized I was absolutely paralyzed by what I knew was going to happen next, namely some Chinese shell was going to slam into CIC and blast us all to hamburger. His message was clear, "Do what the hell you are supposed to be doing or you'll have me, instead of the Chinese, all over you." In an instant I had conjured up my recurring nightmare left over from Inchon and he had wiped it out just as quickly.

Three things needed to happen simultaneously. We were anchored, we couldn't move until that changed, and we had to move carefully if we were to remain in the swept area. Despite that, the ship went all ahead full against the anchor chain hoping to drag us out of position while LTJG Bob Rogers and others from Forward Damage Control as well as BM2 Cernak from one of the gun mounts ran out on the main deck and used a sledge to drive out the pin and 'slip anchor.' While they did this, the sea around them was being covered with splashes from some twenty-five bracketing 76-mm shells. Fragments from near misses seemed to be going everywhere. At the same time our two forward five-inch dual mounts had begun rapid-firing four gun salvos right over their heads.

Second, we had to guess where all this was coming from and try to suppress it. Even if we couldn't hit it surgically, they probably would pull their artillery back into the caves on Kalma Pando if we even came close. Third, it was clear that we had already been hit twice and the details of where and how badly had to get to the bridge and any needed damage control and care of any wounded started immediately. Finally, after we left the impact area, we also had to help *Sperry* and any of the sweeps out of the same gun battle. They emerged without injury.

Initially no one on the bridge had any idea of the source of the fire. We were surrounded by shell splashes that resembled the start of a rain storm on a pond but, knowing that didn't locate the firing batteries. Even my observations from the previous night were momentarily forgotten. Then the bridge released the main batteries to fire at will on Kalma Pando. The two shells that hit us had entered on the port side, which was towards Kalma Pando. Off to starboard, the island of Sin Do was well within reach of our three-inch guns. Although these mounts had been designed as the Navy's response to Kamikaze-type attacks and were primarily intended for use under radar control against oncoming propeller-driven aircraft, they could also fire at surface targets. On a surface shoot, without radar control, they could be fired over the sights. The shells seemed small but a three-inch shell is almost the same size as the French 75 of World War One and almost exactly the same as the 76-mm shells that were hitting all around us. They could be highly destructive on impact and would serve well to suppress fire, even if they didn't hit anything directly.

With that in mind, the skipper authorized me to open fire on Sin Do with any battery that was free. When I said, "Commence firing on Sin Do," no one, including me, was quite sure which island was Sin Do and I suspect that any available island became Sin Do and was taken under fire until we got the hell out of there. Our only worry was hitting something friendly, including our own ship. To prevent that, ships' guns are designed with cut-off stops to prevent the gunner from continuing to fire at a target that had disappeared behind part of his ship. Keeping from hitting anything away from the ship, in the air or where your shot may be falling, was the responsibility of the battery commander. In this situation, 'shoot first, ask later' probably would prevail. It was fortunate there were relatively few friendlies around. We put out 442 three-inch rounds onto or near Sin Do out of three of the four available barrels. One barrel of our twin mount aft was being repaired when the firing commenced. From where I was in CIC looking at a radar repeater and getting ready to plot and defend us against incoming aircraft, my only link with the reality of three-inch action was via sound-powered phones connecting me to the radar room, the three director captains (Chiefs DeWitt and Higgins, and ENS Jarrett), and a talker on the bridge. I also had Jack Blonsick on the phone line. He controlled the two 20-mm mounts from the open bridge. Jack watched three muzzle flashes from the beach, then he saw a fourth. Three measured splashes hit directly in a line walking towards him. The fourth should have hit the bridge and never did.

Neither Jack nor I had anything courageous to do. I could only listen and he could only sight-see. He called out muzzle flashes on Kalma Gak and yelled their bearings, but nobody seemed to be listening. Then, suddenly, he began seeing primary and secondary explosions in the smoke followed by no more muzzle flashes. Generally, in a surface counter-battery shoot, I could only relay commands from the captain on the bridge to the gun mounts. When I received permission to open fire, I was told to release the guns into local control. This gave the mount captains open authority to empty their magazines against the beach—wherever that was. We put Sin Do under heavy fire particularly by the twin mount aft as we moved away from the island, first by the forward starboard mount and then by the forward port mount as we turned in the swept channel to leave. I picked up snatches of information coming in from the other lines to CIC, plus whatever information I could get from those outside, but otherwise I had nothing to do. The gun chiefs had their hands full and were too busy to talk. It was a petrifying three or four minutes. We finally were free of our anchor and by 1244 both *Ozbourn* and *Sperry* were out of danger. Jarrett later told me that as we were leaving, our wake seemed full of exploding 76 mm shells.

As each three-inch gun fired and its cylinder revolved, steel sprockets grabbed each new shell and moved it into the chamber as soon as the gun had recoiled from the previous discharge and had thrown out the empty brass. Handlers kept a chain of new shells moving up from the magazines below to the ready lockers on deck or directly into the open gun mount. As the mount traversed in a circular motion, everyone on it had to hang on. Those within the splinter shield handing up shells had to chase after the loaders to keep up the flow. It was easy to make a mistake and catch your hand in the sprockets if you lost your balance or were careless. When things went well, a good gun crew might put out one hundred rounds a minute from a twin mount. Empty brass piled up in front of the three-inch as well as the five-inch mounts. After each shoot we loaded up the 01 level with empty brass to be returned to the ammunition ship as if we expected a refund for returning empty coke bottles.

I still think we were under fire from Kalma Gak and perhaps even by larger batteries in caves opening from it, but our action report said we were also under fire from Sin Do.[6] Jarrett, on the other hand, remains convinced it was primarily Sin Do but that might only have been small bore automatic and 60 mm mortar fire. Regardless, we must have resembled *Lind* the previous night. Probably no one ashore could even see the ship for the gun flashes and they assumed we were exploding and sank. We probably came as close to earning our voice call— 'Fireball'—as we ever would.

above: Mark 56 Director with empty brass after an engagement with batteries on Sin Do and Kalma Gak, Wonsan Harbor.
below: Inspection of the Mark 56 Director after the Sin Do and Kalma Gak engagement. Note 76mm shell hole in the gyro compartment. February 18, 1951.

After everything calmed down we were able to assess the damage. Our major damage was that the twin three-inch battery aft had taken a shell in the Mark 56 Director hitting the fire control radar operator and battery officer's compartment at about leg height. They both sat in this small metal box and looked out through a hatch on the top. Had the shell hit while we were at GQ, two people would have been sitting there. One was eating and Jarrett, the other, was asleep when it hit.

The second round passed first through the motor whaleboat, plunged through the side of the deck house aft and then exploded against the steel decking in the passageway outside After Officer's Quarters and dimpled it. Had the Chief Engineer been in his bunk when it went off about five feet from his bunk, he would have had a ferocious headache. Instead, he and his roommate were eating with me and had missed it. Jarrett was asleep in After Officer's when the shells hit; one missed his room by about ten feet and the other blew a hole in his GQ station. Fragments from the shell hitting in the passageway did a lot of superficial damage to overhead wiring in the passageway and blew fragment holes all over the place. Although fragments and shell splinters from near misses were everywhere on deck, no further hits occurred. Back aft, the concussion and fragments even hit the executive officer's safe, breaking the small bottles of medicinal alcohol and most of the morphine ampules stored in it. We also had some damage on the bridge. A near miss smashed glass out of our port search light and severed a radio antenna. Chief DeWitt's wound probably came from this shell. An antenna lead on the mainmast was partially severed but that was only found later when we went alongside a tender.

Initially only two people had been hit and suffered minor wounds. For this, they were recommended for Purple Hearts. A.D. Lee, Fireman (Metalsmith) was walking down the after passageway to open the Ship's Store when the shell went off against the deck. He was hit in the shoulder with small fragments. I was talking by sound-powered telephone to Chief DeWitt, at the port three-inch Director, when he was struck in the lip by small fragments. Afterward, he looked more like he'd cut himself shaving and he took a lot of razzing for his Purple Heart. They had been wounded in action and the awards were deserved.

Everyone else had come close. Had Jarrett not been sleeping and been able to find his shoes faster, he probably would have been killed in the Mark 56 Director aft. As it was, he ran most of the way asleep, but with clothes over his arms and dressing on the way, only to find when he got there that his station was useless. He and BM2 Tausche who sat beside him had just missed death.

After it was over, Jarrett picked up his big telephone talker's helmet and brought it up to the wardroom for our inspection; it looked like a road grader had run over it. The Commodore told him to keep it as a souvenir saying, "In fifty years, you'll be telling your grandchildren you had it on when it happened." Jarrett lost the helmet but on the Jarrett's kitchen wall in Pittsburgh is an oak plaque onto which is mounted the nose plug from the shell that hit his Director. It came from a Russian-made 76 mm armor-piercing shell.

Had the explosion in the aft passageway occurred ten minutes later some twenty or more sailors would have been in line waiting to buy candy and cigarettes. Miraculously, fragments from that shell also went on through the bulkhead and traveled just above the deck into our stateroom and the chief engineer's. LT Armond Remmen had three pairs of shoes lined up under his bunk. The left shoe in each pair was destroyed. Blonsick also lost a left shoe of a pair stowed under my bunk. He also found another shell fragment stuck in his pillow. 'Boy's Town' had fiber glass fragments everywhere.

Several days later Seaman Apprentice Stoner told Jarrett that he had a pimple on his face that wouldn't heal. When Doc Ketcham probed it, out came another tiny shell fragment—our third Purple Heart. We had been very fortunate. Except for a sailor who ran three-inch loading sprockets through his hand and fingers during a General Quarters dry-run, these three were the only casualties during *Ozbourn*'s first Korean tour. Ironically, during our first leave period after getting back to San Diego, a sailor drove his motorcycle under a semi-tractor and was killed. Another fell off the pier and drowned.

We were still at GQ, when the ET2 (electronic technician) in charge of the radar units asked permission to leave his post to go to the head. I gave him permission, advising him that everyone else on the circuit had already completed the process right where we were standing. After we had cleared the impact area and had finally secured from General Quarters, everybody was on a giant high. Men roamed around the ship until after midnight telling stories about where they had been and how close they had come to being killed.

I returned later in the afternoon to the bridge and looked up past the 37 Director to the yard-arm of the main mast. There was the American flag full to the truck, standing stiff in the breeze and absolutely riddled from shell fragments. It looked like something out of a movie about Fort McHenry. The sky behind it was bright blue and there was the flag fully extended, pocked, and shredded from shell fragments. Every time I see the American flag standing out against the sky I see the same image and feel the same emotional thrill that went through me on that day in 1951.

By late afternoon, the crew also passed around the Commodore's comment to the captain on the bridge at our battle of Wonsan, "lets get out of here, Charley." We all agreed. In addition to three Purple Hearts, other medals were proposed. The mount captain, R. M. Lauer, Gunner's Mate Chief, USN, of the after three-inch mount, was proposed for a Navy Commendation Ribbon for returning his battery to action after the Director had been knocked out. The Executive Officer, the Gunnery Officer, John Hadley, and John Bond, Main Battery Director Officer, were proposed for the Bronze Star. The captain was proposed for a Silver Star and several other Commendation Ribbons were proposed. I favored John Moriarty's Bronze Star, but it was to be for something that happened later the same day.

The Rescue

Once clear of danger, we immediately sent an action report message to the fleet describing our problems. About 1400, Task Force 77 sent in an air strike on Kalma Pando. One of the planes was hit by ground-fire and the pilot crashed thirteen miles south of the swept channel, deep inside the unswept area and behind some islands. Although a shell hole had just rendered the motor whaleboat *hors de combat*, the undamaged captain's gig was still available. It was launched at 1645 with

John Moriarty again in charge of the boat crew. Night was falling.

Aided by a search plane, at 1926, John reported they had recovered the pilot alive and by 2200, they had returned to *Ozbourn*. During much of those five hours they had been out of our sight but had located and then rescued the pilot from the icy waters, almost losing him to hypothermia before getting him back. This time John had recovered Ensign R. M. Tvede, USN, from *Valley Forge*.[7] We spent the rest of the night alternatively wrapping him in blankets and standing him in a cold shower. John Moriarty was nearly in as bad condition. By the next morning Tvede had recovered sufficiently from exposure to be returned to the *Valley Forge*. John was subsequently awarded the Bronze Star with Combat V and the boat crew were awarded the Commendation Ribbon with V for their successful mission. When we sent Tvede back to *Valley Forge*, they rewarded us with two gallons of ice cream. I found myself envious of John's 'luck,' and secretly wanted to do something similar before leaving Korea, so I kept volunteering as boat officer.

Afterwards

As things returned to normal, I remembered the newspaper publicity when destroyers had been hit at Inchon. I knew that, unlike World War Two when ship damage and losses might be kept out of the papers, anything happening now would probably make the front page of the *New York Times* the next day and ruin my father's breakfast. Still, we hadn't been sunk and I wasn't wounded. I wrote the details to my high school teacher, William Charlesworth, and asked him to tell my parents what had happened if anything came up in the papers. Meanwhile, I decided that I would keep on writing about sunsets and when we were due to leave. If our battle hadn't made the newspapers, then I could delay talking about the whole thing until I got home. None of that worked.

Unfortunately, my Grandmother Seanor was alone while she listened to the Sunday evening news on the radio and heard the Communist version. They reported a US ship with 846 on its side had been sunk in Wonsan harbor. She didn't know whether or not anyone else knew, and finally decided just to keep it to herself, which she did for three days. She, obviously, had the worst of it. As soon as Dad read it next day in the *New York Times*, he telephoned our Congressman who confirmed, first, that we hadn't been sunk and second, that I wasn't one of those wounded.

Meanwhile in Pittsburgh, Mr. and Mrs. Jarrett were also listening to the evening news while getting ready to go out for supper. They heard the same report, that a ship with 846 on it had been sunk with all hands in North Korean waters. The next morning their Congressman also assured them that the report was not true.

We had just completed our first counter-battery suppression exercise. Other gun-fire support missions in Wonsan and else-where would come either against pre-set coordinates such as a night-time interdiction of a road crossing or supply dump, or against coordinates called in by spotters in aircraft. Only occasionally would we be able to see our own fall of shot and do our own spotting. On occasion, someone ashore would take us under fire, but it was never as dicey as that first encounter.

On February 24, the Commodore and the skipper of *Manchester* set in motion their plans to invade Sin Do by landing a platoon of Korean Marines on it. Accompanying them was a US Marine Captain from the *Manchester* and ENS Blonsick from *Ozbourn*. Jack Blonsick's Marine Corps' experience was limited to being a back-seat radio operator. Neither of the two US officers spoke Korean. After greasy pork chops for break-fast, everyone was loaded into landing craft for the early morn-ing assault. They then sat there bouncing up and down for more than four hours, alternating between being scared to death and seasick. Finally, the assault occurred and went without a hitch because nobody was on Sin Do. Jack had conjured up wild images of a landing like that at Tarawa. As soon as they were ashore, he and the Marine Captain hid behind a very large rock, hoping the Korean Marines remembered who the enemy was. Neither Jack nor the Marine spoke Korean and none of the Korean Marines spoke English. I had watched the planning of the landing as it went on in our wardroom during the previous week. Given what went on in our wardroom, how Inchon ever happened escaped me. It seemed to lie somewhere between incompetence and over-planning but in the end it was success-ful.

During time inshore, we remained at a modified Condition III. This meant keeping some of the crew at their GQ stations, most of the watertight doors shut, manning the 37 director and having one of the five-inch mounts ready to fire. There was no need to keep everybody continuously at GQ when firing one- or two-gun interdiction missions. While at Condition III, you could be reading in your bunk or doing paperwork and hear the sharp crack of the five-inch followed by the clang of brass being ejected onto the deck. If you were close enough outside you might even catch the acrid smell of burnt powder or see the peculiar yellow-orange cloud that turns white after emerging from the muzzles. The rest of the time, it was a muffled clang. After a while you became used to a clang now and then and ignored it.

With many of the doors dogged shut, it was difficult to get around but it did improve our water-tight integrity if we hit a mine. General Task Force 95 operating instructions required us to remain in waters deeper than one hundred fathoms (six hundred feet), a depth generally thought to be greater than one in which mines could be moored and be effective. In Wonsan harbor, water was scarcely one hundred feet deep and mooring mines was easy. The instructions applied only when off the coast, not in Wonsan harbor. Mines remained on my mind continuously, but never more so than when operating alone perhaps one hundred miles from help. A mine that didn't sink us at once might well lead to progressive failure of water-tight integrity, permitting more and more water to get into more and more compartments. Finally, you lost boilers, then the ability to generate electricity for pumps and lights and, ultimately, the ship would go down in very cold water. Sinking was far less likely if you were hit with counter-battery fire. Keeping the ship buttoned up during counter-battery fire would also keep people off the weather decks and probably reduce injuries from fragments. While in Wonsan, I remember only once using the weather deck to run to my GQ station. While running, I looked out to starboard and could see tall plumes of water rising several hundred yards away. Explosions in water always seemed innocuous and harmless.

We then went on to independent surveillance and shore-bombarding patrols ranging as far north as Chongjin. The blockade's northern border had been established at 4l-50N which excluded the port of Rashin some twenty miles south of the Russian border. Rashin was then being leased by the Russians; whether it was being used to provide materiel for the North Koreans or Chinese, we never knew. Even if it were, we could still block off the coastal route south by coastal interdiction. Rashin was later attacked from the air.[8]

We watched for coastal road or rail traffic as we patrolled the coast. Normally you would notice traffic at night only when they used lights. However, the random firing at known sites using illumination shells followed by five-inch anti-aircraft common shells might also work. Songjin and the more northern city of Chongjin had been heavily bombed. Both were also usually bombarded as a matter of course during a visit.

Chongjin was suspected as the site from which floating or drifter mines were being launched. The use of drifter mines in war was in contravention to the Hague Convention of 1907 and the London Conference of 1909. According to the Conference, moored mines could be used but they had to be equipped with devices that disarmed them thirty minutes after they broke free from their moorings. Obviously, neither North Korea, the Soviet Union, nor China were signatory to the 1909 London Conference. The mines that were captured during the Autumn 1950 move north, or were inspected after being planted, or collected drifting free, were all Soviet in origin.[9]

On *Wiltsie* they saw small blips on the radar at night when they were in the swept area in Wonsan and concluded the North Koreans were releasing floaters in the harbor. Unlike *Ozbourn*, on which we used the 20-mm machine guns, *Wiltsie* preferred using a rifle to shoot mines. Once while underway, *Wiltsie* discovered a floater dead ahead and had only time to use left full rudder followed by right full rudder to avoid hitting it. Jim and others on the bridge leaned over the splinter shield to watch it drift down the starboard side. There must have been many similar near misses to other ships and often at night. In September while *Ozbourn* was backing down and getting underway in Inchon, John Bond and Jack Blonsick saw an American corpse in the water floating out with the tide. As it got nearer, they also saw a mine partially hidden by the body draped over it. Bond leaned over the splinter shield and held his breath while it too drifted down our starboard side.

Once on the blockade along the northern coast, we found one small boat several thousand yards inshore of us and we fired five rounds of five-inch to warn him back to shore. It was a brisk clear windy day with a strong chop. I can still see this small boat with a Korean standing up in the back trying to scull into the wind while coming at him was our measured fire of single rounds throwing up columns of water that finally fell away with the wind. We never hit him and he never quit doing whatever he was doing out there. Anyone out in the ocean was presumed to be dragging more drifting mines out into southerly flowing currents. Even if he was merely fishing, that also aided the enemy.

By late February, the strategic dimensions of the war seemed to be coming into focus. This war was being limited to the Korean peninsula, although not everyone agreed with that assessment. On 5 March, the editor of the *Beaver Valley Times* reminded his readers that six hundred members of the First Marine Division rotating home were due to arrive in San Francisco along with four hundred wounded, "they are members of the First Marine Division which has played such an important part in the opening phase of World War III." By then it was becoming clear to us, that if World War Three hadn't started yet, it probably wouldn't. The question was how to stop the one we had. Others have said that World War Three was really the Cold War and in fact was due to run for many more years.

As the swept area in Wonsan was enlarged, more ships came in. Finally, LST 799, equipped with helicopters, was brought in to rescue downed pilots and they could move much more rapidly than a captain's gig. When there was nothing else to do, its helicopters overflew the beach looking for targets of opportunity. Later on, they found one for *Ozbourn* and we killed some four hundred troops mustering outside a building. Our normal Condition III with one five-inch mount manned as well as the main director was not enough for that task; this target required everything. I was in CIC when the spotting message with the coordinates came in from 'Windmill Queen' and we immediately went to General Quarters to fire six gun salvos. I was still in CIC when we received a tremendous 'well-done' from the helicopter pilot.[10] LST 799 was to become the only ship eligible for all seven battle stars awarded during the Korean War.

I always wondered who we ended up killing and why they hadn't sense enough not to hold muster in wartime—then I remembered all those personnel inspections we had held. In this war, as any, there were sufficient, unexpected surprises on both sides and enough stupidity to satisfy everyone. As the naval pressure against Wonsan grew stronger, resistance ashore grew stronger.

Ozbourn, remaining in Wonsan harbor until 25 February, was involved in another pilot's rescue and had several more experiences with counter-battery fire, but no more hits. At 1710 on 26 February we got underway for Sasebo arriving on 27 February where we moored next to *Borie* alongside the destroyer tender *Prairie*. We had come back alongside a destroyer tender to repair our damaged boat, rework the wiring, and repair Jarrett's Director.

While in Sasebo for repairs, a message came in one evening addressed to all destroyer divisions asking for volunteers for an extended tour in WestPac. The Commodore read it late one night after returning from a heavy party at the 'O' Club. He immediately released a message saying, "DesDiv 112 would happily remain in WestPac til the cows came home." When he awoke next morning, a big blue flag was flying from the truck with DesDiv 112 across the top and a cow's udder with four teats emblazoned across the bottom. Somebody had worked all night, whom we never knew; the flag came down quickly but not before we had been extended. CAPT Roeder was shocked next morning when he read what he had sent out the night before, but, regardless of his chagrin, we had been volunteered. As soon as I could reach a telephone, I called home on 3 March talking briefly to Dad explaining that it really hadn't been quite the way the *New York Times* had described it. Actually they were accurate enough for not having been there.

This time, *Hollister* was in with us for time alongside a tender; the ships in our Division were gradually falling apart. Brickwork in one of her boilers was failing—too much high speed with the carriers while we were getting into trouble in Wonsan. Each ship was building up a long list of things that would need to get fixed or replaced when we returned to the States and into a shipyard for a major overhaul.

Shortly after we arrived, it was time for the former executive officer's going-away party. When it was over, we sent him off on a thirty-six hour train ride to Yokosuka where he would catch a Northwest Orient flight back to the States. Meanwhile Barr Palmer, the new exec, was trying to get some people off the ship and into the new rest camps outside Yokohama. We probably all needed a little time off the *Oz*. A group of enlisted men and several junior officers were able to get off on a few days R & R at a famous Japanese rest area. Off they went anticipating an idyllic several days full of Geishas, sumptuous baths and lots of booze. The first beers had hardly been opened when three majors from MacArthur's headquarters in Tokyo showed up, took over the entire place, and sent our troops back to Sasebo.

The rumor was that the Commodore would get a second Legion of Merit for his successful tour and that Captain Akers, the Bronze Star with V for his tour. They both had earned them. Dad's letter mentioned that the *New York Times* said we had been down near Yangyang on the 10th of February; I didn't know where we had been then but I doubted it. He was more nearly correct; we were within a few miles of it and the *New York Times* had it right. The word around the ship had been that we had gone south near Pohang to help ROK Marines clean out guerrillas left over from last fall. Instead, those were the days we spent at the Main Line of Resistance (MLR) waiting to be called upon for gunfire support should the Chinese counter-offensive expand eastward from Wonju and reach the coast. Close support of friendly troops is tough; there is no room for error and you can never correct your mistakes.

On 3 March in Sasebo we entertained VADM Andrewes, RN, Commander Task Force 95, as our official guest. We had become his first wounded destroyer from Wonsan. He was then based on board HMS *Ladybird*, which had been an old Yangtze River gunboat. It had been tied up in Sasebo since the previous August and looked more like an Ohio River steamboat or the Albany night boat than a warship. The next rumor was that they were returning us to Task Force 77 for the remainder of our tour.

Someone came up with a new reason for rotating destroyers between the carriers and blockade duty. Just so many shells can safely pass out of a gun barrel before its lands are worn, accuracy drops, and the barrel needs replacing which means a major overhaul. Use everyone's guns a little by rotating your destroyers, just as you should your tires.

While in harbor, destroyers used their motor whaleboats for getting liberty parties into the landing and then back again. A ground fog came in one night during a late return to the ship and Ike Voles and his crew kept on going until they came up on the *Valley Forge*. The next stop would have been open ocean.

On Saturday afternoon, 10 March, we were still in Sasebo harbor and I got a feverish cold. I felt lousy about 1500, and saw Doc Ketcham in Sick Bay. He kindly sent me to bed. Unfortunately, I failed to advise anyone of my illness and when the LT Remmen saw me in the sack during working hours, he yanked me out and sent me back to work. Akers considered him to be the best engineering officer on any destroyer in the Pacific Fleet. Remmen could be an old grouch but it was mostly all bark; I got up and managed to survive for the rest of the day.

I spent most of my time in Sasebo delivering officer messenger mail, getting new charts and doing other 'go-fer' type things. We were due to leave Sasebo at 0200 on 11 March along with *Hollister* and start back north to find Task Force 77. I expected this would be our last time with them.

Meanwhile we were also tracking the destroyer division that would be our relief as it came west. They had stayed only one day in Pearl Harbor but when passing Midway, someone broke down and that delayed them five additional days. It was like waiting for Santa Claus except Christmas kept moving back. Finally, they were due in Japan on or about 17 March. Allowing for overlap, we should be out of Japan by 31 March unless someone decided we needed an April income tax break.

LT Remmen again took over my old iron typewriter to finish his last-minute Engineering Reports. He also sent it to the tender for another complete overhaul this time in. I had bought it in September for twenty dollars from a departing officer on the division staff. From home came word that my eighty-three-year-old Grandmother Seanor had fallen down the stairs and only strained her back. All things considered, this had been a lucky spring.

When we went back to sea, instead of rejoining the carriers one more time, we remained in Task Force 95. By 2300 on 15 March, we were looking for small junks near Chongjin and using star shells to illuminate the waters inshore. At least one of our parachute flares drifted ashore and landed in woods behind the city where it started a small forest fire. You could never know what someone was doing out in a junk, particularly at night, and Chongjin was famous as the site from which most of the floating mines originated. Whenever we found a boat, we had no choice but to shoot. The last time in Wonsan we had been ordered to take under fire several school-houses and a park that the helicopters reported were being used to house NK troops—what a business.

We were somewhere off the coast when a small fishing vessel was sighted. Standing orders were to take under fire any small boats found offshore. Charley Akers was on the bridge with the Commodore when the event began. In order to improve our chances of hitting it, the skipper moved in closer. Suddenly he realized that a young woman with a baby was sitting in the stern and looking at the ship. Akers asked Roeder to take a look and did he really want us to begin firing? Roeder looked and asked the skipper to proceed on our trip elsewhere.

During a small boat search in Wonsan, Jack Blonsick, as the boat officer, was convinced they had captured a small mine layer. It had fishing nets on board which were bone dry, a shiny new winch, and a new wooden shield aft with two oiled railroad track sections which might best be used for sliding mines into the water. The Korean skipper was not very respectful and our crew protested to our Korean interpreter that they couldn't be fishing. However, the final word from Charley Akers was to let them go. Who was correct?

By 16 March, we were still off Chongjin, North Korea and that was as far north as we went. Any further north and you had to speak Russian. This time, we came up with *Missouri* and several other ships. We worked over the town while the battleship tried to drop a coastal bridge. This was one of the few times I could actually see the target. People in our 37 Director above the bridge were higher and had far better optics than bridge binoculars so I climbed up and into the Director to watch. As *Missouri* fired you could follow the shells on their way to the target.

Because *Missouri* was getting a number of premature bursts from shells that exploded about a mile out of the barrel, they asked that no 'small boys' (destroyers) pass between them and the beach and, thus, under the path of their shells. These prematures were spectacular aerial bursts about the size of a shopping mall filled with yellow smoke and making fragment splashes all over the ocean. Troops around the Korean bridge continued working throughout the shelling; rather discouraging on our part. We took up a position about a mile astern of *Missouri* and you could see her move sideways when they fired all guns simultaneously in a broadside. Despite the distance, sailors on the fantail later found shell fragments and pockmarks from the prematures.

People on our bridge and in the Director were unimpressed with *Missouri*'s accuracy. Shells fell so far from the abutments that the workers were not aware they were the target. Finally, 'Alameda Spot 8,' the aircraft spotting the mission suggested letting the 'small boys' do it. With that, *Missouri* stopped and several destroyers moved in close to do the job. Whether we did or not, I never found out because I left the bridge. Shutting down the coastal transportation system by shore and aerial bombardment would also become more difficult because of shore batteries. On this same trip north, someone opened up on us from the beach using a heavy caliber machine gun. We must have been five miles out. About two miles inshore from us you could see a line of bullets hitting the water. Except for this, we were never to experience counter-battery fire except in Wonsan. By the end of the war, anti-aircraft and anti-ship fire could be expected along much of the coast.

Suddenly, we were sent south again. While off Chongjin, we received orders to report back to Wonsan with all haste. The day began at Chongjin with General Quarters at 0600 in the middle of my 04-08 watch. For the first time I was out in the open when I replaced Chief DeWitt on the Port 63 Director while he went below for breakfast. When DeWitt came back, I then relieved the JOOD while he did the same. I had never seen outside during a real General Quarters on *Ozbourn*. All I had done was to stand over a radar and have my ears get sore from wearing sound-powered phones. Outside it was the same, except your ears first hurt and then became numb from the bitter cold.

We raced down to Wonsan but missed out on something very big that had happened two nights previously. A spotter aircraft had seen heavily trampled snow adjacent to a warehouse and the slaughtering began. First, *Manchester* had hit a barracks area, killing an estimated six thousand Chinese. Then one of her accompanying destroyers killed another estimated two thousand with six gun salvos. This harbor had numerous targets because it was on a main road south from China to the front.

By 1130, we were in the inner harbor of Wonsan and in standby, two thousand yards behind the main line of firing destroyers. Nothing happened until 1536 when three splashes erupted near one of the destroyers and the entire line opened up on likely targets ashore. Although *Ozbourn* went to General Quarters, we had been given no assigned targets ashore and were not permitted to fire over ships already on the line. At 1549, we secured from GQ with no shots fired – end of action.

The next day we were to leave Wonsan again. We pulled out from the inner firing lane and anchored outside the islands late on the 18th to allow us to leave and meet the replenishment group on 19 March. Earlier we had been requested to extend our tour by eight more days to assist Task Force 95 but those days were about up and the rest of the Division was finally with us. *Hollister*, who had been up north with *Missouri*, remained with her when we left. At Wonsan, *Knox* and *McKean* were also there, having been in on the 'turkey shoot' two nights previously. We had missed all the excitement but everyone felt more useful in the harbor doing this than we did dancing with carriers. On the 18th, *Ozbourn* had fired over two hundred fifty five-inch rounds. Every morning, helicopters lifted off the LST, toured the beach and then came back with fire missions for us. There was a wealth of damage to be done there and we shared targets with Navy Panthers and Air Force B-26s and F-80s.

Jack Blonsick saw other air traffic in the area – assorted B-26s, F-80s, and F-86s from bases in South Korea, plus Navy and Marine aircraft including AD-4s, F4Us, F9Fs, and PBMs. Even the MIGs weren't that far away. One evening, on the bridge as JOOD, I was admiring a spectacular sunset over the darkening mountains as we steamed five miles offshore south of Songjin. Suddenly a pair of blue Navy Panther jets slipped low over the mountains and roared out of the setting sun, passing over us at little more than masthead height. They were on us and gone in a climbing turn in seconds. No one on the bridge had seen them, nor had CIC spotted them on radar, we had been caught flatfooted. Had it been a real attack, we would have been dead meat. No MIGs ever attempted anything similar, but we were certainly vulnerable to such an attack.

On another evening while moving south, the clouds over the mountains to the north behind us were being colored off and on with heat lightning flashes. Thunder rumblings went along with it and together they could have masqueraded as a distant rainstorm until one remembered that *Missouri* was behind us and that her sixteen-inch shells were causing grief rather than rain somewhere along the North Korean coast. We steamed on, gradually the noise lessened, the clouds continued to darken, and night fell on our way south to Wonsan.

We began 20 March with another Dawn Alert but that would be followed by a full day outside taking on provisions, mail, shells, and oil. That could be our last time provisioning. Our relieving destroyer division had already arrived and was now working offshore with Task Force 77; we were now shorttimers. The rumors were that we would now be released and likely escort *Missouri* back to Yokosuka. The word was that all our mail, and hers too. was being held at the Yokosuka Mail Center beginning 20 March. After we escorted *Missouri* to Yokosuka, we would begin the trip back to the States.

Instead, on 20 March we again reentered Wonsan through the swept channels and took up a standby position about two thousand yards behind the firing line. At 1851, splashes were observed near HMNS *Evertsen*, the Dutch destroyer, and we commenced firing at battery positions on Kalma Gak moving back and forth across four known sites. At 1901 our shells created a large explosion followed by flashes and several smaller explosions at one of the sites on Kalma Gak. The explosions, fire, and smoke continued for over forty-five minutes and appeared to have been an ammunition dump.[11] When we were no longer required, *Ozbourn* and *Hollister* were ordered north to Songjin with Commodore serving as Task Element Commander of TE 95.22. We left the inner harbor at 1911. Royal commandos were on reconnaissance as part of a plan for a massive British special forces land assault from ships on Song-jin, and we might be needed for close support.

We returned to Wonsan on 21 March but about dusk, we were under orders to leave and again patrol north to Songjin. I had gone to sleep prior to the midwatch when the General Quarter alarm went off one more time. I grabbed clothes, and shoes and bolted up the inside passage towards CIC and, again, missed seeing any of the splashes. Fortunately, there were only splashes and no hits but it was difficult to go back to sleep afterwards.

Four destroyers were now on the firing line parallel to Kalma Pando. From north to south they were *Forest Royal, Hollister, Evertsen*, and *Zellers*. We were lying to off Sin Do and *English* was anchored further east in the swept channel. When helicopters made their morning sweeps of the beach they found the North Koreans had been busy during the night improving old and digging new revetments and emplacements for gun positions. They had dug completely through Kalma Pando and could supply the shore batteries from the landward side of the hill.

We were taken under fire just about the time we were also supposed to leave for Songjin. The firing on both sides was dilatory until about 1700 when it picked up, focusing on a small mine-sweep but also firing at *Evertsen*. At that point, the Dutch captain came up on the TBS announcing in heavy accent, "All ships...Dis iss Trendt, dey ar shooting ad me, I am clozing de rangh." With that, he cranked on power, moved directly toward Kalma Gak and, from all indications, left the swept area in order to get close enough to effectively suppress the fire. It was certainly heroic, if foolhardy. The Commodore, on the other hand, was watching his wrist watch. The Dutchman's words had scarcely sunk in when the Commodore came up on the same circuit and requested permission to leave with *Ozbourn* and *Hollister* on 'duties assigned.' The Task Element boss came back with a "Permission granted, Mobilize Dog, I think the rest of us can handle it." An innocuous enough statement, except for the tone I thought I heard in the message. After that, I never really wished to meet anyone from the Dutch Navy and tell them I knew 'Mobilize Dog.' It seemed an embarrassing way to depart a gun battle. It was like being called home to supper during the last quarter of a football game. The *Evertsen* later was inducted into 'Charley's Lost Anchor Club' when she, too, slipped her anchor to avoid being hit. At least one other ship left behind an anchor before the long siege of Wonsan was over.

This time the NK also shelled the departure path. Jarrett, sitting in his Director aft as we wended our way out the channel, provided me with a running account of the near misses creeping up our wake. People watching the splashes said these were bigger than before (76 mm) and we thought they had brought in guns up to 155 mm to get us out of there. This was to be our last visit and I was very glad to be out of Wonsan, although we might have been able to leave a little more gracefully. One really doesn't leave a fight before its over no matter what. Suddenly we were out of Wonsan and probably on our way home after a short visit to Songjin. On at least one counter-battery attack, *Ozbourn* and the other destroyers got underway, leaving behind our motor whaleboat which was out investigating a suspicious small boat. For about an hour ENS Blonsick became SOPA (Senior Officer Present Afloat) Wonsan until we returned for him, Ike Voles, and the rest of the boat crew.

By 0700 on 23 March we were again interdicting targets ashore at Songjin. During this mission, we destroyed two fifteen foot-long fishing junks by gunfire and dispersed the fishermen around five others by firing air bursts. We were eight thousand five hundred yards offshore and could not get much closer and still remain outside the one hundred fathom line. That had to be our last effort. Now we could go home.

Early 24 March, *Ozbourn* and *Hollister* departed Songjin at twenty-three knots en route to Yokosuka and from there to CONUS—or that was the scuttlebutt. Rumor now was that we would meet *Boxer* in Van Dieman Straits off the southern coast of Japan as she rejoined Task Force 77 after her stateside overhaul. There we would take on board fifty-four passengers for further transit to Yokosuka. When we reached Yokosuka we would, of course, join *McKean* and *Knox* who were already there. They had arrived three days earlier. We were sure we would only be there a few days before leaving for home.

Another version of 'That Rumor' was that we would stay in Yokosuka until *Valley Forge* or *Missouri* left the operating area after they had been relieved by *Boxer* and *New Jersey*, respectively. We would then escort either one or both home. That too would be good because there would then be no need to stop for fuel except at Pearl. If we had to stop in Pearl, it would probably be a very short stop. Throughout the ship, people spent considerable time sorting out the various versions of these arrangements with the help of the people in the Ship's Laundry and even the yeomen in the Ship's Office; unfortunately they were all wrong.

Instead, we returned to Wonsan. About 1330 we were all lined up on the firing line when CIC reported a 'May Day' over one of the aircraft emergency nets we monitored. Within minutes we had our plane crash detail out and our newly re-paired whaleboat lowered to deck-level in case we had to help. About the same time, 'Windmill Queen,' returned to LST 779 from a spotting mission for some of the destroyers. We believed it would not be available immediately to go out on a rescue. *Hollister,* underway from her gunfire position, was ready to take on the rescue, as were we. Just as people on the bridge saw the damaged F-80 flying overhead in a beautiful blue spring sky, its pilot radioed, "This thing is breaking up," and bailed out over the harbor.

His chute had just opened when 'Windmill Queen' lifted off the deck of LST 799 and started in the direction of the para-chute. The pilot had scarcely hit the water before 'Queen' was over him and pulled him in. Meanwhile, the F-80 did a falling leaf tailspin and hit the water about three miles away. The flight leader stayed overhead to watch it all. When they had the downed pilot safely on board the LST, he thanked everyone and went on his way. We had finally seen another side of Wonsan.

In the previous six days we had been everywhere from Chongjin to Songjin to Wonsan. There had been little change to Wonsan except less snow although, on 24 March, the North Korean gunners blasted another ROK minesweeper. The rest of our time there seemed quiet. Finally, we really were on our way home.

Reprise

In December 1951, I was home for Christmas leave and ran into PFC Harold Smith, USMC, a friend from Emma-Jean's high school class. Smitty was due back in San Francisco at Treasure Island before being sent to Korea. A few weeks later both of us met in San Francisco and tried to find Pete Partridge in the naval hospital. Pete had become the second Scout from the Wolf Patrol, Troop 406, wounded in action. Pete spent seven months on the front lines through the 1951 Spring Offensive and battles in the 'Punch Bowl,' but had been wounded in October while unrigging a booby trap. Smitty was later stationed on one of the islands in Wonsan and was wounded during counter-battery activity. Now, when we meet at Emma-Jean's class reunions, we retell the same old Wonsan stories over and over again and sound like old GAR veterans remembering Gettysburg.

Wonsan remained under siege until 27 July 1953, the longest continuous investment of any enemy-held harbor in naval history. Of the eighty-seven ships damaged during the Korean War, forty-four were hit by shell-fire in Wonsan Harbor. Although two US mine-sweeps were sunk there in October 1950, the North Koreans never achieved their objective of sinking an American destroyer.[12]

After the US Navy left on July 27, 1953, Wonsan was next visited by USS *Pueblo*, following its capture offshore in January 1968. *Ozbourn* returned to the vicinity of Wonsan on 23 January 1968, when she and the nuclear-powered carrier USS *Enterprise* patrolled the Sea of Japan for forty days in case force was needed to free the *Pueblo*'s crew. President Johnson had a plan prepared for sending a destroyer into Wonsan to rescue the *Pueblo* crew but it was never implemented. It would be been fate at work had it been *Ozbourn*.

If I ever return to Korea, I want to see Inchon and Fankochi Point again, but I would also like to see Wonsan as well. Things have changed in South Korea, and in the rest of the world, but somehow North Korea seems stuck in the concrete of the past. Wonsan harbor characterizes it for me. It was indeed a very bloody place. Somehow I don't imagine I, or any American from that era, would be much welcomed.

Endnotes:

[1] Cagle and Manson (1957:281-373) discuss the formation of TF 95 and its subsequent duties in considerable detail. This chapter is the source for information and events not personally experienced.

[2] Cagle and Manson (1957:281) quoting the 4 July 1950, Presidential announcement. Whelan (1990) joins other recent writers (Alexander 1986 and Blair 1987) in focusing solely on ground events and passing, too lightly, over the blockade implications.

[3] Cagle and Manson (1957).

[4] Unlike an embargo, which is not an 'act of war,' a blockade is one under international law. However, it must first be deemed 'effective' before the blockading force can legally exercise force to turn away ships of a neutral nation attempting to pass through the blockade.

[5] Cagle and Manson 1957:401. Author's letters. USS *Ozbourn* War Diary and Action Report.

[6] Cagle and Manson (1957:401) quote from the action report and also mention two wounded and that our starboard searchlight was destroyed as well.

[7] Personal correspondence from CDR Tvede, USN-Ret. Tvede kept looking for the *Ozbourn* throughout his military career to thank them for his life and was recently able to do so. CDR Tvede now lives in retirement in Memphis, Tennessee; the whereabouts of LTJG Moriarty is unknown. Robert Whitten published the contents of a letter from Tvede describing the event in more detail in *Fireball*, an *Ozbourn* Association Newsletter, November 1994.

[8] Cagle and Manson (1957:243-247).

[9] Cagle and Manson (1957). Chapter 4 describes the October 1950 Wonsan minesweeping operations; Chapter 5 describes the October 1950 Chinnampo events, and Chapter 7 describes mine warfare from 1951 to 1953. See also Lott 1959, for further details.

[10] Thornton (1981) describes helicopter operations while working off LST 799 in Wonsan harbor in late March 1951. He was shot down on 30 March and spent the remainder of the war as a prisoner.

[11] Action Report: Wonsan, East Coast, Korea, 20 March 1951. USS *Ozbourn*. Closely paraphrased.

[12] Cagle and Manson (1957:528-531) for details of ships damaged.

BACK TO THE WEST COAST

No early liberty greeted us when we arrived in Yokosuka. By the time I reached Tokyo all the stores were closed. Several of us walked the Ginza, wandered into one or two bars, and then came back to the ship; I had seen Tokyo. It was hard for sailors to do anything else but get drunk and/or in trouble under the circumstances, but, even had someone scheduled a Gray Line tour of Tokyo for the crew, many would still have been out looking for bars, women, and trouble. When you joined the Navy to see the world, 'the world' tended to end about a mile from Fleet Landing. For some sailors, everything beyond the first bar was irrelevant and who could get beyond there before liberty expired anyway?

We left Yokosuka, Honshu Island on 29 March and by 3 April, we were about eleven hundred miles from Pearl and four hundred miles south of Midway. We had departed a day late because another tropical storm hit the Honshu coast, and we endured a week of gales and rough weather as we traveled east. Finally we emerged into clear, trade wind-dominated weather. Charley Akers had hoped for about a week of calm sea time for chipping and painting topside to make us look presentable for entry into Pearl; he wasn't going to get it. After a week of storms, the entire ship had rust runs coming out from behind paint bubbles. Even my poor typewriter looked rusty. Its keys stuck and there would be no more free repair trips to the *Dixie*.

We were due into Pearl on 6 April which crept up on us at the pace Christmas comes to children. Even the Commodore seemed itchy and announced that he didn't want to spend more than six hours in there refueling. This meant no chance to see my fraternity friend, Dickson Pratt, as we passed through. Many of the crew had never had liberty in Honolulu and wanted a chance to get ashore. 'Smiley' Higgins, the Torpedoman Chief from the port three-inch Director, talked about the last time *Ozbourn* had been in Pearl. Coming back from Operation Reach with the USS *Norton Sound*, the *Ozbourn* sailors had found trouble ashore. 'Smiley' had been on Shore Patrol duty. He was about six-foot-three, looked like John Wayne, even had his mannerisms, and smiled about as often. He did well on Shore Patrol. Nothing ever rattled him and he kept his sanity on my telephone circuit during counter-battery fire; his was the only voice remaining at the same pitch when we were being shelled. Everyone else got rattled and became instant tenors, including me.

Upon departing Pearl, we expected to arrive in San Diego the morning of 11 April. I would sneak ashore and call home that evening even though I expected to get the duty and allow married guys the first night home. The ship was expected immediately to go out of service for a thirty-day leave period which would be divided in two parts: the first, 11-26 April, the second, 27 April-12 May. I was slated for the second.

The trip back across the Pacific was just long enough to begin a decompression process. Although we had scarcely been under heavy combat conditions, we had been under long periods of stress. During the past ten months, we had grown quite close in ways that I failed to realize. After standing four on and eight off with multiple General Quarters, looking out for mines and watching for planes for nine months, the long trip back allowed us to gradually come off that edge. By the time we docked at Pearl, Korea was becoming a memory. The ship's port holes were open at night and our running lights were on, as were lights on deck. From the bridge on the return trip, you could watch the crew lounging on deck while the sun set. At the same time, over the PA system in the background, Doris Day was singing "Canadian Capers" or, at least, her record was. By then we were back on a watch in four, mostly sleeping all night, looking at sunsets and watching the evening movie out under the stars either on the 01 deck or on the fantail. The Navy had once again become 'three hots and a flop.' What more could you ask? At the same time we were decompressing, the crew was also growing apart. That became clear in San Diego as leave parties left, new officers and men reported on board, and old hands went elsewhere. The team was evaporating in front of us.

Upon arriving in Pearl, officers exploded off the ship in all different directions on all sorts of made-up jobs while Charley Akers and the Commodore made their official visits as appropriate. At the Ships' Service near Baker Docks across from the Submarine Base, I called Dickson, who got down to the ship about a half hour before we left. Dickson had been in the Navy for a short time at the end of the war and was still worrying whether he would be recalled. Although he still had some Reserve time left, he had few military skills and experience then needed and was not likely to be recalled unless the anticipated Chinese Spring Offensive really got out of hand. If that happened, all of us would go back to the Sea of Japan just like *Valley Forge*. All too soon, we were leaving Pearl for home.

The four destroyers in the Division left Pearl Harbor in a column and, at the same time, shared the channel with an inbound fleet oiler, one of our friends from Sea of Japan Replenishment Group days. She pretty well hogged the channel and was much more difficult to maneuver than the destroyers. The entrance to Pearl is always treacherous with reefs on either side; this time, it got a little too snug. *Ozbourn* passed her safely but, while maneuvering around the oiler, *McKean* suddenly slowed and drifted onto the reef. She had water in her fuel and lost a boiler. Losing power, she had ended up in a temporary grounding. The Commodore was concerned about what damage had resulted. As soon as we could, the three lucky ones came about and reentered the harbor.

Everyone on board saw at least a night's liberty in Pearl at *McKean*'s expense. We were scarcely inside Pearl when Commander-in-Chief Pacific Fleet ordered the three undamaged ships to continue our departure. Reluctantly we left *McKean* to an underwater inspection by divers, its own devices, and a probable late arrival; for once it wasn't *Ozbourn* in trouble. *McKean* was fortunate to get away with only some

left: USS *Ozbourn* in dry-dock at Hunter's Point (also the San Francisco Naval Shipyard), early January 1952.

below: Liberty party from "O" Division at Honolulu, October 1951.

scratched paint, dented plating, and nothing more serious than an embarrassed captain, followed shortly thereafter by a worried black gang in the fireroom. We didn't expect her captain, CDR Weatherwax, to come to any grief over this.

By Tuesday, 10 April, we were within four hundred miles of San Diego and plans were for us to arrive at 1400 on 11 April. I was now definitely in the second leave party, leaving on 27 April and coming back on 11 May. Once the leave period was over, we were to begin anti-submarine exercises on 13 May, thus rebuilding for our next deployment.

We continued to make better progress home than planned and had to slow down to keep from making our grand entrance earlier than already announced in the San Diego newspapers. That gave us time to paint on 'battle ribbons,' make our 'Homeward Bound' pennant, and clean up the ship, making ready for entering port. *McKean* trailed us by only one hundred miles and our slowing should allow her to catch up. There was a growing sense that this cruise was really over, a feeling of returning from night into day. The ship was full of plans being made, details about flights home, people to see, and a chance to find out what has really been going on stateside for the past ten months.

We arrived Wednesday, 11 April, and picked up Buoy 26 in the middle of the harbor just off the Fifth Avenue landing. On my first liberty in San Diego I walked around in a daze until I found a hamburger stand and then had two with a thick milkshake. I can still picture the pickle slices on the side of the plate. Les Paul and Mary Ford, with their echoed electric guitar sound, were new. Their "All the world is waiting for a sunrise" didn't come out until later that summer, but ours had just happened.

By Sunday, 15 April, we had begun to adjust and had received 1300 liberty two days of three; those not on leave were on a one-in-three duty section. Travel plans east had not yet matured, but Jarrett and I worked on them with Barbara and Hattie at the TWA desk downtown in the Grant Hotel. We learned they were also willing to cash personal checks for us; I was still using the Fort MacIntosh Bank in Beaver.

Our arrival in San Diego hadn't made quite the splash we thought it might; there was too much service around. Everywhere you went ashore you were surrounded by Marines and sailors with Purple Hearts, Bronze Stars, and other ribbons. Just having been to Korea didn't make us look very special. With so much Navy in town, as well as Marines from Camp Pendleton, it was difficult to be anything except just another serviceman. It was also not a good idea for an officer to come ashore in uniform. With both Navy and Marine boot camps in the area, you would work your arm to death returning salutes to privates and seamen recruits. At least the town no longer seemed to be crawling with nervous anxiety as it had been the previous July. By April 1951, everyone seemed to know what was going on in Korea and the likelihood for the future. A rotation plan out and back now existed and the process wasn't the secret it once had been.

We became acquainted with the other half of *Ozbourn's* family—all the wives and children associated with people on board. While we were gone, they kept in close touch with each other and knew more about who was where and what we were doing than we did. San Diego was full of females at this point, most of whom were more or less attached by a long thin line of letters to someone somewhere in the Pacific. A few, less attached than others, were available in the bars and there was much potential heartache available from that.

As payday was close, I was reduced to watching evening movies on the 01 deck, along with others either out of money or on board for the duty. This time it was *Task Force* with Gary Cooper, which seemed appropriate. I was one of the duty officers, as well as one running out of money. We now met ensigns from the next class. We had just received a new NROTC ensign, our first from 1951. Others would follow. By Sunday, it was now very quiet on board. Jarrett and I planned to leave San Diego for Pittsburgh on Saturday, 28 April. Not only had we bought tickets at TWA but had managed to begin dating Barbara and Hattie, the women selling them.

Wonsan made the San Diego paper. The siege had just become the longest in the history of the US Navy—sixty days. Even Vicksburg, in 1863 during the Civil War, had been only forty days long. Our small part in history was that we started it.

Jarrett and I arrived at the Old Pittsburgh Airport just after noon, Saturday, 28 April and both families were there in force. Two weeks seems like forever until it starts; the time was actually very short. Dad had again rearranged his car pool and I had the family car. I intended to use it to drive the 'college circuit,' going first to Penn State to see Emma-Jean who was still in school and then on to Cornell to see other people.

This leave became something like a 'see old girlfriends' week. While at Cornell, I walked across the quadrangle and found one who actually asked, "Where have you been this year? Hadn't seen you around." How could you answer that in a sentence? I wasn't in uniform or it might have been unasked. Korea did not seem to be a big issue on campus. I wandered around campus staring at buildings and trying to recapture how it had been there just a year before. I talked to Dr. Raney and Howard Evans, among others, and even had trouble talking to my friends on the faculty. I felt strangely out of place with all these World War Two people who were still talking about the real war, no matter what they had or had not seen of it. Later LCDR Palmer commented that he had seen more action in the six weeks he had been on board the *Ozbourn* than he had throughout World War Two.

Korea had become something indescribably different. I knew I hadn't done much, but others had. I also felt secretly guilty about missing what had happened ashore. During the trip from Penn State to Cornell, instead of being overwhelmed with spring and the beauty of the hills of Pennsylvania, I listened on the car radio to General MacArthur's "old soldiers" speech to the Congress. Had someone told me in May 1950 what would transpire in the coming ten months and that I would be part of MacArthur's Army-Navy group in a war someplace, I would never have believed them. In May 1950, he seemed like a controversial, elderly American institution that would go on forever; not so by May 1951. I finally left Ithaca en route to Beaver and stopped at a beautiful trout stream to spend an afternoon fly fishing. Korea seemed a forever away. The afternoon was already a success before I caught a superb trout. That afternoon had been necessary.

Back in Beaver, I walked around town by myself and met several '46 high school classmates, but the women were either married or otherwise spoken for. Everyone I knew was engaged. All the guys were either in the Army or still in college. One morning, I sat on a bench in the park overlooking the Ohio River and read the papers. I looked everywhere in the *Beaver*

Valley Times for something about Korea and it was nowhere. Subconsciously, I had expected to return to coffee and gasoline rationing and windows with blue-star flags. That was the Beaver I remembered during the Big One—not this time.

In April-May 1951, people had other things to do and unless your son was there, nobody seemed to care much about Korea or WestPac. There seemed neither a need nor the will and I wasn't much interested in describing what we had done, which of course paled into insignificance compared to most. So *silence* seemed the message. Korea just didn't seem to exist. That reaction in Beaver was strange, but maybe neither they nor I knew what to say.

Meanwhile, others were coming and going to Korea and some didn't make it back. Robert Gillespie and Emma-Jean had become friends after meeting at a local YMCA camp. Instead of going to college, Bob joined the Navy after graduation from New Brighton High School in 1947. He had intended to become a pharmacist after his tour but that plan ended somewhere in Korea on September 17, 1951, when he was killed serving as a Navy Corpsman with the Marines. Several days after the telegram had come, Bob's father listened incredulously to an interview on the radio in which a Marine, just back from the fatal patrol, described Bob's death to a correspondent.

Dad and I went fishing once before I left. We never talked much about my involvement. Perhaps the letters had covered whatever emotions had been running through the mind of a twenty-two-year-old. Neither of us caught anything but the memory of that warm May day lasts. It would be five or six more years before all the father-son barriers broke down and we could talk together as adults but at least it was beginning to happen. All too soon the days had run out and it was again Saturday and time to fly back to San Diego.

By next Monday, not only was I back in San Diego, but I had been moved unceremoniously and precipitously into a BOQ near the Fleet Sonar School, where I was to be a student for the next five weeks. While informally nosing around the ship after my return, I discovered that someone had requested a five-week sonar school for me, and I was to report ASAP.

The following Saturday night, we attended a big Navy party at the Athletic Field for all the officers and crew attached to the destroyers, cruisers, and tenders associated with CruDesPac. We ended at a club outside La Jolla, closing it down at 0200.

Another Monday came and I was still at Sonar School. Many of the junior officers in the Sonar course, as well as those at the CIC School at Point Loma, lived in the BOQ, so there were plenty of people to do things. Transportation was our biggest problem--followed shortly thereafter by finding dates and having money. Without a car you either went along with other people and their plans, or stayed in and played ping-pong by yourself. Going out two or three times a week was expensive. I was now reading *The American Mind* by Henry Steele Commager; the Base had a good library and at least I could walk there. *Ozbourn* was now out all week acting as plane guard for *Rendova*, a small recommissioned escort carrier; that meant no contact with officers on the ship.

We had a Division Officers' cocktail party at the Admiral Kidd Officers' Club next door to the Fleet Sonar School and the TWA foursome again made the scene. We had planned on dinner somewhere else after putting in a short but proper appearance. Instead it turned out to be so nice that after the cocktail party we stayed through most of the dancing. The Club was full and those from *Ozbourn* included the Hadleys, the Moriartys, the Palmers, the Akers, the Roeders, Jerry Solomon and his date and us. Charley Akers and the Commodore had begun the evening in rare form, but were fading by the end of cocktails. The rest of us finished the evening at the Hadley house on Mission Beach about 1:00 a.m. for bacon and eggs. The party ended when we managed to wake up Betty and John Moriarty's little girl; she had been spending the night and sharing the Hadley's sitter.

Sonar school dealt with something we never had to use in WestPac—our capacity to kill submarines. Whoever sent me to this one managed to miss sending me to the correct one. A three-week basic school had preceded it and, immediately, I was in over my head. The first course covered basic equipment and simple one-ship attacks. When I began, they were doing advanced hedgehog and depth charge attacks from single-, as well as dual-ship patterns on submerged submarines using the mock-up attack trainers. Everything was new to me. Most of the class had some shipboard experience in sonar and anti-submarine warfare.

We used 'attack teachers' that were quasi-analog units plotting ships' courses and speeds; they also had built-in turn transfer distances and time needed for descending charges to reach submarine depth. We plugged in the bearing and slant range of the target and they reproduced fairly accurately what a ship could do in an attack. This was another exercise in relative motion except the sonar officer operated from the bowels of the ship and made recommendations to the captain on the bridge who carried out the attack. Unlike the sonar officer, the captain could look out at the ocean and easily visualize the attack as it developed. Down in the sonar room, I could only visualize the attack in my head and I had trouble following the rapidly changing situation. I probably would not do well as a sonar officer.

The operational speeds of submerged submarines running on batteries then had capabilities of up to ten knots, but most World War Two submarines of the *Balao* class, when evading a destroyer attack, moved most quietly at submerged speeds of three knots or less; at least they did for us. The guppy or snorkeling capability introduced by the Germans in 1944-45 had been adapted to US fleet submarines. This allowed submarines to use their diesels while submerged drawing surface air through a surface device. They could then reach speeds of twenty knots submerged, but any use of the snorkel gave their position away to ships or aircraft.

Gearing and Sumner-class destroyers in 1951 were equipped with late World War Two sonar technology suitable for countering submarines similar to the last German fleet submarines. We probably could have coped with the Soviet Navy submarines had they entered the Korean War. However, by the late 1950s nuclear submarines operated submerged at speeds in excess of twenty knots. A Gearing destroyer could keep up, but its own sonar's return signal would become muffled in the noise of water driven against its sonar dome. When I finished the course, I returned to *Ozbourn* and relieved Jack Worden, this time of his General Quarters job as sonar officer.

Jerry Solomon moved into the BOQ as my roommate while he attended Air Controller's School at Point Loma. He had replaced Dave Thornhill as CIC officer and was also going through the Ensign assignments on board. While we were off,

Ozbourn burned up a generator at sea and went to Mare Island Ship Yard for two weeks to get it replaced. They would be short-handed with five officers ashore in San Diego going to these various schools. There was still no word yet on when our big yard period would begin, except it was still likely to start in December.

By Sunday night, 27 May, I was still at the BOQ but, just as I became adjusted to being ashore, it all ended. The last two weeks of sonar school were to be spent at sea on Destroyer Escorts (DE) practicing those tactics against submerged submarines. We were due to get underway at 0700 and return at 1800. It would be a long day because you had to allow time for travel to and from the ship anchored somewhere in the harbor.

Memorial Day was also coming and shortly after, 12 June, marked the end of my first year on active duty. Jarrett left the ship before they went north and was now attending a two-week Cryptographic School at the Destroyer Base in San Diego. After Jerry Solomon completed the Air Controller School, he was to go to CIC Basic. Even so, both would still be back on board before me. We were now attending the short-term specialty schools we should have had before going to WestPac; Korea had changed all that. Solomon, Jarrett, and I had learned on the job and now they were sending us to schools to validate our record.

Ashore, I was becoming spoiled, falling asleep to the sound of cars, trains, and crickets and being able to watch the sun rise and set through a window. San Diego was nearly Camelot as far as the weather was concerned. The days were always bright and beautiful and it only rained at night, at least in May and June.

Monday, 4 June, began the first week of riding ships. We were on *Weeden*. She had just come out of mothballs and was serving as a school ship while getting her own crew and officers into shape. Although we spent nearly twelve hours a day looking for a slow moving submarine, sonar conditions off San Diego were often so poor that we didn't get much good experience. The sonar operators were also students going through the enlisted school and what they managed to find we managed to bungle during the attacks. The equipment on this ship was quite primitive compared to what we would be using on typical fleet destroyers.

Good luck still played a large part in being able to find and then to hold a submarine contact throughout the attack. If you couldn't hold him right in to about one hundred yards before you passed over him, you would never get an effective depth charge hit. Getting a solid echo from a three-degree-wide beam of sound spreading out and bending in the water and then using it to track a submerged object while differentiating a submarine from whales, fish schools, water knuckles, and sound layers was only part of the problem. A good operator not only could stay on the sub but also detect up or down doppler noises allowing you to know whether it was coming at you or going away and whether it was moving to the left or right. After much practice with a submarine an operator and sonar officer became proficient. The game plan was to determine the submarine's course and speed and then arrive over a spot of water such that your dropped depth charges arrived around him just as he passed through. His turns, speed changes, or anything else made that difficult.

Still no word on what was to happen to DesDiv 112's yard time. *Wiltsie* and Jim Tregurtha had come back a month earlier and they expected to be in the yards in October. We thought we were still set for either Mare Island (Vallejo) or Hunter's Point (San Francisco Naval Ship Yard) in January. The big worry going through everyone's mind was who would be kept on *Ozbourn?* Yard time was an excellent time to transfer people.

I had turned in my first request for a reassignment and had been turned down for Underwater Demolition Teams (UDT). They held several classes each year and for this one, they had too many applicants. My application was 'in the files,' whatever that meant. After being turned down, I went to the amphibious base in Coronado and talked to some UDT officers. I left wondering whether applying had been as wise as I had thought it to be. At least they had been fighting in a real war.

The Bureau of Naval Personnel and CruDesPac were beginning to move many 1950 ensigns off operating destroyers and onto DDs and DEs coming out of mothballs. After seeing *Weeden*, I was not interested in a move onto a recommissioned ship, be it DD or DE. If I couldn't get into UDT, I would try to ride *Ozbourn* back overseas on her second tour. Promotion to LTJG was nearly automatic at the end of twenty-four months of active duty. By now we all expected the Navy to extend the Regular NROTC commitment on active duty to three years given the Korean problem and its worldwide impact.

The next Monday, I was on another destroyer escort, *Currier*, also fresh out of mothballs. *Ozbourn* had come back Sunday afternoon from her stay in the yards and had brought the rest of my clothes. The ship looked good. More can be done to a ship in the shipyard than can ever be done alongside a tender, as necessary as tenders are. Once *Ozbourn* had arrived at Mare Island, someone decided the ship also needed a dry-docking. *Ozbourn* had been working with *Rendova*, as plane guard during flight operations the previous month. One day, while Jarrett had the conn, *Rendova* turned right and *Ozbourn* couldn't; he nearly hit the carrier. Jarrett closed to about two hundred yards and could hear them passing the word on *Rendova*, "stand clear of the starboard quarter and prepare for collision." *Oz* had been acting sluggishly for the last several months but no one suspected it was as bad as that. Some suspected it was further damage from near misses in Wonsan or the beating from the typhoon. When they dry docked *Ozbourn*, engineers found most of the pins holding the twin rudders had sheared off and she was about to drop both rudders.

Sonar School ended on 15 June and I expected to be back on board. It had been nice, but expensive, ashore, yet it was good to be back on board. By now even some of the LTJGs on board were broke and ready to return to WestPac to recoup.

Shortly before we left for Hawaii, Hattie and I broke up the TWA foursome by coming to a natural parting of the ways. By 5 August we were again alongside *Dixie* for two week's tender availability before going to Hawaii. Both Don Abbott and John Hadley had orders transferring them off *Ozbourn*. Abbott left after only thirteen months on board and by November, LT Remmen was also transferred. Someone had heard from Dave Thornhill; he was now back in Wonsan on shore bombardment duty. By 13 August Jack Blonsick also left the ship to go to flight school and Jerry Solomon would leave later. Things were changing and San Diego was beginning to lose its charm.

On 20 August, *Ozbourn* deployed to Hawaii for advanced operations and shore bombardment practice on Kahoolawe, then a Navy gunnery range. Liberty in the islands could get out of hand. One night most of the wardroom managed to get drunk in Trader Vic's and all of us were tossed out when someone climbed a palm tree. Shortly afterward, one of our new ensigns passed out on the street and as duty teetotaler, I had the task of getting him home. As a result, I missed a further celebration downtown in honor of another ensign's 'Dear John' letter.

I now had another job, 'O' Division Officer, and found myself responsible for fifty enlisted men, ages seventeen to forty-eight, which was a startling transition to have made one year after college graduation. I made decisions for people who could not read, but wanted advanced Navy schooling. Others had divorce problems, people too young—or not ready—to get married, and on it went. This experience was not time wasted. I had fought in a little war, and with this level of responsibility, I had matured some.

When we arrived in Pearl Harbor and I could get ashore, swimming and playing volley ball were the first exercise in a year. After sweltering in Pearl for twelve days, we got underway 6 September to work with a submarine. I actually dropped one mock depth charge pattern within twenty-five yards of the submarine, but it had occurred on a slow stern chase that anyone could have done. Akers was not very impressed with his new sonar attack officer. In these exercises, when you arrive at the center of the planned depth charges, you drop a hand grenade and a bag of green dye marker into the water. The submarine then sends up an air bubble when it hears the grenade explode. The bubble and dye marker should coincide if you have done it correctly. After six hours of frustration, we came back in, off-loaded some bad five-inch shells, and had a surprise audit of the crew's recreation fund.

As time passed, his OODs and JOODs gained more experience and Charley Akers gradually began to trust two somewhat experienced ensigns to stand the top watch during daylight hours—Jarrett and me. But mistakes, due to lapses in attention or inexperience, could still be made. I found myself working as a semi-qualified OOD underway with a new ensign as my JOOD while *Ozbourn* was undergoing refresher training with a carrier. We had just been ordered into a plane guard station aft and to the right of a carrier. Under my expert hand, we had maneuvered there in good shape. I then turned the 'conn' over to my

new JOOD, having just shown him how we did it for real with
TF 77. Just as I did, the carrier announced it was altering her
course more to the right. I listened absent-mindedly as my
JOOD sang out, "left standard rudder," which was dutifully
executed by the helmsman. Inattention or cloud-watching on
my part got us well into our swing counter to the carrier's new
course and we came seriously close to her before I realized he
had meant "right" when he said "left." I had 'heard' what I knew
he wanted to do which was the reverse of what he did. I quickly
took the conn back, shifted rudder hard right, and the ship
heeled sharply in response. At that instant, Akers appeared on
the bridge and observed us make a close aboard inspection of
the backside of an aircraft carrier with all those nice sailors
waving to us from its fantail. I don't remember Akers' unpleasant comments but, as I had come perilously close to ruining his
naval career, I deserved whatever it was he said. He and I both
realized I might not yet be ready for full standing as a qualified
OOD underway.

My roommates changed almost daily. I had acquired a
Naval Academy ensign, Robert Brodie, III, and then Rob Roy
Farnam who graduated from the Agriculture School at the
University of Nebraska—what different backgrounds. Less than
a year later Brodie was transferred to submarine school. They,
and others coming on board, replaced the recalled reservists we
would soon be losing when their two-year obligations had been
completed.

We had a liberty weekend in Hilo before departing and the
ship got underway late Sunday afternoon with almost no one
sober enough to be responsible. By 21 October we were on our
way back to San Diego, six days later we were home again. I was
now scheduled for Christmas leave from 19 December to 9
January, but only if the captain would put a replacement
Custodian in place. I laid plans to have that happen. A disturbing rumor surfaced that all Cruiser Destroyer Pacific officers
could expect to be transferred after about twenty months on
board. If true, I probably would be transferred before we went
west again.

Shortly after our return to San Diego, *Boxer* returned from
her WestPac deployment. She had arrived in WestPac the
previous March, just as we were leaving. The cycle was coming

around for us and it scarcely seemed as if we had been home that long. It would soon be time for *Ozbourn* to return to Korea.

By the end of October, our schedule for the ship yard was now firm and the number of planned modifications would require several months in the yard. Bob Whitten had momentarily replaced LT Remmen and was responsible for all the job orders. During the yard period, further changes were bound to happen. Officers and crew staying on the ship's roster would have to be moved ashore for classes, while others were scattered to other commands or discharged.

I was now standing duty officer watches while we were tied up at the Destroyer Base in San Diego. Our gyro compass specialist just returned from a twelve-week school. The gyro had failed once while we were in the vicinity of the mine field in Wonsan. When the gyro 'tumbles,' or fails, the helmsman begins following a faulty course; trying to stay within Wonsan's swept paths required accurate navigation and a gyro compass that worked. Wonsan was no place for that kind of trouble. Meanwhile, Christmas leave plans for those getting it were building.

In late November 1951, *Ozbourn* sailed from San Diego to the San Francisco Naval Ship Yards for overhaul. The Division had sailed up the coast at fifteen knots through a dense fog in order to make our arrival time. Fortunately, the radar worked the whole way. I was JOOD on the bridge the night we came into San Francisco en route to Hunter's Point and I sensed that things were ending. During an overhaul, people first moved off the ship as it went into dry-dock and then, normal daily routine was replaced by workmen working round the clock. All ship's services were gone, no water, no heads, and a maze of lights and wires and welding going on day and night, all intended to bring the ship up to specifications and to replace aging equipment with newer radars, sonars, fire control equipment, radios, etc. It was also a breaking up experience for officers and crew. After it was all over, not only would the ship need to be broken-in again, but it would take several months to rebuild the new crew. I was also coming upon an anniversary; December 1951 would mark the half-way point in my three years of active duty. The previous June our active duty had been extended to thirty-six months.

Someone started a poker game in the wardroom and each night the stakes were higher. Finally, I bowed out and was back reading. I was just getting into Morison's *Operations in North African Waters* when I realized I was reading about the father of my roommate. CAPT Robert Brodie, II, won the Navy Cross by running his destroyer up a river during the invasion. Robert Brodie, III, represented the next generation in an honorable family lineage among Academy graduates. This was another reason why NROTC graduates felt somewhat outside the system—the Commodore and your roommate's father might well have been Academy classmates. Brodie's style of leadership was somewhat more authoritarian than mine; I preferred the Dave Thornhill model. Jerry Solomon now had orders. Then, just as suddenly, they were canceled, but he expected new orders to flight school any day. The Navy was relaxing its rule about serving three years on a surface ship before going to subs or flight school; it needed pilots for Korea. My friendly competition with Jerry—NROTC versus the Academy—was about to end. Doubtless some NROTC graduates might believe themselves to have been discriminated against but it hadn't happened to me on *Ozbourn*. I was sorry to see Jerry leave.

Just before Christmas, we had an awards mast. O'Brien, one of my quartermasters, received a Letter of Commendation for getting us safely out of Wonsan in February. John Moriarty's Bronze Star Medal also came through as did his Coxswain's Navy Commendation Medal. Likewise, so did the Commodore's star representing his second Legion of Merit as well as a Bronze Star for CAPT Akers. The highest award in the division was a Silver Star awarded to a sailor on *Hollister* who jumped into wintery Wonsan harbor and saved a wounded pilot. I still wanted to become a small scale hero. It wasn't to happen.

The poker game noise in the evening was getting worse but the hammering and other shipyard racket on board was even worse. Soon we would all have to leave the ship. The Custodian's audit and transfer occurred just in time to allow me to pick up my leave papers and go to Moffett Field. Our new Operations Officer, LT Pitcher, had just left duty at Moffett Field. He pulled some strings for Jarrett and me and got us rides east on a courier plane going to Washington. Beaver by train from Washington was easy. I took my two weeks

Christmas leave and came back to see *Ozbourn* stripped in dry dock. Next to the pain of seeing a parent hopelessly confined and irrational in bed, comes seeing your ship in a dry-dock. If ships are female, being around during a dry-docking and a major overhaul is like being at some woman's dissection. I felt someone had disrobed and dismantled a friend and then laid her open for all to see and fix.

I was happy to be home for Christmas. Everything had pointed to another winter and Christmas being spent again chasing carriers off Korea. The typical first tour for new ensigns was still three years on sea duty. Although I had again volunteered for Underwater Demolition Team, also a sea duty assignment, I still expected to finish my normal tour on board this or some other CruDesPac ship.

Shortly after Christmas, while still on leave, my orders came. I was being transferred east to Underwater Demolition Team #4, US Naval Amphibious Base, Little Creek, Virginia. Following satisfactory completion of the basic UDT course, I could be called a 'frogman.'[1] I had always assumed that, if selected, I would undergo UDT training on the west coast and then be assigned to a west coast team. Of course, I had asked for the east coast but it had never occurred to me they would actually do it. Don't ask for what you don't want, they might give it to you.

My leave expired in early January 1952 and I returned to San Francisco. There I turned over my remaining duties as sonar officer to another junior officer and left my old friend, *Ozbourn*, in her agony in the dry dock. One of the major 'ticket punchings' out of an ensign's first tour at sea was to become qualified as OOD underway. I still said 'right' when meaning 'left'—probably some kind of learning disability—but my final fitness report from Charley Akers said I was 'deck qualified underway.' By the time I had left the ship, being 'qualified underway,' had indeed become more important than medals. I had begged him to put it on my final fitness report. Although I probably wasn't, he finally agreed and did it. Had I gone to another ship, the next skipper would still watch me carefully until he was satisfied that I knew what I was doing because he would remain responsible for any mistakes I might make as one of his underway OODs. I departed *Ozbourn* with mixed feelings and reluctance. I was not happy to see the end of my relationship with her, and I never saw her again. Ultimately, though, it happens to every sailor, and so, it was on to Underwater Demolition Team #4.

Endnotes:

[1] The term 'frogman' was never used by members of the Teams. You were either a UDT or a Demolitioneer. 'Frogmen' was a term limited to those plastic prizes in cereal boxes.

PART III

UNCONVENTIONAL WARFARE

UNDERWATER

DEMOLITION TEAMS

World War Two and UDTs

Although D-Day at Normandy was the biggest assault landing of World War Two, the Pacific War from 1942 to 1945 had
seen many landings beginning with Guadalcanal, during which
joint Marine and Navy assault landing teams had became highly
skilled. Although pre-assault reconnaissances had occurred as
early as the 1942 landings North Africa,[1] no units existed with
this as an assigned mission until Underwater Demolition Teams
(UDTs and NCDUs) began in June 1942 at Fort Pierce, Florida. Initially, they were called Naval Combat Demolition Units,
and both NCDUs and UDTs existed throughout the war. Only
NCDUs participated in the Normandy invasion of France, but
UDTs and NCDUs were used throughout the Pacific War. The
invasion of Tarawa in November 1943, was a costly 'fiasco'
because of uncharted coral reefs, unexpected anti-boat mines,
and inadequate hydrographic information. To provide pre-
assault intelligence, and to remove obstacles, Teams and Units
were used before every assault landing after Tarawa until the
end of the war.

By late in the war, one hundred or so swimmers from each
Team, during daylight, were dropped in a line parallel to and
five hundred yards off the beach using small high-speed landing
craft (LCPR, Landing Craft Personnel, Ramped). The distance

to the beach would depend upon bottom contour, available fire support, enemy defenses, and long-shore currents, etc. The swimmers then slowly swam inshore, stopped on signal every twenty-five yards, and measured depth to the bottom with a weighted fishing line. Each man recorded depth on his plexiglass slate, made notes on obstacles, coral reefs, and then, on signal, swam to the next. Meanwhile, Japanese gunners ashore kept swimmers under rifle, mortar, and machine gun fire. Once each member was close enough to shore and had the required data, on signal all returned to the pick-up line and were snatched out of the water by the same speeding boats.

Obstacles anticipated for the Normandy invasion were concrete blocks and large steel structures called Belgian gates. Each was equipped with anti-tank mines. In the Pacific war, coral reefs, anti-boat mines, cribs constructed of coconut palm logs and filled with coral rubble were more likely. These obstacles required varied demolition techniques and equipment. Sections of light-weight pipe, called Bangalore torpedoes, could be used to clear barbed wire and other lighter obstructions. Sections of four-inch rubber hose, packed with explosives and tetryl packs (satchel charges) had to be brought into near-shore waters and packed onto rock-filled cribs. None of these satchels floated. Placing them under incoming small-arms and mortar fire from the beach was "a horrible job."[2]

A typical pre-landing mission identified where and what was in the water, as well as the condition of the beach and its approaches for landing craft. Beach sand needed to be firm enough to support tracked vehicles. If obstacles were found in the initial swim, there would be a second swim. This time each swimmer brought four or more satchels loaded with twenty pounds of tetryl. The satchels were kept afloat with air-filled rubber bladders. Swimming in with them was relatively easy unless a mortar round hit close enough to cause a sympathetic explosion. Planting them on a submerged obstacle or an offending coral reef might be a different matter. To attach the charge, the flotation bladder was stabbed and the sinking satchel was then hung on the obstacle. The charges were linked together by a network of primacord, a line suggestive of plastic clothesline but filled with explosive. When all swimmers had tied their individual charges into the primacord network, all but two swam offshore to the recovery line to be picked up by a high-speed LCPR. The last swimmers had a flotation bladder with a known-length of water-proof time fuse wrapped around it leading to a blasting cap he taped into the net. The swimmers then lit the fuse with an waterproof lighter – all sealed inside a condom. When the fuse was lit and burning, they swam like hell out to sea for pick-up. The blasting cap set off the primacord and, nearly instantaneously, all of the charges tied into the network exploded. Getting away from a lit time fuse was the task given to the Team's fastest crawl swimmers. Being in the water and near the explosion of several tons of powder would rupture intestines and damage other body parts.

A single Team with one hundred swimmers in the water might clear five hundred yards of beach in a two-mission operation, depending on the density of obstacles. Six Teams from ten fast-attack transports (APDs) had been used in the Lingayen Gulf landing in the Philippines.[3] By the end of the war, the Navy had some twenty-seven Teams composed of three thousand five hundred trained swimmers[4] preparing for the assault on the Japanese mainland. They had participated in a number of landings, but like other elements of the wartime Navy they, too, were rapidly released from active duty. By 1946, all World War Two Underwater Demolition Teams had been decommissioned and anyone remaining on active duty was reassigned. The number of combat swimmers on active duty in the Navy had been reduced to several hundred.

As post-war requirements emerged in the Caribbean and Mediterranean, as well as in the Far East, four new Teams (1, 2, 3, and 4) were commissioned in May 1946. Teams #2 and #4 were then transferred to the Atlantic Fleet, Commander Amphibious Forces, Atlantic Fleet (ComPhibLant) and stationed at The Naval Amphibious Base, Little Creek, Virginia. At the same time, Teams 1 and 3 (#5 was added later) were assigned to the Pacific Fleet and stationed at the Naval Amphibious Base, Coronado, California. During the midshipman cruise of 1948, we watched the Pacific Teams put on a mock landing reconnaissance on the beaches at Coronado.

By the start of the Korean War, the primary UDT mission remained unchanged; it was still pre-assault reconnaissance. However, except for the landing at Inchon, which required intelligence of a different sort, most UDT duties in Korea involved mine removal, coastal reconnaissance behind the lines, and tunnel destruction missions. During the Korean War, many of the combat missions involving the West Coast Teams, as well as mission development activities by either West Coast or East Coast Teams were highly classified. In the mind of a young sailor or junior officer serving on a ship, becoming part of UDT was a physical, as well as, mental challenge to be surmounted. Although the beach reconnaissance swim was now well known, its other operations were still highly classified and thus was also part of an intriguing mystery.

By 1952, Teams 2 and 4 at Little Creek had small deployed groups supporting Marine landing exercises along the east coast and in the Caribbean, while others were on assignment in the Mediterranean. The Atlantic Fleet Teams were also involved in experimental programs involving the aqualung and other SCUBA devices that used pure oxygen. They also experimented with lock-out from submerged submarines, cold-weather swimming systems, parachute training, and miniature submersibles—including equipment captured after World War Two in Europe. Further, there was a natural linkage between the Team's combat intelligence capabilities and the more covert intelligence activities that might involve CIA responsibilities. Experienced sailors and officers who had acquired these skills and experience were invaluable throughout the intelligence community, if not in the mainline Naval Establishment. The Navy needed to retain them but that was hard to do.

In 1952, when I joined Team 4, pre-assault reconnaissance was still its primary mission. Memories of how it had been done at Okinawa remained fresh in the minds of senior petty officers as well as the officer leadership. Although, it was too early to see the impact of the emerging Cold War and the changing field of unconventional warfare, these two events ultimately lead to the SEALs. These were experiments with the future and were not the same as spending twenty years at sea with the fleet and moving up to Department Head, Executive Officer, and, finally, to Captain of something before being selected for Rear Admiral. That was the route to an admiral's stars, not floating around learning how to blow up coral and senior officers charged with the process of selecting the oncoming senior officers knew it.

As a result, for Regular Navy—officers as well as enlisted—any time spent in UDT was viewed as time wasted off the promotion ladder and thus likely to be considered adversely when an officer's file was reviewed for promotion. Until far later, there was scarcely any way for an enlisted man or officer to make a complete naval career out of being a 'frog.' At least that was the conventional wisdom.

Basic Training

My orders were to report to Commander, Underwater Demolition Unit Two "no later than January 21, 1952" for the start of the Basic School and, if I survived the course, I would then be assigned to UDT 4. Commander, Underwater Demolition Unit Two, (ComUDU 2) was in charge of Teams 2 and 4 and, in addition, ran the Basic Training Class. Officer and enlisted instructors for the Class were selected from the two Teams. In the following year the course was transferred to the Amphibious Training Command at Little Creek. Finally, it evolved into the basic course for Teams (and now for SEALs) on both coasts and is conducted at one location—Coronado. Thus, my Basic Class evolved into the Basic Underwater Demolition Class (BUDs Class) now followed by a number. Upon graduation, you would be forever identified as a member of BUDs-14 or 15. At the yearly reunions of the Fraternal Order of UDT/SEALs, the standard introduction question is, "what was your BUDs number?" Anyone from the Korean Era can only wonder, "have I forgotten that too?" I thought we did not have one, but we were Class #8.

Upon graduating from the basic class, a sailor or officer was qualified to carry out beach reconnaissance and demolition operations similar to those used at Iwo Jima and Okinawa at the end of World War Two. Early Team work in the Pacific had not stressed swimming but, by 1952, the graduate needed to show long distance swimming capacity as well as skills with fins and face mask sufficient to propel you to depths up to twenty feet to plant charges. Superb physical conditioning was behind everything. Athletic ability was important, but motivation, intelligence, and perseverance were essential.

I arrived in Little Creek early Sunday evening, 20 January 1952, checked into the BOQ, located UDU #2 and reported to the Duty Petty Officer in an old quonset hut. He politely advised me that I was two weeks' late for the start of the class. From his look I could easily read, "Where the hell have you been, you idiot Ensign, sir?" I had missed not only a week of physical conditioning but also Hell Week.

Hell Week had become a UDT tradition during World War Two training and resembled a week-long fraternity initiation. It featured C-rations, no sleep, carrying around a rubber boat, incessant running and push-ups, crawling through mud and swamps with instructors wearing white helmets continuously ragging and insulting everyone. To top it all, So-Solly Day featured half-pound blocks of TNT and worse exploding all over the place. Those who came from the fleet were conditioned to explosions from muzzles of guns, not from a block of TNT exploding close to your right foot. No one was ever truly 'in' a Team until he had been subjected to the Hell Week experience. No enlisted or officer was really trusted around explosives until he had demonstrated good sense and extreme tolerance in their presence.

Training started the next morning with Physical Training (PT) at 0530, runs on the sand dunes, demolition classes, and more and more runs. The uniform for everyone, officers and enlisted men, was green navy fatigues, web belt, and a helmet liner painted red to identify you for what you were to anyone on the base at Little Creek. Being an officer did not help. Being twenty-three did, somewhat, even though I was badly out of condition and fifteen pounds overweight from eighteen months of eating well on *Ozbourn*. Although I caught up on the class work and was finally able to keep up physically with the rest of the class, I would still be required to go through all of Hell Week with the next training class.

Although I had joined my training class only two weeks after it had started, it was already reduced to seven officers and fifty enlisted. Most classes started with ten officers and one hundred enlisted. Early attrition was always high and Hell Week and So-Solly Day routinely took a high toll. Most officers in our class were NROTC Regulars or reservists and none was planning on a naval career. The enlisted men in the class were predominantly young seamen or firemen. Although a few were third-class petty officers, almost all were on first enlistments. Whether they had careers in mind, I never knew. Whether any of us would last the week and get through the next Saturday morning exit screening was more often asked than whether we wanted a life's work centered around unconventional warfare. Just getting through each day was what this place was really all about. I had no more idea why others were there than I had about myself. I simply knew they would have to 'fire' me. I wouldn't quit.

Our basic course ran for six more weeks in Little Creek and then finished with six additional weeks of demolitions, long-distance swimming, and beach reconnaissance training at St. Thomas in the Virgin Islands. Just before we departed, the entire class—officers and enlisted men—pitched in and loaded several tons of forty-pound boxes of C-3 explosives and then ourselves onto USS *Bowers* (an APD or high-speed attack transport, built in 1943). *Bowers* was an example of a good recalled ship with a good recalled crew.

Once loaded, we sailed for Charlotte Amalie, St. Thomas, a beautiful place to finish a basic training involving swimming. Upon arrival, *Bowers* tied up to a small pier and the trainees and instructors moved ashore to live in the old Submarine Base barracks. We ate our meals, took showers, and had our laundry done on *Bowers*. The rest of the time was spent either ashore running up steep hills or being ferried around in the *Bowers'* LCPRs for swimming, reconnaissance, or demolitions training. We used every bit of the several tons of powder. At the end there was a rumor that the empty boxes had been refilled with bottles of Virgin Island rum and returned to the magazine for return to the States. That probably didn't happen because, of course, that would have been smuggling.

The daily energy expenditure with so much time in the water was incredible. I was losing weight while seemingly eating nearly eight thousand calories a day. Those true athletes among us were now in superb shape and could spend all night on liberty in Charlotte Amalie if they didn't get caught. Some barely made it back by 0500 in time to get into greens for PT and the run up the hills before the morning swim.

The basic mission of the Team—pre-landing reconnaissance—could be done either by swimming or by rubber boat. The seven-man rubber boat (IBS) was also a part of Team

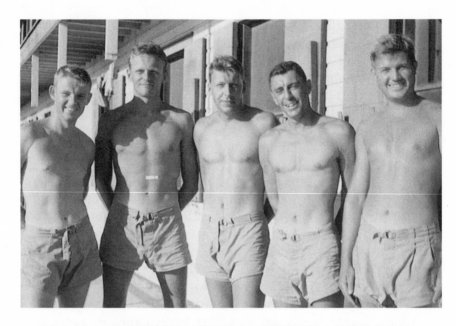

above, l. to r.: ENS Cole, ENS Duke, LTJG Hora, LTJG Palmer, and LTJG Hodge at St. Thomas during the Basic Class in March 1952. *below:* Instructors and trainees rigging a water-proof firing assembly for use off Roosevelt Roads, Puerto Rico, March 1953.

tradition. IBS stood for Inflatable Boat Small. It might have been small but it was not light. We spent a lot of time carrying them around. Its use in coastal reconnaissance pre-dated the later swimming reconnaissance missions of World War Two. In Korea, it was used by UDT detachments to land behind enemy lines and also as a platform from which swimmers could conduct mine removal operations.

The class was organized in seven-man boat crews with three enlisted men per side and an officer in the stern acting as coxswain, navigator, and general anchor. Teams were judged on how well they were led and who was doing it. This was one of the first instances I saw where the Navy was interested in who emerged as an 'emergency leader.' Sometimes it was not the guy with gold on his shirt collar. At St. Thomas, we made several night-time insertions onto Water Island, located in the middle of the Charlotte Amalie harbor and at that time overgrown with shrubs and brambles. A night visit to Water Island seemed like something from Korea. One of Team 4's new officers, LTJG Karl Christoph, USN, had made several such insertions behind the lines in Korea for which he had received the Navy Commendation Ribbon. He and I were the only people in Team #4 with any recent experience on both coasts and the only two with Korean War time. Christoph later made Rear Admiral which weakened my assessment that unconventional warfare experience, such as UDT, was a professional dead-end. No one, however, could afford to spend much of his career in UDT. Christoph had an extremely varied career before retiring.

There was one black enlisted man in Team #2 and we had another in our class. He was harassed by some instructors who used terms like 'boy,' 'night-fighter,' and similar slurs. At the time, it didn't seem much worse than what I was getting from instructors as I ran at the rear of the line or failed to complete the fourth set of twenty push-ups. Finally, he disappeared. I never heard him give his reason. Someone said he left when the instructors decided he couldn't float. One of us officers might have done more but none did. It took a lot just to keep yourself in the 'system.'

From 1947 to 1952, east coast Teams usually ran two classes a year in which attrition averaged fifty percent, although one entire class was reportedly washed out. This was probably due to a lack of officer leadership. People left for various reasons. Physical injuries due to falls, ear damage, sun poisoning, coral poisoning, or an inability to meet progressively more difficult swimming standards probably were the most common reasons. Others that quit simply did not have the will to stay and take the verbal abuse. Some were claustrophobic or scared of explosives, and the list went on. A few who refused to quit, were screened out on Saturday morning following a careful review of their behavior by the instructor staff. During the week, all you had to do was hold up your hand and you were on your way back to the fleet. 'Back to the fleet!' That phrase defined a real gap between us and them. This was so different from the Navy that at times I really felt no longer in the Navy. Having to go back from this would have been very embarrassing.

I knew my own athletic weaknesses from trying and not succeeding at several sports at Cornell, but I also knew how not to pay attention to fraternity-style verbal abuse and hazing. I might not make it on athletic talent, but they were going to have to fire me. I would not get insulted and quit. At twenty-three, I was also somewhat older than most enlisted people in the class. In addition, I had combat experience, was reasonably intelligent, patient, as well as experienced in and willing to turn a deaf ear to all manner of abuse that officers got in Basic training which, if anything, they got more heavily than enlisted. They needed some officers and wouldn't likely get rid of all of us. Although I usually found myself at the back of the line of runners going up and down sand dunes, I managed to convince myself that I was doing some good back there as I tried to encourage someone else not to quit. It took my mind off what I wasn't doing very well.

In distance swims, inevitably, I was also in the back of the pack along with my swimming partner, an over-aged Hospitalman Chief.[5] The Team needed corpsmen and often they were assigned rather than volunteering. One way or the other, they went through the class. At least once a week at St. Thomas, we had to swim from the Submarine Base and around the point to Brewers Bay, a distance of some three miles. At Red Point, just as you entered Brewers Bay, it was possible to swim as hard as you wished for about twenty minutes after which you could look down and realize you were still swimming over the same hunk of coral. I simply could not get into the Bay any faster than the current was coming out and there I remained—no matter how hard I worked. Meanwhile those in front got further ahead. How they managed I didn't know. One reason was that I did not learn to flutter-kick with swim fins until three months after training was over. Although basic training was often long on verbal hazing, it seemed short on teaching people how to overcome problems. Despite this, at least one enlisted man in our class taught himself to swim during the course; human will is indeed remarkable.

On one long swim, when the chief and I were again bringing up the rear, the LCPR with the skipper of Team Two came up. I wasn't dogging it, I just couldn't go any faster. Going over and over in my head was the phrase, "they can throw my ass out but nobody will get the satisfaction of seeing me quit...they can..." and so on. LCDR Hoyt began with, "You are the most sorry-ass swimmer in this whole lot. I wouldn't have you as an officer in my Team." After that, he got insulting. Unless I was ordered out of the water, my intention was to keep on swimming while saying, 'Yes Sir,' as often as appropriate. Finally he left in disgust. I never saw him in the water, but then he had been captured by the Japanese, had made the Bataan Death March, and had been held prisoner for nearly four years. His dues were paid in full even though he wasn't very nice. I was just thankful I had been assigned to Team #4 and not to his Team #2.

Submersible-Operations Platoon

In addition to the basic class, UDU simultaneously ran an advanced underwater swimmers' course in St. Thomas using instructors from the then secret Submersible-Operations Platoon (Sub-Ops), LT Robert Fay in charge. By 1952, UDU was selecting experienced graduates of the basic course and training them to use the aqualung. There were several oxygen rebreathing units also being considered for combat swimming operations. The Costeau aqualung, invented during World War Two, uses compressed air and is not suited for combat insertions against an alert enemy because it leaves a characteristic string of exploding air bubbles on the surface. However, in spite of the bubbles, the aqualung was an appropriate first step in the training of free underwater combat swimmers. The aqualung had many advantages and incorporated some of the diving medicine principles used in hard hat diving, only you weren't attached to the surface by an air hose and safety line.

Oxygen-recycling lungs had been used by British and Italian frogmen when they operated midget submarines during World War Two. However, swimmers going too deep on pure compressed oxygen were subject to oxygen poisoning; the entire issue of swimming on mixed gases was just beginning to be investigated. Every user of an aqualung learned he could rupture a lung with an air embolism if he ascended without exhaling enough expanding air, also, he could get the bends by working deep with multiple tanks and then not ascending according to the Navy's diving table. In general, the aqualung was an acceptable first step and had practical, non-combat uses all of us could appreciate.

Conducting a complete, undetected, pre-assault reconnaissance underwater was clearly better than surface swimming under fire onto an enemy beach. Such a mission could even involve submerged night-time swimming on a fixed course to a fixed point and then back again. Latent claustrophobia, tendencies to panic, or to become disoriented in the dark, were all negative behaviors that might limit one's future usefulness in submersible operations. Use of SCUBA (Self-Contained Underwater Breathing Apparatus) opened the door to other activities. The ability to conduct such operations was the beginning of changes that ultimately resulted in formation of SEAL Teams ten years later.

USS *Sealion* (APSS-315), a submarine then equipped to carry troops, appeared one evening in the middle of the advanced course and tied up to the dock. *Sealion* was to be used for practicing underwater lock-outs and subsequent reentries by aqualung-equipped swimmers as she lay submerged on the bottom off Brewer's Bay. All these procedures were then heavily classified and we in the basic class were not supposed to know they were taking place. The advanced class also practiced night-time deep ditchings of aqualungs followed by free ascents in the dark and underwater swims following compass courses.

To become a candidate for sub-ops, one first had to pass the pressure test in a diving chamber at Little Creek. If your ears and sinuses tolerated changes, the next step was a week of free ascents in the Submarine Escape Tower in New London. This required being locked out first at fifty and then at one hundred feet below the surface and finally making a free, controlled ascent to the surface. Once through this step, if judged psychologically suitable, and sufficient time remained on your enlistment, you could be picked for the advanced class. A submarine medicine specialist was attached to Sub-Ops operations to assist in evaluations.

Selection for the advanced course happened behind closed doors in the Sub-Ops Operating Area and only those making the Navy a career probably had much chance. Reservists, either officers or enlisted, would at most serve two to three years with the Team before being separated and thus were not likely to be chosen. An enlisted man on a regular six-year enlistment might stand a better chance and anyone on a second enlistment was probably on a career track and had the best chance.

As a basic class member, I had all I could handle and more just keeping up with what was happening to me, although we all heard parts of these stories. None of these advanced procedures could be ever absolutely safe and several years later GM2 Tom MacAllister, one of my favorite people in Team #4, was killed during a day-time training swim in St. Thomas. Murphy, a member of my platoon came back from New London with the bends. He was small and after a problem getting a control valve unstuck in the lock-out chamber, everyone else bigger got out before he did. As a result he stayed too long under pressure at the one hundred foot depth, absorbed too much nitrogen, and a nitrogen bubble dislodged somewhere in his lower spine after he reached the surface. However, considering the opportunity for problems, these training exercises were remarkably free of them.

Other Medical Problems

My class made several night-time surface swims from offshore into Brewers Bay and we were always under close scrutiny by instructors in an LCPR. I found it very easy to become disoriented when swimming in the dark. I also disliked skin diving at night and probably would have been a poor sub-ops candidate. Furthermore, some instructor was always willing to describe a night-time surface swim he had made in Guantanamo Bay which was interrupted by bumps from porpoises he thought were sharks. It was only part of the hype but it worked on me. We carried flares in case of emergencies but swam without the inflatable life vests which would come later. A cramped leg in the darkness might be all one would need to drown despite the presence of your swimming buddy. I often cramped but never saw porpoises and only one shark, although I spent a lot of time looking for them.

Far more serious was the combination of sun, black sea urchins, and coral. Several classmates either sat on or were thrown against urchins by wave surge. Urchin quills would break off inside the skin and fester with infection. Coral was nice to look at but swimming in or over it, or trying to set explosive charges in it while being thrown onto it by waves inevitably caused cuts that usually became infected. Navy coral shoes were made of light canvas with thin soles and the fins fit over them. The shoes were a nuisance and not much used.

By itself, the sun was the worst. In days before sun-screen, the only help with the sun was to wear a field jacket and cap and swim with zinc oxide plastered on your nose. Only the small Voit fins were then available and the hard green Voit masks you shaped to your face with a knife were also unhelpful. Fins usually rubbed sores and the face masks leaked. As newer, soft, face-fitting masks, no matter the color, came on the market, they were substituted, even if you had to buy your own.

Our skipper, LCDR David C. Saunders, USNR, later was severely injured during parachute training and was finally given a medical discharge. His accident, MacAllister's death and Murphy's case of bends, were the only serious training accidents I knew about. Occasionally people picked up small wounds from copper splinters from blasting caps or were hit with small rock fragments in explosions, but our safety record was surprisingly good despite the apparent risks being taken.

People in the training class were carefully watched, particularly when around explosives. Some trainees who did the physical activities with ease blanked out around explosives, which was one of the reasons they wanted me to go through So-Solly Day. So-Solly Day was full of things going off and some people simply froze. I didn't mind the noise, and unlike my Korean experiences, I knew the instructors in white helmets weren't trying to kill us.

Underwater Demolition Team Four

Despite everything, I graduated in April 1952, joined Team #4 and became one of its fourteen officers. Eight were LTs or above, seven were recalled reservists and five had Pacific Theater UDT experience. The remaining six, LTJG or ENS, were regular Navy, two from NROTC, and four from the Academy. Of our four Annapolis graduates, all were LTJGs; two were from Class of '48 and two from '49. Bobby Hodgson, (Georgia Tech, 51) and I were the two NROTC Regulars.

LCDR Saunders had been recalled and now wore two hats, Com UDU 2 and Com UDT 4. He had graduated from the University of Pittsburgh in 1940 and spent much of the war on a carrier as an Explosive Ordnance Disposal Officer. Late in the war, he had been assigned to a Team as its commanding officer. We all knew him affectionately—albeit behind his back—as 'Cement-head.' Although we had suspicions, none dared ask why. Saunders was rock-hard, tough, and well respected despite the sobriquet. Had he ever come walking directly through the walls of our quonset, instead of through the doors, no one would have been surprised. His executive officer was LCDR Francis Kaine, USNR, described by Orr Kelly as MacArthur's UDT man.[6]

The Team then had about one hundred enlisted men, many of whom were third-class petty officers or above and many on second and third reenlistments. We seemed top-heavy in chiefs, and in ratings such as gunner's mates and boatswains' mates. Any wise destroyer captain would have traded a better-than-average executive officer for four or five of these people. Many of our enlisted had Pacific Theater experience from World War Two and often were also decorated. Joe Dimartino had even survived the pre-assault work at Normandy. Everyone who had survived a UDT pre-invasion reconnaissance mission in the Pacific Theater seemed to have earned the Silver Star if an officer or the Bronze Star if enlisted.

Many enlisted men were also qualified either as salvage or first-class divers. Several of the chiefs were master divers with

significant hard-hat diving experience. Others had graduated
from Explosive Ordnance Disposal School and some had received Raiders training with the Marines or, more recently, had
done things that nobody was supposed to talk about. It was a
challenging group of men with whom to be confronted, even
though a few were living on past glory and others were active
alcoholics. Some also seemed past their physical prime. That
people could continue to do these activities into their early
forties was incomprehensible to my twenty-three year-old mind.
Only the excellent athletes among us could continue meeting
the on going physical requirements.

By 1952, deployments to the Mediterranean of combat-
ready ships with Marine battalions on board had been underway for several years. A platoon consisting of two officers and
twenty-five enlisted men from Team #4 alternated with one
from Team #2 on the Med cruises. The Platoon and the APD
on which they were berthed would be attached to the Sixth
Fleet and then stay overseas for up to six months before being
rotated back to Little Creek. During a normal tour, the Platoon
would support Marine landing exercises.

Usually nothing more happened. A similar West Coast
detachment had been in the Far East when Korea began and
thus, any deployed Platoon could quickly become front-line
troops. A Med cruise might become boring and officers had to
watch for people jumping ship and joining the French Foreign
Legion. If interminably watching Marines come ashore
becomes too boring and you really wanted a fight, the Legion-
naires were always involved somewhere. At least one 'frog'
jumped. Mediterranean operations were also the only platoon-
sized swimming operations Team members normally encoun-
tered after basic training. Whenever possible, the deployed
Platoon consisted of bachelors; I missed my trip January 1953
by getting married in December. In addition to showing the
flag, a Med cruise could offer a variety of social experiences,
perhaps more for those on cruisers than those riding around on
APDs.

Detachments also went to Labrador and Greenland to
support the construction of the Dew Line, an early warning
radar system. Smaller deployed groups of five to ten men
served as lifeguards, assisting Marine landing exercises at Little

Creek or at Onslow Beach in North Carolina. I made five or more practice assaults with Marines in the following months, none of which was ever preceded by a pre-landing recon and demolition training mission assignment. Instead, we worked primarily as lifeguards or as in-the-surf handymen to the Beachmaster, the naval officer in charge of troop movement across the beach.

The Amphibious Base at Little Creek

The Naval Amphibious Base at Little Creek, Virginia in 1952 had not changed much since 1945. The recent increases in taxes had gone directly to supporting the war. Cut-backs in the Navy from 1947 to 1949 which I had seen as a midshipman, had had negative impacts everywhere. The Base seemed temporary and somewhat shabby.

The Base surrounds a small harbor halfway between Norfolk and Cape Henry. Until completion of the Chesapeake Bay Bridge and the Hampton Road tunnel, the harbor also served as the southern terminus for the ferries to Hampton and to Newport News. It was usually filled with mine sweepers and smaller landing craft as well as LSTs and high-speed attack transports or APDs such as *Bowers*.

The Japanese had made heavy use of destroyers to deliver troops and supplies at night during the Guadalcanal campaign in 1942-43. The US Navy created a near equivalent when it converted several old 'four piper' destroyers from World War One (*e.g.* USS *Belknap*) into APDs. Following the Pacific War, these older conversions were scrapped. Late in World War Two, many excess Buckley-class destroyer escorts were converted into more modern APDs. Although ninety-seven APDs existed at war's end, many had been placed in mothballs until 1950.[7] By 1952-53, at least the following nine had been reactivated and were in Little Creek: USS *Bowers* (APD-40), USS *Carpellotti* (APD-136), USS *Hollis* (APD-86), USS *Klinesmith* (APD-134), USS *Laning* (APD-55), USS *Liddle* (APD-60), USS *Lloyd* (APD-63), USS *Ruchampkin* (APD-89), and USS *Weiss* (APD-135). All had been laid down from 1943-45 as 1,650-ton destroyer escorts but before completion were converted to transport UDTs, Marine Raiders, and other small party operations as well as supplies. Other ships of the Atlantic Fleet, not

deployed to the Mediterranean or on training or landing operations elsewhere—destroyers, cruisers, and aircraft carriers—
were either tied up to piers at, or anchored off, the nearby
Norfolk Naval Base. Others were in Narragansett Bay, Rhode
Island, or at Charleston, South Carolina.

Without giving my own move much thought, I had become
part of the 'Gator Navy' now made up of slow moving LSTs,
APDs, AKAs, APAs, and a long string of odd looking landing
craft and strange units such as my own.

The Atlantic Fleet

Not only had I left destroyers and entered the amphibs, but
I had come to the East Coast. Had I been contemplating a
naval career, I probably had made an unwise choice on at least
one account. The route upward to Admiral's stars still seemed
to be submarines, air, perhaps surface, but never amphibs, and
certainly not 'unconventional warfare.'

Further, except for the Essex carrier, *Leyte*, and several east
coast destroyer divisions sent to West Pac for duty in Task
Force 77 early in the Korean War, there did not appear to be
any further deployments to WestPac from the Atlantic Fleet.
Several officers from earlier swimmers' classes had been transferred to UDTs at Coronado. That no longer happened. For
better or worse, Korea was the 'other Fleet's Problem' just as
the growing Russian problem and maintaining stability in the
Mediterranean were the Atlantic Fleet's. These were very different issues and the fleets were quite separate.

A decade later I would hear regular Navy and Marine officers describing Vietnam as, "..the only war we've got...," to justify
their requests for combat assignments. Steaming in harm's way
had always seemed the way up the promotion ladder. When it
was available, combat experience was essential to any military
career. If so, we ought to be swapping units and spreading
combat experience into both Fleets. Perhaps, in the final analysis, it simply cost too much to move ships and people.

As a result, the Atlantic Fleet seemed to remember World
War Two, but be unaware of Korea. It seemed asleep, or if not
that, at least at peace. Contingents of enlisted men and officers
regularly went in to see the skipper requesting duty in Korea

but were always turned down.[8] Spreading around the strengths of each others' experience just never happened. Meanwhile, the Pacific Fleet was confronted with a limited, though real enough, war that nobody back east cared much about. I had no way of realizing this before coming to the Atlantic Fleet. As the Korean War became more and more politically unpopular, the difference festered.

♨

Professional Futures in Unconventional Warfare

Given the limited vision of the UDT mission, Regular Navy officers served only a two- to three-year tour with a Team before being reassigned to the next billet they would need on their way up the ladder. As recalled reserve officers from World War Two returned to civilian life and Regular officers and men were reassigned or transferred, the future for longer-term retention of skills and experience within the Team did not look good. Furthermore, regular petty officers who chose to stay with the Teams were being hurt professionally because their new skills were not related to any needed in their next rating examination. Electronics Technicians and Radiomen would forget more than they learned in a two-year tour with a Team. Several highly skilled operators finally asked to be reassigned because they were not keeping up with the technical changes in technical rates. To move up in the fleet, they needed daily experience with the newest equipment. Staying with the Team usually meant slower promotions which, ultimately, discouraged reenlistments.

During Vietnam, I spent two training duty tours in the Pentagon in an unconventional warfare group. While on my last tour, the skipper of one of the Little Creek Teams was killed during a riverine insertion mission. By then, CDR Robert Fay, former Sub-Ops platoon leader, had been killed. Others I knew from Teams 2 and 4 who stayed on would be killed or wounded in Vietnam while serving either as UDT or as SEALs. The Navy had finally recognized one of the few benefits of a war to be the opportunity to put people in situations they will never see in training.

At times I considered staying, but by summer 1952, I decided that I could not adjust to the peacetime Navy. After completing two years of service and a promotion to LTJG USN, in

August, I requested a transfer from USN to USNR, which would then allow me to be separated from the Navy at the end of my three-year obligation.

Other Changes

Between 1953 and 1962, changes to the UDT program included the creation of a career path.[9] To evolve from a World War Two doctrine suited for the landings at Iwo Jima and Okinawa to the doctrine used to insert SEALS by air in Panama and later in Desert Storm, the Navy needed non-orthodox thinkers and planners. They began with Robert Fay, David Saunders and Frank Kaine, among others. Al Hodge was the only officer in my class who remained involved in unconventional warfare. UDT to the mainline naval establishment must have seemed more like something for grown-up kids that were still playing with fire-crackers.

Night insertion and reconnaissance behind the lines became important in Korea. That meant rubber boat training and night-time infiltration training as well as small arms training. When I realized I was going to the Teams, I had asked one of the *Ozbourn*'s gunner's mates to teach me how to field-strip a 45 automatic pistol. Although it, the M-1 carbine, 38 caliber pistol, and the 45 caliber grease gun or Tommy gun with the 'coat hanger' stock were standard issue in the Team gun lockers, I had never fired small arms during basic training. Although our unorthodox behavior bothered the real Navy, UDU 2 was still behind the times and seemed somewhat unaware of what Korea was bringing about. In many aspects, the Korean War seemed a rerun of World War Two by using its equipment, its recalled people, and its tactics. This led to an unsatisfactory end which, more than forty years later, still frustrates its veterans. However, out of the Korean experience would come change as the US began to confront counter-insurgency problems in the 1960s. Just before Vietnam, the SEALs were formed and many experienced Team swimmers transitioned into SEAL Teams. UDT remained separated units throughout Vietnam but they were finally disestablished in 1983.

Sinking Ships

The Italians and British had used midget submarines to deliver limpet mines inside enemy harbors during World War Two. My own experiences convinced me that no destroyer anchored off Korea was prepared to defend itself and would have been easy to sink with limpets. It probably could even have been captured by a rubber-boat load of well-armed people. *Ozbourn* and others bombarding in Wonsan Harbor had been lucky. We had no plan to counter an assault boarding; all our small arms were securely locked up. We were lucky.

During 1952-53, Team swimmers were first used at Guantanamo Bay, and then in the Norfolk harbor area, to conduct 'sneak attacks' on anchored naval ships. Ships swinging at buoys in the Norfolk or San Diego harbors were frequently embarrassed when UDT swimmers climbed up their anchor chains on assignment to test security. Our people climbed on board without being noticed, left notes in unlocked magazines, stole things from captains' cabins. It was all too easy.

Life and Death at Vieques

Immediately after graduation 12 April, 1952, I was assigned as assistant platoon leader to a platoon going south on an LST to Vieques east of Puerto Rico for TraEx II, a battalion-sized training operation. Vieques had been used by Marines for amphibious training since the 1930s. After the initial landing, I remained behind as officer-in-charge of five swimmers and attached to the Beachmaster. A boatswain's mate second (BM2), a machinist's mate second (MM2), a boatswain's mate third (BM3), a fireman (FN), and a seaman (SN) were in my detachment. The first administrative landing put Marines and equipment ashore for jungle training. Later, the second simulated a combat assault.

The administrative landing went off without a hitch. We set up with the Beachmaster, observed SeaBees putting in the mobile piers, watched Marines land tanks from LSTs, and watched LCUs and LCMs bringing ashore Marines after which we were out of work watching. The six of us settled down for five weeks of enjoying the tropics before the combat landing.

It was my first experience as a field leader and I was not quite up to the challenge. My first mistake was letting my five enlisted people set up camp down the beach away from the Beachmaster tents where they basically went native. Beards, too much time free to wander the island or spend at the Marine NCO slop-chute (bar), plus a general lack of control plagued me most of the time. To keep occupied, they corralled a squadron of free-running horses and used them to harass Marine encampments like a band of marauding cavalry. Finally, they swiped a DUKW (amphibious truck) after midnight from the Marine motor pool and then used it to raid supply dumps. I'd see them once a day at 0800 for muster and then their fun began. I wasn't particularly regulation, but the title of their game was, 'beat the Marines and their shore patrols, fool ENS Cole, and get away with everything you can.' I was clearly outclassed. Even my BM2 seemed out of shape and we didn't agree on much of anything. I had not yet put anyone on report but he came close.

After a few loud discussions I learned yet another painful leadership lesson not taught in NROTC classes about controlling people. I was not very good at independent duty assignments and these were not ordinary sailors. However, I spent hours swimming from one end of the beach to the other and finally learned how to flutter-kick with swim-fins.

Despite my problems, I found a good friend in Richard Matheny, my machinist's mate. Dick had enlisted in 1948 after high school and then played football at the Great Lakes Training Center before joining the Team. We looked like Mutt and Jeff. He weighed 220 pounds and I, 150. He helped most by keeping me blissfully ignorant of trouble with the Marine Military Police (MP), kept the peace when I learned, and taught me how to skin-dive under beached LCM landing craft and remove line twisted up in the propellers.

About once a day, an LCM coming in from the transports offshore beached in front of us and, inevitably, picked up a length of discarded line, wrapped it around the prop and shaft, and stalled out. Someone discovered that you could swim carefully in from the boat's stern and then duck under the boat's counter and come up in a pocket of air just above the skids protecting the propeller. That air pocket resulted from cavitation during the landing. Assuming the craft didn't roll over on you, you could wrap yourself around the rudder post and breathe from this air pocket until you got the line unwrapped. If some idiot coxswain forgot you were under there and started his engine, you might also come out in the wake, a piece at a time, and looking like hamburger. It was the only practical skill, except how to blow up bridges and land behind enemy lines, that I had learned. None of them I ever had an opportunity to use later.

While I was sitting on the beach and they were getting into trouble, the Marines conducted field problems. The Marines finally finished and reloaded onto the transports waiting offshore, to be re-landed several miles away in a mock assault. This larger beach in Vieques was used later in the film *Away All Boats* starring Jeff Chandler.

When not otherwise raising hell, we swam offshore to skin dive twenty to twenty-five feet for conch shells and to look at eel grass and coral. It was an idyllic way to spend five weeks. What I didn't know about things going on down the beach was fine — most of the time. Three times a day, we loaded into the Beachmaster's DUKW and were driven to a Marine mess tent to enjoy B-rations. Each evening after it began to get dark, the Marines sent a truck to spray our tent site at the beach. To be certain of yet another night's sleep free of mosquitoes, I stood in my skivvies in the wafting fog of DDT. When sufficiently covered I went back in and climbed into my cot for a quiet night. What it did for our long-term health was something else. Read the mail, write a letter, read a book, fall asleep, and soon another day began with a spectacular Caribbean sunrise. It certainly beat riding around on a destroyer.

To keep his Marines happy, their colonel scheduled swim calls off the Beachmaster's beach. This colonel assigned his own life guards. We were not on duty on the beach when a Marine drowned, but for the next three days, he let us dive for the corpse. Late on the third day, while we were off eating supper, the corpse floated to the surface. Even though we had not found him, I keep this mental image of swimming up into his face. I hated looking for corpses.

To Marine Colonels — It Is, "Yes Sir"

During the summer and early autumn 1952, I made several similar training landings in North Carolina, at Virginia Beach, and at Little Creek. One evening after the landing at Onslow Beach was completed, I stood with a former midshipman friend from *Boxer*, now a Marine Second Lieutenant and listened quietly as he went over a long list of wounded and dead people our age who had made the choice I almost had made—namely become a Marine. A depressing end to an otherwise pleasant summer evening also spent listening to waves and watching evening descend on Onslow Beach.

On most of these exercises, we were there in case heavily loaded Marines had trouble in the surf or a landing craft broached. In July, John Bakelaar, BM3, and I were assigned to help at a landing at Little Creek. We arrived on the beach during the middle of the night and were required to stay up and send back reports on the state of the surf. Someone somewhere then used our report to decide whether conditions were safe enough for the landing to proceed. After staying up all night and watching the surf, we would be on the beach and ready to meet the first boats.

Our instructions were to wait in swim suits with fins, face masks, belt, and a sheathed knife ready to go in the water. As wave after wave came in and after sitting in the sun for four hours, we usually covered ourselves with Navy fatigue jackets and a Marine field cap. After eight hours in the hot Virginia sun waiting for a landing exercise to finish, I would have been cooked without some protection.

During this particular landing, while landing craft ramps were coming open and Marines were stumbling into a low surf, John and I sat and watched. Wearing swim suits and ball caps, we apparently looked like ignorant sight-seers who had wandered in for a swim. Suddenly an angry Marine MP confronted us and ordered us to come with him. We followed him, all the while looking over our shoulders at more incoming boats and possible victims. Finally we entered the Beachmaster's tent and were greeted by a Marine bird colonel close to apoplexy. He then proceeded to chew me out every way to Sunday for being out of uniform during his amphibious assault landing. If we were going to be on his beach, we would be there in the uniform of the day or off to jail. He wasn't at all interested in whether life guards ought to be dressed to stand inspection or dressed to save Marines. If I was going to be on *his* beach, I'd be in uniform or in a hell of a mess. My response was a series of verbal and respectful, "Yes sirs," but with a lot of, "You dumb shit," thoughts passing through my head.

Nobody died and the whole thing was very silly, but it was difficult knowing that obedience to his order was contrary to those given me by my commanding officer. Had a landing craft broached and heavily weighted-down Marines been unable to get ashore from ten feet of water, someone probably would have drowned even had we been right on the spot. Getting out of the uniform of the day and into swim gear would have only made it worse.

The Colonel was in no mood to put his order in writing. Left with little alternative, John and I returned to our perch on the berm and put on whatever we had of a legitimate uniform. Strangely, that one event helped me make up my mind to get out of the Regular Navy. Several weeks later I put in a request to have my commission changed from Lieutenant (jg) USN to USNR. By then (1952), recalled reserve officers who had accumulated six or more years of prior active duty were deciding they might as well stay on active duty and retire on twenty. To do this, they felt they had to become Regular Navy. Every USNR officer I knew thought I was nuts to want to go the other way.

Demolition Dumbness

During the same summer, I began working with John Hostilio, GM2, and also EOD (Explosive Ordnance Disposal) qualified. He, John Bakelaar, and Dick Matheny were the people with whom you trusted your life. Conversely, you often had theirs in your hands. Following one of the Team's explosives training exercises, Hostilio and I remained behind to police the site and gather up and dispose of all unexpended explosives. Any typical demolition operation usually threw unexploded pieces of C-3 or TNT around the site. They could neither be left nor returned to the magazines. Someone had to detonate them.

We scoured the area and then made a nice pile at the edge of a swamp. John stuck an electric blasting cap in the midst of the pieces of C-3, TNT, and miscellaneous primacord fragments and we stepped behind a nearby pine tree. He yelled, "Fire in the hole," and twisted the handle of a hell box to create the electric charge that fired the cap. We had vastly underestimated the size of the pile. I can still see parts of a rubber boat plus other miscellaneous trash we had also collected from the site come rocketing past the tree. I probably came closer to killing myself doing stupid stuff during those days than ever off Korea.

Life on Beach #7

It was fun playing with half-pound blocks of TNT, primacord, and pieces of Bangalore torpedo. Beach #7 at Little Creek, where much of it happened, holds many strange memories. Beach #7 then had replicas of many of the World War Two beach obstacles, from those huge Belgian gates used by the Germans at Normandy to concrete tetrahedrons with steel spikes used by the Japanese in the Pacific. All were constructed of concrete or of old railroad iron or iron channels. Each was used in training demonstrations. My favorite was a three foot high cement tetrahedron with four-foot sections of old railroad track extending from its top. Tetrahedrons were planted underwater and were intended to drive holes in oncoming landing craft to prevent them from making it ashore. Anything under water might also be rigged with anti-tank mines that would explode when the craft hit.

In Dick Matheny's training class, someone hung a twenty-pound pack on one of the tetrahedrons on the beach and then proceeded to demonstrate how twenty pounds of TNT would destroy it. Everyone dug in. Someone yelled, "Fire in the hole," and then set off the charge electrically. As soon as any charge went off, you always looked skyward for ascending things that might ultimately land on you. If you were alert, you usually could avoid falling rocks and dirt clods.

We had a reputation for underestimating explosions. If the handbook said ten, we used twenty pounds to be sure. When this charge went off, in addition to completely shattering the concrete, the blast also threw a piece of railroad iron skyward on a high looping path that you could follow like an upper-deck home run. Those on the beach watched with dismay as it went up and then finally down disappearing behind the pine trees lining the back of a swamp over three hundred yards behind the dune line. When it was finally found, it had traveled well over four hundred yards before falling through the roof of the Admiral's Quarters. It had gone through his living room ceiling before embedding itself in the floor next to the coffee table. The admiral and family were out at the time but when he came home, he was quite unhappy. As the years passed, demolitions training on Beach #7 grew more and more sedate and tame. Finally, because of the noise, it was forbidden entirely. The NIMBY (Not In My Back Yard) problem soon overtook UDT as well.

Not Our Finest Hour!

A far more tragic event occurred in Boston on September 29, 1949 during a mock landing of several thousand Marines at Carson Beach, South Boston. Seventy-five swimmers were participating in a demonstration of swimming-in under simulated gunfire. The show was to end with underwater explosions after recovery of the swimmers. Although it was a big exercise, it was still a relatively routine demonstration. To liven it up, someone decided to use a signal mortar, and, instead of using regular signal pyrotechnics, substituted TNT blocks with lighted fuses to simulate air bursts when they exploded in the air. Several charges were launched successfully and then a block stuck in the tube where it then exploded, shattering the mortar tube and killing a Boston news photographer. Several others were severely wounded. When he realized the tube was about to explode, LT Hugh McStay threw himself on top of the mortar absorbing much of the explosion.[10] Such behavior in combat might have earned him the Medal of Honor. Following that fiasco, pieces of TNT and other explosives kept turning up on the beach according to the Boston newspapers. It was not UDT's finest hour.

Later, during a demonstration for President Truman, several people in a landing craft were assigned to drop half pound blocks of TNT with lighted fuses into the water behind the LCPR. When they exploded, they simulated mortar explosions. Upon receipt of a signal to "cease fire," a junior officer, without thinking, obeyed the order and returned an already lighted charge to a nearly full box of TNT. Someone else alertly grabbed it barely getting it out of the boat before it too exploded. The next day LCDR Hoyt had that officer transferred out of Team #2.

In all of these things, good and bad, there was a residue of war and rebellion below the surface amongst the Team people. They were highly capable and often nearly self-destructive. The days were filled with football and volleyball games or running to keep in shape. Detachments went to the Caribbean and new people were trained, but nights were often spent getting drunk. Why did we do all that? I, and perhaps others, never made the mental shift from the previous or even the ongoing Korean War to one of thinking about and planning for the next one. How do you get a Team ready for the next football game, when one isn't on the schedule?

There was some planning for the future in the Sub-Ops Platoon and it ultimately evolved into a new mission and the SEAL Teams in the early 1960s. Meanwhile, many felt we were training day after day for something that would never happen. A tour in Korea would have put some of us past that.

Getting Killed Fooling Around

Once a month we were required to handle explosives to qualify for hazardous duty pay. On one of those days, we played with home-made shaped charges on Beach #7. Shaped charges could be made by molding plastic explosive around the outside of little metal cones that stood on three wire legs. When ready to be fired electrically, they resembled metal ice cream cones with the ice cream on the outside and standing on a steel plate with the pointed end up. The containers came in various shapes and sizes. We would select one for the task at hand and surround it with C-3 plastic explosive. When it exploded, a fire ball jumped from the inside of the cone and instantly bored a nice round hole into the steel armor plate. Shaped charges depended on the same physical and chemical principles used by the bazooka to bore holes in tanks—the Monroe effect. We did this for several shots and then someone wondered what would happen if we bent the legs to make the axis of discharge horizontal rather than vertical. If it worked, we could aim fire balls out into Chesapeake Bay, rather than down at a piece of steel. It worked perfectly and a white hot ball emerged like a shot from a Roman candle arcing at least a thousand yards from shore. It would have bored a hole in any steel it hit. However, when we realized that we had also nearly scored a direct hit on a passing LST even that game was over. These stories became part of the Team's memories but they were also stupid things. Further, how could one conduct war training with all this noise?

Hemispheric Mines and No Sense

Just before leaving the Navy, I was placed in charge of a group assigned to test Mark 57 anti-boat mines at a beach just south of Virginia Beach. These hemispheric mines were designed to be planted in shallow water where they would detonate when a landing craft hit them. We planted mines without explosives close to shore and practiced driving landing craft and DUKWs into them. After they had been run into, we recovered them for analysis by someone.

We were also required to detonate several active mines using approved demolition methods; that was John Hostilio's job. He set up the charges but also deactivated them if something went wrong and they did not explode. It was difficult being in charge when someone else has to take a chance with his own life. Rather stupidly, I tried to provide moral support by standing next to him hoping to pass tools while he was working. That sounded sufficiently heroic to me, but John refused to do anything until I left. He worked on the mine until it finally exploded properly and I was denied the opportunity to get killed watching something close at hand that I had no business being involved with in the first place. Good sense always dictated only one life on a one-person task. Somehow it seemed that if it went up, I ought to be there too. This philosophy only made his job more difficult. Some superb trainees during Hell Week bailed out because explosives scared them. I do not remember any fear of explosives. I believed everything I had been told about how difficult it was to explode something accidentally. My secret fears were claustrophobia and swimming at the surface in very deep water or underwater at night. Those were the things I had to force myself to do. As a result I doubt that I could ever have locked out of a submarine at night, but that was the next step and only those in the Sub-Ops Platoon were then doing it.

On the last day of the Mark 57 mine operation, six of us stood in a drifting DUKW taking turns skin-diving in fifteen feet of water trying to find a live mine with an unexploded detonator. Something else had failed to work. Finally someone found it and, as we muscled it aboard, I thoughtlessly reached out for the detonator device intending to yank it off the horn of the mine. Just in time, someone batted my hand away preventing me from blowing us all up. My only response was, "Thank God you did that." Those were the things that got around among the troops. "Don't work with LTJG Cole. Did you hear what that idiot almost did?" I never had a sense of fear while working with explosives because I felt myself to be very methodical—or had been, until then. I can still see that group of sailors standing around this over-sized half basketball and someone batting my hand away just in time.

Rubber Boat Stupidity

One pitch black night, we were running rubber boat extraction drills. Boat teams departed through the low surf on Beach #7 and then paddled west into the shipping channel and then up into a swamp. First team in won. What, I don't remember. I got us into a race with Bobby Hodgson's rubber boat and we led the race across the channel, passing right into the wake of some large vessel that had just passed. When we were dead astern of it, I looked up and realized it was a tug. Its tow rope snapped over our heads. Not only had I committed us to a sprint with Hodgson's seven-man rubber boat but we were now also racing against the arrival of the tug's barge which was rapidly coming up on us. We just cleared the path as it rumbled past. Again, I had nearly killed us all. At that point I was twenty-four years old, a combat veteran, qualified OOD underway on destroyers, and nearly the senior officer in my training class. No wonder people die.

For years after playing these games, practicing night-time insertions, and blowing up things, I would idly think about how best to blow up a building in which the disliked dean worked, how to take out that bridge abutment, or even how to defend the church choir loft against armed terrorists during choir practice. War does tend to cripple the mind—even if only playing at it.

East Cuff Beach, Labrador

In November 1952, LTJG Sam Deal and I took a contingent on board an APD en route to Labrador where we would support yet another Marine landing exercise. The trip northward was uneventful as we proceeded up the Gulf of St. Lawrence. We were then attached to the tractor component which included the LCIs, LSTs, and all the other slow-moving landing ships. We made a short stop in Newfoundland to put ashore a medical problem. Newfoundland in November was cold and gray; it was going to be an icy landing.

Most of the transit I spent in the bunk reading or sleeping, or on deck looking at marine birds, watching the Northern Lights, or in the wardroom at meals or the movies. There was also a continuous cribbage game going on in the wardroom that was reluctantly interrupted for meals and movies. This was the last time I played cribbage. I also read three volumes of Freeman's *Life of George Washington* during the trip. Sea trips always pointed out how much of each day we use doing things. Sailors have a lot of time they can't fill with mowing the lawn or driving to work. Going to sea limits what you do with your hours and reading helps pass time; I read most of the books in the Amphib Base Library before getting out.

Off the Labrador coast, weather conditions resembled those off Korea in 1950-51. The days were short, the waters were frigid, and there was a continuous cloud cover, although no snow. We made one administrative landing and then moved up the coast to make a second several days later. The second resembled a combat landing but again, no beach recon. The first time, elements of our detachment went ashore buttoned up in a Marine amphibious personnel mover called an 'alligator.' The second time, we went in one of the APD's LCPRs. Sam

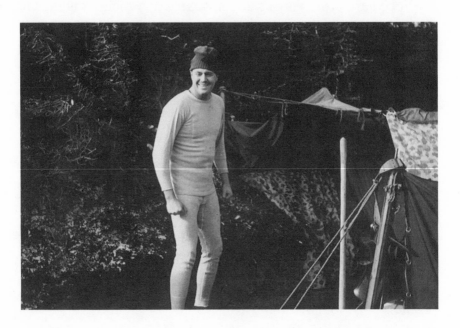

LTJG Sam Deal in his diving underwear at the UDT Hobo Camp,
East Cuff Beach, Labrador, November 1952,
during Operation NORAMEX.

and I had the responsibility of finding the correct beach before
daylight with no lights ashore. Sam was in charge. I picked one
beach and Sam the other. He was correct. My choice would
have put an entire battalion ashore in the wrong place.

Once the Marines had completed the landing and set up
tent camps ashore, we were again assigned to the Beachmaster
to render assistance as required. During our two weeks ashore,
half of us lived on the APD several miles out while the other
half lived ashore in a pyramid tent equipped with a space
heater. It was cold enough to sleep in arctic bags while wearing
woolen diving underwear under fatigues. We also had the latest
insulated combat boots.

Considerable frost bite occurred in Korea during the winter
of 1950-51, so a new winterized boot was devised to prevent it.
We were provided a supply. Marines who had been in Korea
during the winter of 1951-52 said the new boots arrived at the

front only after all the rear echelon people had received them. These heavy rubber boots looked like they belonged on Mickey Mouse but they were great. You could wear them in the icy surf, get your feet wet and still keep warm. However, when we worked in 30-degree water, it took more than boots.

Rubberized dry suits with a zipper up the back were then available for swimmers in arctic waters and they took about ten minutes to get into correctly. If all went well, you stayed absolutely dry but, inevitably, the zippers leaked and you felt you had been stabbed. It probably was too cold for wet suit swimming; no matter, they were still in the future. Wet suits allow water to gradually enter next to the skin where body heat keeps it warm. Dressing in a dry suit and then swimming under those conditions was something of a last resort effort. Unless it was cold enough to absolutely require a dry suit, the only other option was to swim wearing diving underwear tops or old sweatshirts which we did even when water temperatures were in the 50s. Hypothermia was poorly understood at that time and cold water was exhausting.

Ashore, it was cold enough that we usually wore Navy green fatigues over suits of woolen diving underwear. Even better were Marine Corps fatigues and their fatigue caps—I liked working with Marines—even looking like them. On this landing, nobody cared how we looked and, after awhile, our shore side base resembled an ill-kept Boy Scout winter camp. For amusement, I walked around looking for shore and tundra birds but most had already migrated south. Meanwhile, life ashore with the Marines resembled what life behind the lines in Korea must have been like. I was finally getting my fill of camping out and eating C-rations. When life became too bad Sam and I exchanged contingents and cycled back to the APD with its hot showers, warm meals, mail, and movies. It may have looked like Korea but it wasn't.

While we were ashore, someone discovered a small stream nearby that was loaded with Arctic char. My worst military sin was to accompany a 'midnight working party' into the Marine ammunition dump looking for hand grenades. Hand grenades stolen from a Marine ammunition dump would have allowed us to go fishing for char and change our diet. We held a midnight recon or 'sneak and peak' on a dump, entered, and spent a half hour looking for grenades. It was surrounded by Marine guards with loaded carbines and, I suppose, orders to shoot. We never found hand grenades but then no one got shot.

For daylight diversion we could also sneak onto the 105mm howitzer range and listen to artillery shells warbling as they passed overhead. By the time you were wise enough not to do stupid things, you might no longer be physically equipped to do the job—another Team problem.

Our only useful activity during the entire landing consisted of putting on drysuits and rescuing cases of C-rations that had fallen out of a landing craft and into the surf. Our prime role was to be of assistance to swamped boats, drowning Marines, and whatever else the Beachmaster assigned us. Usually there was little to do in administrative or mock-combat landings except 'stay close.' Near the end of our stay, while Marines were again being transported back to the landing ships, an 'alligator' loaded with Marines swamped and sunk in some hundred feet of water. It went down like a rock with Marines locked up inside. There was nothing we could do—we didn't even have aqualungs with us. It was impossible to conduct salvage work without aqualungs or other diving gear and it was far beyond anyone's ability to surface dive. We just were not equipped to help. Even if we could have gone down, it would not have made much difference to the drowned Marines inside. I didn't like looking for corpses.

We left Labrador stopping in New York on the way back for a liberty weekend. This gave me time to visit my Aunt Elizabeth. Next was a few days leave in Beaver for Thanksgiving and a chance to pick up a marriage license; Emma-Jean and I were married 23 December 1952. Dick Matheny was also on the Labrador trip and returned in time to be married at Thanksgiving.

That trip was the last time Sam Deal and I worked together. Until he was separated, I saw Sam frequently because he lived in the BOQ next to me. Sam saved things. In April 1953, just before he returned to Texas and civilian life, he asked me into his room and showed me his closet. Most people had shoes on the floor; Sam collected old, unexploded pieces of C-3, hunks of primacord, and other things from a number of training operations at Beach #7 and elsewhere in Little Creek. He probably

had twenty pounds of explosives. The BOQ would have vanished had it gone off. When Sam left for Texas, it was all
locked in the trunk of his car. I never heard from Sam and can
only presume he had the best Fourth of July fireworks in town
when he got home – if he got home.

There was an implicit anti-establishment code built into
Team behavior. Some of it was due to the pride of having
proved that you could do all these bizarre tasks. Some of the
behavior was also a way of telling the Navy its orthodox system
had a lot of holes. How to keep officers and men unorthodox in
their thinking, keep up useful combat skills, maintain their
willingness to take chances, and yet keep them out of trouble
must have been a challenge for the senior leadership in the
Team.

After *Ozbourn* returned to San Diego from Korea, I sensed
that I had left something behind – a band of people satisfied
they could do the mission. Something had happened that made
my being part of a ship's crew and of the Navy an unforgettable
experience. My military experiences had differed greatly from
those of Marines returning from the Chosin Reservoir or Corsair pilots returning to carriers. Nonetheless, *Ozbourn*'s crew
had become bonded in a way that people bond while enduring a
common adversity. We had developed into a team by experiencing something different from that undergone by those ashore,
but it seemed to vanish when we returned to the States. I never
sensed it again while on active duty. Some of the Team's irrational behavior seemed to be the residue of a 'bonding that no
longer had anything to stick on. Also, the need every day to
prove yourself better than anything or anyone every day took its
toll.

Life As An Instructor

For me, the trivial pursuits of peacetime service ended as
anger which spilled out during a minor event. While returning
from a Caribbean deployment in Spring 1953, I exploded and
very nearly physically assaulted the executive officer on the
Liddle. Those who knew me scarcely believed it possible.

My good friend, LT Joe Worthington, had been recalled to
the Teams. Joe was assigned to the Amphibious School in Little

Creek and was designated as Officer-in-Charge of the basic underwater demolition training class beginning January 1953. He had earned the Silver Star for a pre-invasion swimming mission at Iwo Jima. With his maturity and World War Two experience, Joe had all the credentials needed to lead the training program. He held the respect of all his instructors; he certainly had mine, his senior officer instructor. The course would take fourteen weeks, culminating in eight weeks of infiltration training, combat swimming, and demolitions in the Caribbean. The *Liddle*, an APD, would be our home base.

After four weeks of physical training and Hell Week at Little Creek, our team of officer and enlisted instructors boarded the APD along with ten trainee officers and fifty enlisted trainees. UDT people became a little touchy when asked to do what they perceived to be work that ship's company should be doing. Usually there would be at least one fist fight between enlisted men to define things below decks. Our enlisted people generally kept the officers out of those discussions. From an officer's perspective, our people kept their own spaces clean, provided mess cooks, and kept our personnel squared away like normal transients. Our officers, when asked, were expected to take care of the troops first, last, and always.

Because there were no officer's prerogatives on a combat swim, we tended to become close to our enlisted men. They had to know they could rely on you as well as you could on them. Some officers on the transporting ships took perverse pleasure in assigning our junior officers to the bridge as JOODs, putting our seamen on garbage details, and even putting our enlisted people on report wherever possible.

Most APDs were superb. Some were awful. Inevitably, on those ships something would happen between ship's company and the Team people unless everyone paid close attention. Because all East Coast APDs were home-ported in Little Creek, the reputations of the troublesome APDs were well known to all. We kept book on them and I had been warned about *Liddle*.

In February 1953, we traveled uneventfully to Roosevelt Roads, Puerto Rico. An unfounded story about the ship circulated in the wardroom and concerned the former gunnery officer who had just been elevated to executive officer. Next, the

above: Others from the St. Thomas Basic Class. *l. to r.:* Bronson, unknown, Gough, Casey, Noble, and Gravitz. *below:* ENS Robert Hodgson, UDT #4, at Roosevelt Roads, Puerto Rico, March 1953.

skipper moved the assistant gunnery officer up as gunnery officer. After this naval game of musical chairs, the new exec immediately confined the new gun boss to the ship until all gun mounts and magazines were brought up to inspection condition—something he had obviously failed to do. No UDT officer was sure whether this actually had happened, but the personalities seemed to fit the story. It seemed like something out of *Mr. Roberts*. Before the cruise was over, I learned yet another important leadership lesson the hard way.

During our return to Little Creek, one evening just before movies, I was reading in the wardroom when an irate senior enlisted instructor asked to come in and speak to Mr. Worthington. The instructor had just left the fantail where movies were to be shown. Not only were our enlisted people from the training class being ordered away from the movies but so were our officer and enlisted instructors. The ship's Master-at-Arms said there was only sufficient space for ship's company. Watching evening movies at sea was second only to being fed. No one had ever been excluded before and it wasn't about to start now.

"Mr. Cole, you got to do something," came like an order from our First Class Gunner's Mate. For some reason, this latest piece of naval stupidity characterized everything outrageous and chicken about this 'peacetime' scow and the whole damned Atlantic Fleet. "Didn't anyone know there was a war on?" These black thoughts sent good sense elsewhere.

In a fury, I tried to rouse poor Joe Worthington to help me fight, but Joe was deathly seasick and lay immobilized in his bunk. Any battle to defend the honor of the Teams was now in my hands alone. I agreed to take on this particular windmill and get our fair share of the seats.

Unfortunately, I did not carry it out in a thoughtful manner, and my enthusiasm for the cause far exceeded good sense. One thing led to another and a lot of irrelevant stuff about a lousy peacetime Navy came out before the exec. All of it came boiling out of the closet. Some might even have been true. I found myself expressing guilt over being over on the East Coast knowing that I had voluntarily left the West Coast Navy which was where the real war was and where real sailors were. I had deserted *Ozbourn* and all my shipmates on their return trip to Wonsan and so on.

By the time I had finished shouting at the ship's XO—later even at the CO—I had been placed in hack for the three days remaining in the trip back to Little Creek. I'd never even seen an officer placed in hack, or 'confined to quarters,' until it happened to me. That non-judicial punishment assured me of a bad concurrent fitness report from the skipper of the APD. Despite an off-setting letter and a concurrent report from the commanding officer of the Amphibious Base, as well as one from the admiral about how good I was, I probably had ensured that I had blown large holes in whatever remained of my naval career. After three days spent staring at the overhead from my top bunk, I cooled down.

It was clear to all that I had done damage in spades to any potential naval career. Before the explosion, I had even thought about staying in the Navy. Although becoming an admiral had never occurred to me, I might have made captain. Those wiser than I thought even that might be unlikely. On the other hand, but for that blunder, I might have made a more serious one later, and, at some higher rank. Perhaps I was seeing the military version of the Peter Principle at work—maybe even in the mirror. Far worse, our people did not get their movie seats. Further, they didn't even thank me for trying something that personally had become very costly. Most of them must have been too embarrassed by the defeat suffered by one of their 'leaders.'

Memorial Day, 1953

A month later, just before my separation from active duty, I went to Beaver for the Memorial Day weekend. I was asked to wear dress whites and command the American Legion unit for the rifle salute at the Memorial Day ceremony. This was an honor but, instead, I felt as if only the World War Two guys had been in the real war and declined the offer. There was a blackness falling over the end to the Korean War; somehow those of us there had not done it right.

When Memorial Day weekend was over, Dad and I drove to Little Creek while I went through the separation process. I walked out of the Team's quonset huts and into a near fight with a very big Navy doctor who persisted in using a tongue depressor. Depressors make me gag, but I was not ready to be arrested for assault. He and his stick prevailed. I left regretting that I had not lost my breakfast all over his dress khakis to top off my departure.

By 6 June 1953, I had picked my way through the final processing and Dad and I drove back to Beaver. As we drove away from Little Creek, first going south towards Smithfield before turning west toward Richmond, something large was over and I felt somehow diminished. It was bright and sunny as we passed tobacco fields and then saw the Smithfield hams hanging up at gas stations. Gradually we drove through Petersburg, into Richmond and then on west towards Pittsburgh and Beaver; the Navy was now behind me.

Endnotes:

[1] See Dwyer (1994) for details of the origin and mission of the Navy's Scouts and Raiders who took part in landings in North Africa, Sicily, and Anzio, among other landings. The Naval Combat Demolition Units participated in Normandy, but UDT was particularly Pacific Fleet in development. See also Riker (1993 and 1994) for the first two books, in a fictionalized version, of the origins leading to the SEALs.

[2] CAPT Francis P. Kaine, USN-Ret. Letter to author, 6 March 95.

[3] Morison (1975:304); Kelly (1992) has many of the details of UDTs during the Pacific campaigns. See also, Riker (1993 and 1994) for fictionalized versions.

[4] Dockery (1991:45). See early chapters for additional details on operations in World War Two.

[5] Hospitalmen (HM) were also called Corpsmen and were assigned to combat units to provide on-site first-aid during battle. Many corpsmen were assigned to Marine units and most of the Navy's casualties during Korea were hospitalmen. One HM Second Class in the Little Creek infirmary had won the Navy Cross during the Chosin Reservoir withdrawal in December 1950. The Team needed a Hospitalman Chief far more than it needed another Ensign.

[6] Kelly (1993) describes Kaine's World War II exploits. Frank Kaine was a nice, taciturn leader who seemed somewhat a foil for Saunder's blunt, hardheaded behavior. Frank followed Saunders to become Com UDU 2.

s

[7] *Janes* (1947-48:388).

[8] Personal communication with MM2 Richard Matheny. Some felt a personal animosity between the two UDU Commanders that may have made this more unlikely.

[9] See Bosiljevac (1990) and Dockery (1991) for additional information. Also *Newsweek* (June 17, 1991:20-28) for SEALs tactics and work in Desert Storm, 1991.

[10] The *Boston Herald* (September 30, 1949). For several days after the incident, this item made the front page. LCDR F. D. Fane, would later advise the Board of Inquiry that a half pound of TNT had been substituted for a standard smoke signal.

PART IV

AFTERMATH

IT WASN'T OVER

Emma-Jean and I spent our first summer together living in Massachusetts where I worked as morning janitor at the Wood's Hole Aquarium. I was also responsible for raising the American flag and feeding the fish—my first authority comedown. One week, I was someone in charge of things and responsible for people's lives; the next, I was in charge of a broom.

I shared my summer with Dr. Wilbur Bullock, then on the faculty at the University of New Hampshire. Wilbur had been a combat engineer in France following D-Day and I dutifully listened to his war stories; somehow mine were different and far less interesting. Joe Worthington had a friend and ex-Team mate, Jack Colton, at the Lab and several former Marines worked there as well. They still awed me. On top of everything else they had won *their* war. Perversely, the comparison seemed to be that of a football game—"they won, we lost, or was it a tie?" No matter, logic said they were better. From those days forward I carried around a feeling that somehow we hadn't given it the same effort. That was certainly an easy enough conclusion when all you had seen was seawater from the bridge of a destroyer with an occasional counter-battery flash on some distant shore. Those who had survived the Pusan Perimeter or the Punchbowl had given nearly everything; those that hadn't survived had nothing more to give. Perhaps Korea disappeared so quickly for me because I had other things to do or maybe just because I was tired of comparing myself as I listened to stories about 'Big Two.' Somehow the older guys had done it right and we hadn't.

Gradually I came to realize how different the rules were as I tried to measure our results against theirs. One evening I watched television footage from modern Korea. Until then Inchon had never changed in my mind from some old dingy fishing village near a mud flat with a burned out locomotive, a destroyed brewery, and a corpse still on the dock. By then Hyundais, Gold Star TVs, and other South Korean products were flooding the US markets and yet I had separated out my own memories and kept them unconnected to the present. It finally occurred to me that the people of South Korea remained thankful for our efforts. Indeed, no rational person able to contrast North and South Korea in 1994 should have any difficulty determining who won over forty years earlier, and, if not won, certainly, at least, who had lost. At the same time, I also began to understand what the war had cost not only South Korea but also North Korea and China. Furthermore, my friends Howard Johns and Pete Partridge from Beaver, Bob Gillespie from New Brighton, and thousands from other towns elsewhere had paid a substantial part of the bill.

The announcement of the end of the Korean War came on 27 July, 1953, as I listened to a radio while looking out a window and onto the ferry slip at Woods Hole. I stared across the bay with confused thoughts going through my head, and then I returned to doing what I had determined to do with my life. It was an otherwise black moment on a bright clear day late in July 1953.

After a summer on Cape Cod, we returned to Ithaca and to Cornell University where I began graduate school, naively expecting that returning Korean veterans would soon flood campuses and that we would reprise roles played in 1946-50 by returning World War Two veterans. It was not to be. Cornell was then deeply enmeshed in the battles of the McCarthy era and several prominent faculty, including Dr. Marcus Singer in Zoology, had already been implicated.[1] I had classes to pass, a working wife, car payments to meet, and professional friends to make. I did not have time to sort out the McCarthy problem and also keep afloat in graduate school. Fortunately for Cornell, others fought that battle. It was enough surviving the first year of classes, adjusting to being a student, and to being married.

During my first year back, Emma-Jean and I went to homecoming at Theta Xi, my fraternity. Most of the evening was spent arguing why we hadn't 'lost' in Korea with an older fraternity alumnus, an ex-World War Two infantryman. The rest of the evening was spent wondering who all these young kids were and why hadn't they been drafted? Emma-Jean and I never went back. While in Ithaca from 1953 through 1957, I never sensed that Korean veterans were there in large enough numbers to know and recognize each other, nor did I sense the same feeling of respect from students or faculty accorded the World War Two veteran. Perhaps the prisoners-of-war, 'brainwashing' and the turn-coat issues, in addition to our 'losing' had affected attitudes. Certainly everyone was glad it was over. The Korean War vanished from view like a lost football game. I was through arguing with people about Korea, the Navy, or anything else. It may have been my earliest contribution to our generation of silence leading to our Forgotten War.

The Reserves

I became sour and stayed away from the reserves for several years. Finally, I joined a small Naval Research Company during my last two years in Ithaca. I was the only Korean War vintage officer there and was again completely surrounded by World War Two officers.

In November 1956 during my final year in graduate school, the Hungarian 'problem' arose. The Soviet Union was taking over Hungary by force. I was now a card-carrying LTJG, USNR, and could see myself being recalled for something in eastern Europe for which I was no longer mentally or physically prepared. I was out of shape for going back to being a 'Frogman,' was in my last year of graduate school, had a wife, a fifteen-month old son and a daughter on the way. Late one evening, I walked with some other veterans from our laboratory to the parking lot. We were certain that President Eisenhower was going to have to recall some or all of us and I, for one, would never get my damned dissertation finished. Painful as it was, there was nothing Eisenhower, the American military, or anyone else could do to help the Hungarians, this side of starting World War Three. There seemed to be little any rational people could do, so we Americans wisely pretended it wasn't happening. This was to be the first of several times when membership in the reserves almost became a hazard to career and family. Hungary was followed by the Berlin Wall, the Cuban Missile Crisis, and, finally, Vietnam. In September 1957 I received the PhD and began my teaching career at The University of Arkansas.

By 1962 we had moved and I was teaching at the University of South Florida in Tampa by day and on Wednesday nights commanding a reserve unit in St. Petersburg, Florida. The training center was directly on Tampa Bay and we had a reserve destroyer escort, USS *Greenwood*, and an old yard craft tied up behind us. Wednesday nights seemed like Navy again. We even had a pre-submarine group attached to us. Civilians wanting submarine duty would enlist, spend up to a year with us and then be assured assignment on a submarine during their active duty tours. The night after the nuclear powered submarine *Thresher* sank off New Hampshire with all hands, we were overwhelmed with new volunteers. President Kennedy's admonition to, "Ask not what your country can do for you, ask what you can do for your country," was being answered by twenty new sailors. Within five years, those days of Camelot would disappear into the deepening gloom of Vietnam.

In 1964 I moved to the University of Massachusetts at Amherst and began drilling with reserve units in Springfield. We had hardly unpacked before Vietnam began to grow like a malevolent cancer and those of us with Reserve units began planning our personal lives anticipating a call up. I had done enough volunteering but I spent the years of 1964 to 1967 expecting to be called. As years passed at the university everything Vietnam stood for met increasing student anger, ending with the 1969 riots. During the day I dealt with the avoiders, the returnees, the volunteers—even conscientious objectors.

In the evening, I also served as Commanding Officer of several more reserve units. Progressively, like college campuses, they also became places to avoid the infantry. We had no trouble meeting our enlistment quota but many of those who joined did as little as possible. If attendance at drills became unsatisfactory, our instructions were to recommend that the Naval District Commandant order them to immediate active duty. Usually, the Naval District refused to call up the offenders. That was the limit of my authority. It became the most depressing of experiences.

The Springfield Training Center was a 'museum' of archaic equipment, most of which did not work and little that was relevant to the current fleet. After the USS *Pueblo* was captured outside of Wonsan while on intelligence missions, the word came down to run training simulations on our mock-up bridge and CIC. Phone lines snaked out across the floor, bridge talkers, lee helmsmen, the wheel was manned, and for a brief moment, I was back off Wonsan as the commanding officer of the *Pueblo*. No other experience following my return in 1951 was so vivid. I heard shell-fire, the realities of possible boarding from North Korean gun-boats that must have been in the parking lot. Suddenly, the flash-back was over and I awoke to the realization that people were staring at me. I turned over the command to the next commanding officer in training and returned to the office paperwork. Here I was signing things. Elsewhere, another Navy officer was putting his life on the line.

Enough time has now passed for me to realize how closely those days of personal despair mirrored the attitudes and emotions of the larger American society. We had begun in Vietnam what had seemed to some like a noble idea with the enthusiasm that said we couldn't fail. Somehow it had gradually turned evil and awful, and then we had failed. Through all of it, the Navy had changed. It wasn't the Navy that I didn't like or what the Navy could be used for or even those in it; it was what misuse of military capability during the 60s had turned the Navy into that bothered me. When I was certain that I had twenty satisfactory years for retirement purposes, I simply quit going at age forty-six. It would be fourteen years before the retirement checks began.

Sometime during my tour as commanding officer, I had a very heated discussion with the reserve captain over me about how we faculty were tenderly treating all those commie, pot-smoking kids on campus. I don't think my response helped my fitness report as I first looked at his World War Two ribbons, saw no battle stars and then said too much. Nobody should ever be promoted beyond Ensign who has no notion of the cost of war.

After being turned down for promotion to Captain, I almost left before even completing my twenty years. My last commanding officer, Ronald Fredrickson, had just been promoted to Captain. He was the exception to my rule that no one should attain a rank higher than Ensign who hadn't been shot at at least once. Ron had spent five years on active duty from 1955 to 1960 serving on a cruiser making trips to the Mediterranean. He had been my training officer, my executive officer, and now, as my commanding officer and friend, had convinced me to come back and finish the twenty.

In addition to being reserve co-workers, we were both faculty members at the University of Massachusetts. He introduced me to the two ROTC programs on campus (Army and Air Force) by recruiting me onto a university sub-committee. The University Senate had acquired veto power over all officers nominated for duty as ROTC instructors and had created a Military Affairs Sub-committee to screen all incoming officers; Ron had become its chair. If officers met university standards, the committee would certify them to the Provost as qualified to hold ROTC faculty positions during their two to three years on campus. These officers had first been selected by the Army or Air Force, had at least an MS degree, and had completed a military instructors' course but they might not always be 'appropriate.' Of greatest concern, however, were the credentials of and the impressions made by the Air Force and Army colonels nominated to be in charge of their programs. They had sensitive roles to play if ROTC programs were to reemerge on campus. I joined the sub-committee in 1974 and chaired it from 1978 to 1980.

In 1971, when Ron took over, the campus ROTC program on campus was a shambles. Both units had barely survived an attempt to destroy the ROTC building and student numbers had dropped precipitously but, by 1980, both ROTC programs were alive and well. In addition to our interviewing potential instructors, Ron and I, as reserve officers, were called upon to explain ROTC to a sometimes antagonistic faculty and staff.

We also had the task of explaining what incoming officer instructors might expect from a university. Further, as faculty, we also served on the selection boards for the Army and Air Force Scholarship programs. Only ROTC programs could repair themselves, but we could be of assistance.

By 1970, I was convinced that the services would never in my lifetime recover from the damage to their prestige done by Vietnam in all its ramifications. Somehow they, rather than the civilian leadership, had become solely responsible for Vietnam. A chance to interview potential officer candidates seeking Army and Air Force scholarships went a long way toward showing me how rapidly things can change. Either I was watching youth's resilience or merely its ignorance. Vietnam rapidly disappeared from students' minds like a bad dream. Their reasons for wanting ROTC scholarships included the following: "The folks think it's a good job," "The pay's great," and "I'll get a chance to be in charge of people," or "I need the scholarship money." It sounded very familiar; I had used some, if not all of them myself, in 1946. Behind these, as in 1946, was a willingness to be there if, and when, needed. Perhaps that was a return of patriotism.

In 1980, Emma-Jean and I left Amherst, moving to Columbus, Ohio so that I could accept a professorship at The Ohio State University. Times had changed. It was also time for me to get out. Finally, in May 1981, I walked into the Columbus Naval Reserve Training Center and applied for retirement. After nearly ten years of little direct contact with the Navy, the whole system had become strange and somehow different to me. There were several enlisted petty officers in the Training Center whose rating badges I didn't recognize. I never did understand the ribbons and medals from Vietnam. Nonetheless, breaking ties that had lasted thirty-five years was a painful experience. I felt very strange when I returned to the parking lot as a civilian.

Quite by accident, while I was in San Diego in 1987, I rediscovered now Captain James Tregurtha, USN-Ret. We had begun our midshipman days in 1946 and had not seen each other since 1967. His own naval career had begun with a Bachelor's in Dairy Science and he had frequently assured all of us midshipmen that he had every intention of getting right back to the farm to use it. Instead his naval career had extended across thirty years from destroyer duty in 1950 to submarine command.

Our careers seem to capture what Rear Admiral Holloway had intended when the NROTC Program was created in 1946. My own lopsided military career, along with Tregurtha's, symbolized two parts of a national need. During Jim's final separation interview, he was asked what it was he wanted to do with the rest of his life. His answer was, "to get back on board something going to sea," but we were both beyond that. Our love of the sea had started with two destroyers. His had extended to submarines and mine had become somewhat diminished while experiencing Vietnam—New England style. But both had essentially remained unbroken.

We both began that love under the Holloway Plan in peacetime, had both graduated from a good university and, with many others, had been quickly swept into a strange war that would mark the beginning of forty years of strife—warm and cold. Although few others seem to remember, nobody our age needs be reminded that almost as many American lives were lost during three years of the Korean War as were lost in ten years of Vietnam. For those of us who spent a winter in the Sea of Japan chasing carriers with Task Force 77, watching Panthers, Corsairs, and Skyraiders go out whole and come back with holes, or not at all, and, on brief occasions, missing mines or shore-bombarding, it was an experience of a lifetime and we had been there. Although I wouldn't wish it on my children or theirs, I am honored to have served.

Endnotes:

[1] Schrecker (1988:150-160) for the physicist Philip Morrison case at Cornell; 215-217 for the zoologist Marcus Singer case.

POST-SCRIPT

The US Navy's missions, units, ships, and people have changed markedly since the Korean War. USS *Ozbourn*, UDT 4, and ENSs Blonsick, Cole, Jarrett, Solomon, and Tregurtha, all have ridden off into the sunset to be replaced by other weapons and other Ensigns. Only the Korean War remains, stalemated along an Armistice Line called the DMZ and, given sufficient time, perhaps that too may change. Other changes have occurred.

USS *Ozbourn*

Once the refit was complete, *Ozbourn* underwent another training cycle and then returned to WestPac and Korea in Spring 1952. ENS Jarrett made the second trip as well but was released early while she was still overseas in order to return to Law School at the University of Pittsburgh. Just before going home, he was the officer in charge of a whaleboat crew that captured an armed NK vessel in Wonsan harbor. His crew included Newell, Gunner's Mate First, an impressive black giant. Newell was credited with stopping the North Korean crew from beginning a hand grenade shower by leveling his Thompson sub-machine gun at them. The capture had occurred with no injuries. Jarrett was an example of the large number of reservists who volunteered or were recalled in 1950 and who would begin to leave active duty in 1952 after completion of their two years of service.

Life along the Korean coast would go on with destroyers doing what we had done up until the end of the war. *Wiltsie,* without Jim Tregurtha, was shore bombarding in Wonsan on 27 July 1953, the last day of the siege. By then, Jim and Bob Brodie, III, had entered submarine school to begin distinguished careers in submarines. Jim's plans for graduate school and college teaching had turned into something else; the Holloway Plan was working.

After many discussions that had restarted at Penn State in May 1951 and continued in December, 1951, Emma-Jean Way and I were married on December 23, 1952. By then Jarrett had been separated from active duty and was in law school at the University of Pittsburgh. He served as an usher in our wedding. Before the wedding, he and I sat upstairs at home talking about the 'old days,' how *Ozbourn* had changed, who was still there and who wasn't. I heard about the second tour to Korea but I couldn't relate to it; those were his war stories and not mine. The next year he married Emily Engle from Beaver and I served as usher in their wedding.

After Jarrett completed law school, our trails did not cross for years although I heard he had returned to Pittsburgh and become a judge. Somehow our standing together on *Ozbourn's* open bridge quietly singing college beer songs while watching for floating mines seemed a more appropriate memory than thinking of him as some imperious old man in a black robe. We did have more fun days than hard days on *Ozbourn* and so,when I met him after forty years, I was pleased he was the same old Jarrett. The days in Wonsan, Hong Kong, San Diego and Pearl Harbor were now well in the past, but 'Tiny' hadn't changed. He also was not now, nor ever had been, a judge.

Jack Blonsick completed flight training but never returned to Korea. After his release from active duty, he went on to a long career as an airline pilot. Jack retired several years ago and he and his wife are now living in the Seattle area. There they can encounter CDR John Hadley, USN-Ret, and William Ellis. Once Ellis got off Hadley's watch section on the *Ozbourn's* bridge, the two became good friends. Charley Akers retired as

CAPT, USN as did Barr Palmer. Both are living in retirement in California. 'Commodore' Bernard Roeder went on to a distinguished career in the Navy, retiring as a Vice Admiral before his death. Some one hundred shipmates of the USS *Ozbourn* (DD-846) formed an *Ozbourn* Association which held its first reunion in 1993.

By 30 June 1951, two-hundred fifteen US destroyers and destroyer escorts were on commissioned service. That number grew to two-hundred fifty one year later and then to three-hundred forty by 30 December 1952. The Navy planned to modernize two-hundred six of them.[1] Although the Korean War would continue seven additional months into 1953, the days of reduced fleet size and obsolescent equipment seemed past. To fight a war, to modernize the fleet, and to begin new construction, naval appropriations rose quickly from $3.7 billion in 1948-49 to $4.4 billion in 1949-50, to $12.4 billion in 1950-51, and then to a recommended $15.1 billion for 1951-52. A 'Hot War' in the Far East as well as the 'Cold War' in Europe, the Atlantic, and the Mediterranean were all underway. For better or for worse, the austere defense budget of the Truman Administration was finished.

In 1954, during another cruise to the Far East, *Ozbourn* was involved in the evacuation of Nationalist troops from the Tachen Islands close to mainland China. While acting as a screening destroyer she picked up a solid contact on sonar, determined that it was not moving, and finally called for divers to identify it. Down they went and back came the message, "This thing is a destroyer bow with the numerals 846 on it." Six years after the collision, *Ozbourn* had found her own lost bow!

After her second trip to Korea in 1952, under CDR William Fargo, USN, *Ozbourn* dropped out of my mind. Occasionally I'd wander into book stores selling the latest Jane's *Fighting Ships* to see what had happened to her and to realize she also was growing old. Charley Akers, by 1964, was at sea as a Destroyer Squadron Commander and all his Gearings and Sumners were old and tired. Charley was also getting tired. During the fourteen years from 1950 to 1964, he had spent much of it at sea.

Although new aircraft carriers were replacing the Essex class carriers, the lives of destroyers were being lengthened by extensive rebuilding. By 1964, seventy-nine Gearing destroyers had undergone significant conversions called 'Fram 1'[2] to extend their lives with the fleet. Sixteen underwent further 'Fram 2' conversions which changed their looks so much that few of us with 1950-53 destroyer experience would recognize our Gearing friends. *Ozbourn* was also 'frammed.' A number of structural and equipment changes extended her life for four or five more years, but time and change were catching up with her.

Although Gearings initially were as alike as peas, eight years after leaving *Ozbourn*, Jarrett took his wife and children on a frammed Gearing to show them around and he couldn't even find the wardroom. I, on the other hand, made a reserve cruise in 1965 on an unmodified Gearing and it was *Ozbourn* all over again—just older and more tired. Without impossible changes in radar and sonar and new air and submarine defense missiles, they could no longer defend carrier groups against jets or against nuclear submarines using the methods I had learned in 1951. However, their five-inch mounts could still be used for shore bombardment and they could still rescue downed pilots.

As Gearings went through the aging process, I had this image of an old girl friend having so much done to herself that she had become someone else. In her new condition, *Ozbourn* made several tours in Vietnam and again spent time on the gunline as well as rescuing downed pilots. She was part of North SAR (search and rescue unit) during carrier and Air Force strikes against Haiphong and Hanoi on May 10, 1972.[3] During these tours, she was again hit by two shells during a shore bombardment mission and, this time, suffered two fatalities.

The inevitable happened. On March 3, 1975, Navy Secretary J. William Middendorf announced plans to retire thirty-two ships. On the list for scrapping was USS *Ozbourn* (DD-846). The *Agerholm*, decommissioned in 1978, was the last Gearing serving with the Active Fleet, although several frammed destroyers lasted a few years longer with the Naval Reserve. No non-frammed Gearing or Sumner class destroyers became museum ships although, USS *Joseph P. Kennedy, Jr.*, a frammed Gearing, made it.

A trip through the foreign navies section of the yearly Jane's *Fighting Ships* in the decade from 1965 to 1975 gave hints as to where else to look. Obsolete American ships were being distributed around the world and, somewhere, in foreign ports, you could still find the old familiar lines of a Gearing or a

Sumner. You might have reconstructed much of Task Force 77's old destroyer screen out of ships anchored in tropical harbors. When asked, I used to say that *Ozbourn* had been converted into razor blades, but my personal feeling was that the only proper burial for a warship was to be sunk in a thousand fathoms. It seems disrespectful, even immoral, just to turn them into steel scrap or give them away, no matter how justified the need.

NROTC

The Regular NROTC Program designed by CAPT Adams and RADM Holloway has changed very little and has become eminently successful, producing more regular line officers yearly than the Naval Academy. The two years of active duty initially required of Regular NROTC scholarship holders became three years in 1951 to accommodate the Korean War and was then extended to four during Vietnam. For graduates choosing flight training, the commitment now might be closer to eight but that begins only after certification as an aviator which takes up to two years.

During Vietnam, several universities abolished their NROTC Units because of student and faculty pressure, but they were soon replaced by other institutions who wanted the Program. As the revised NROTC Program envisioned by CAPT Adams and ADM Holloway approaches its fiftieth anniversary, it has, with relatively minor modifications, survived as a highly cost-effective system for producing officers.

Post-Cold War cut-backs are being implemented. Although the Navy proposed to reduce the number of NROTC units, Congressional action restored the number. By July 1996, in addition to closing five of the present sixty-six units, sixteen additional units were to have been reduced to eight consortia. Sixty-eight of the current one hundred twenty-four 'cross-town arrangements' are to be closed, thus preventing students from liberal arts schools such as Otterbein College from participating in the program. Other plans placed on hold included commissioning all NROTC and Annapolis graduates beginning 1996 as Ensigns, USNR. Upon completion of one year of service, they would be screened for regular commissions. In 1990-91, 8,783 students were enrolled in the Program, a number being reduced yearly to match the declining needs of the service. Despite cutbacks, competition for scholarships is even more intense.[4] Similar cutbacks are also occurring in the Army and Air Force programs.

Although Naval Academy graduates were favored in career and advancement opportunities during and after Korea, those biases began to fade during Vietnam. Although NROTC has yet to produce a Chief of Naval Operations, it has produced four-star admirals and one general. General P.X. Kelley, USMC, Commandant of the Marine Corps was a 1950 NROTC graduate of Villanova. The retention and career patterns, as well as advancement opportunities, are about as good today for NROTC graduates as they are for USNA graduates. Some might say even better.

United States Naval Academy

Annapolis has also changed and is no longer the 'trade school on the Severn.' An early change occurred in 1930 when the US Naval Academy first awarded Bachelor of Science degrees to its graduates. From then until 1959, however, all midshipmen followed identical academic programs weighted heavily with mathematics, physical science, engineering, and practical experience. Following considerable discussion, the entire curriculum was revamped in 1963. Since then, the curriculum has evolved into eighteen major fields of study. Although Annapolis remains primarily an engineering school, it is possible to select oceanography, political science, and English from among its majors. There is still a core curriculum but it now blends engineering, mathematics, and computer science with the humanities and social sciences. Its graduates now must serve six years of active duty. The Academy's Class of 1990 contained 1,008 graduates of which 236 men and 9 women chose Surface Warfare, 226 men and 10 women chose pilot training. Twenty men chose SEALs. Special Warfare is now an acceptable career track for Academy graduates.

Not every Academy graduate survives to retirement. We lost Dave Thornhill in 1954 and in 1967, CAPT Roger Netherland, USN, was killed leading his Air Group over North Vietnam. In Beaver, a Roger Netherland memorial tree now grows in the park near the Post Office.[5]

Shipboard Experience and Schools

It took about six months at sea on *Ozbourn* for me to catch up with my Annapolis-trained counterpart, Jerry Solomon. Our differences in shipboard skills and knowledge characterized most of us then graduating from these two sources. The pre-1963, hands-on, 'trade school' education at Annapolis easily provided far more experience with ships and naval procedures than could Cornell. To rectify the NROTC deficiency, the Navy began sending its NROTC graduates to a special six month's Surface Warfare School somewhat analogous to the Marine Corps' Basic School. Ironically, and partly because of changes in the Annapolis curriculum, when these NROTC graduates entered the fleet, they were better equipped for shipboard duty than Ensigns from Annapolis. To compensate, the Navy now sends all its newly commissioned Surface Warfare ensigns to Surface Warfare School. This School also solved another problem. As shipboard command and control procedures in the missile era became increasingly complex, no longer could OODs such as John Hadley adequately train junior officers on the job. This course standardized the training of deck officers as well as educated officers for another important career path–Surface Warfare. A not particularly friendly competition still exists between officers from air and submarine backgrounds to which has been added those with Surface Warfare experience. Although perhaps not equal in prestige to flying or submarines, the cruiser and destroyer route is acceptable; unfortunately, duty in the amphibs is still not.

The Navy's Mine Force program virtually vanished after World War Two, was vigorously rebuilt during Korea and then languished again, to be rebuilt in the 1980s. Currently, command of a modern minesweeper is a major plum for the junior Lieutenant Commander on the way up. Mines remain a low-cost way to force hostile naval units to stay well off your coast. The two minings during Desert Storm reminded me why I moved aft on *Ozbourn*. It is the threat of mines, whether or not they are actually present, that is a major deterrent to any in-shore naval activity and mine warfare should remain an important consideration in the Navy's future planning.

Reserve Officers

Although the Holloway Program provided for production of regular officers and some reserve officers, a major source of reserve officers was also needed. The Officers' Candidate School (OCS) at Newport, Rhode Island, started in 1951, began to provide reserve officers who were required to serve three years active duty followed by an additional three years in the Ready Reserve. They would begin to replenish the pool of reserve officers recalled during Korea. After active duty, whether or not serving in a paid drilling unit, OCS graduates would remain eligible for recall in time of national emergency for the rest of their obligated time. Officer programs were always attractive to college graduates wishing an alternative to the draft and the infantry, even if it cost an additional year's service.

Reserve Units and the Recall Process

From World War Two until post-Vietnam, enlisted men and officers in Naval Reserve drill units, if recalled, could expect to be spread at random across the fleet to bring ships and shore facilities up to required wartime levels. Although recall assignments would be based on qualifications, there was almost no chance that all members of particular unit would ever be assigned to a single ship. Only those reservists already serving as crew for a Reserve Fleet ship, attached to an air squadron, or in a SeaBee Unit could expect to remain with their own units if recalled. Accordingly, the larger Surface and the smaller Electronics Units functioned primarily as training schools for pre-active duty recruits and used officers and post-active duty petty officers for instructors. Yearly active duty for training was an individual event for each officer and enlisted man in these Units. In time, failure to provide modern technical training for post-active duty petty officers brought about their gradual obsolescence, making it difficult for them to be advanced. Although officers running these units were promoted by a selection board process, often they too had not acquired shipboard skill levels comparable to their active duty counterparts. If recalled, they would have been useful only if their civilian skills were transferable.

Fourteen years after the Korean War began, President Johnson chose to fight in Vietnam using only regulars, volunteers, and draftees. Initially, either he hoped this little war would not require a call-up, or he wished to keep mobilization as a potential poker chip to be used later, as he implemented his step-by-step policy for turning on the heat. Although not mobilizing might have been intended as a message to North Vietnam that we really didn't need to mobilize to win, it also sent a message to American reservists that either what they were doing was irrelevant or that they weren't good enough. Even though we expected to be recalled, few of us in units wished for it; however, we all knew it represented the commitment on the other side of a reservist's paycheck. But, instead of being recalled to augment fleet needs, we became either a Johnsonian pawn to be played later or some sort of miscellany on a back shelf in the President's strategic reserve.

President Johnson understood very well that the UN-sanctioned Korean Conflict had become 'Truman's War' in less than a year. Calling up significant reserve components could easily become political suicide.[6] But for those of us expecting to be called up in time to participate in a legitimate war, the line of reasoning behind this decision seemed both cynical and one that, in time, placed an unfair burden on regulars as well as on draftees and volunteers. Irrespective of whether Vietnam was necessary, part of the cost of fighting a war we either couldn't or wouldn't win, included a long term rise in cynicism in both the reserves and regular components.

After Vietnam, an all-voluntary military was developed and the draft was abolished. Thus, in 1990, President Bush had no option but to fight Desert Storm with regular forces augmented as needed by national guard and voluntary reserves. Anticipating that potential demand, the Naval Reserve Program was vastly modified from its pre- and post-Korean War configuration. Following World War Two, the Reserve Surface Divisions (Large, Medium, or Small called Electronics) became grounds primarily for pre-active duty seaman and most had obsolete equipment and thus poor programs for keeping post-active duty sailors ready to serve. A Large Surface Division might contain one hundred fifty sailors and fifteen officers. The smaller units were distributed into smaller communities. Were a call-up to occur, enlisted men as well as officers would be scattered throughout the fleet. As a result, there was no reason to train together against that eventuality. This system characterized the recall of reservists during the first years of the Korean War and would have been followed during Vietnam. Other specialized units such as Seabees, Aviation Squadrons, and crews on reserve ships did drill as a unit and would anticipate recall as a unit. Several SeaBee groups were recalled later during Vietnam but there was no generalized recall characteristic of Korea.

Following Vietnam, this format changed and the Surface Divisions were reorganized into smaller units with a primary mission of meeting the explicit needs of individual ships or shore commands. These units worked together, went on training duty together, tended to know each other and were likely to better serve potential needs for shipboard wartime complements. As an example, seven Naval Reserve Special Warfare Units now exist providing an opportunity for former active duty SEALs to remain within the Special Warfare community. Treating these reserve units as part of the regular fleet also better serves the needs of individual reservists by providing them with access to current equipment, doctrine, and procedures which they need if they are to be promoted and remain interested in the program.

Underwater Demolition Teams and SEALS

Underwater Demolition Teams, in 1962, gave birth to SEAL Teams with an expanded mission that included clandestine, behind-lines operations similar to those in which West Coast Teams had engaged during the Korean War. Subsequent to 1962, SEALs were to play important roles in Vietnam, Grenada, Panama, and, most recently, in the Persian Gulf. Because SEALs, if need be, can also perform pre-assault reconnaissance, Underwater Demolition Teams were decommissioned in 1983.

Concerned about loss of unconventional warfare officers and enlisted men either back to the fleet or to civilian life, the Navy established a fourth career path for line officers. Special Warfare joined Air Warfare, Submarine Warfare, and Surface Warfare. The challenge to learn unconventional skills continues to attract people different from the rest of the Navy. The success of future SEAL missions will inevitably depend on retention of such highly trained, unconventional people who can be assured of a twenty-year career. The Navy is recognizing that it takes all kinds and is now doing a much better job at accepting us weird folks than it did in 1950-53.

Finally

Aunt Izzy's green wool sweater had arrived on *Ozbourn* in time for Christmas 1950 and it became one of the many layers needed for bridge watches during that winter. I kept that old green sweater for years. Any time I wore it, I could see a gray horizon and carrier operations underway in the distance. Then one day it vanished from its drawer to the tune of, "Why do you want that old thing, you never wear it anymore...."

Gradually I have left the pain of Korea behind and, as its symbols have departed, only the fading memories recalled above remain.

Endnotes:

[1] *Janes Fighting Ships, 1950-51* (1951:438).

[2] "FRAM" is the naval acronym for Fleet Rehabilitation and Modernization.

[3] Ethell and Prince (1989).

[4] *Chronicle of Higher Education*, (February 13, 1991: A35-37).

[5] Gillcrist (1990:235-241) describes the mission in which CAPT Netherland was killed.

[6] Mitchener's *The Bridges of Toko-Ri* describes the fictional loss of LT Brubaker, a reserve pilot operating off Korea with TF77 and describes much of the declining political support at home for the war. This gradually developed as the battleline became stalemated after *Ozbourn* had completed her first tour.

SOURCES

Alexander, Bevin. *Korea, the First War We Lost*. New York: Hippocrene Press, 1986.

Appleman, Roy E. *South to the Naktong, North to the Yalu: United States Army in the Korea War*. Washington, D.C.: US Government Printing Office, 1961.

Berry, James. "Operation Fishnet," *Proceedings US Naval Institute*. December 1990: 107-108.

Blair, Clay. *The Forgotten War: Americans in Korea 1950-1953*. New York: Times Books, Inc., 1987.

Blanton, S. L. "Damnreservists," *Proceedings US Naval Institute* October 1990: 83-86.

Bosiljevac, T. L. *SEALs: UDT/SEAL Operations in Vietnam*. New York: Ivy Books. 1990.

Brady, James. *The Coldest Winter: A Memoir of Korea*. New York: Orion Books, 1990.

Cagle, Malcolm W. and Frank A. Manson. *The Sea War in Korea*. Annapolis, MD: United States Naval Institute, 1957.

Calvert, James. *The Naval Profession*. New York: McGraw-Hill Book Company, 1971. (Revised edition).

Carey, RADM J. J., USNR. "Wither the Naval Reserve?" *Proceedings Naval Institute* 101 for 1975: 95-97.

Carter, RADM, E. W., III, USN (Ret.). "Blockade," *Proceedings US Naval Institute*. November 1990: 42-47.

Collins, Robert F. *Reserve Officer Training Corps: Campus Paths to Service Commissions*. New York: The Rosen Publishing Groups, 1986.

Cummings, Bruce. *The Origins of the Korean War*. New Jersey: Princeton University Press, 1981.

Davis, Vincent. *The Admirals Lobby*. Chapel Hill: University of North Carolina Press, 1967.

Detzer, David. *Thunder of the Captains: The Short Summer in 1950*. New York: Thomas Y. Crowell Co., 1977.

Dockery, Kevin. *SEALs in Action*. New York: Avon Books, 1991.

Ethell, Jeffrey and Alfred Price. *One Day in a Long War: May 10, 1972*. New York: Random House, 1989.

Fane, CDR F. D., USNR and Major Don W. Moore, USA Ret. "The naked warriors," *Proceedings US Naval Institute* 82(9) for 1956: 913-922.

Field, James A., Jr. *History of the United States Naval Operations: Korea*. Washington, D.C.: US Government Printing Office, 1962.

Fisher, Captain William G., USN. "Reply to Major Morgan's letter," *Proceedings US Naval Institute* 73(8) for 1947: 977-978.

Friedman, Norman. *U.S. Destroyers: An Illustrated Design History*. Annapolis, MD: Naval Institute Press, 1983.

_____ with ship plans by A. D. Baker, III. *U. S. Aircraft Carriers: An Illustrated Design History*. Annapolis, MD: Naval Institute Press, 1983.

Gillcrist, Paul T. *Feet Wet*. Navato, CA: Presidio Press, 1990.

291

Goncharow, Sergei, John W. Lewis, and Xue Litai. *Uncertain Partners: Stalin, Mao, and the Korean War.* Stanford, CA: Stanford University Press, 1993.

Goulden, Joseph C. *Korea: The Untold Story of the War.* New York: Times Books, Inc., 1982.

Guthrie, Jr., RADM Wallace N., CAPT Hugh Baumbardner, and CDR Mel Chaloupa, USNR. "The Reserve is ready and waiting," *Proceedings US Naval Institute* September 1990: 46-51.

Hagen, Kenneth J. *This People's Navy: The Making of American Sea Power.* New York: The Free Press, 1991.

Hall, CAPT R. A., USN. "In defence of the trade schools," *Proceedings US Naval Institute* 73(7) for 1947: 801-812.

Hallion, Richard P. *The Naval Air War in Korea.* Baltimore, MD: The Nautical and Aviation Publishing Company of America, 1986.

Hastings, Max. *The Korean War.* New York: Simon & Schuster, 1987.

Heinl, Robert D., Jr. *Soldiers of the Sea: The United States Marine Corps, 1775-1962.* Baltimore, MD: The Nautical and Aviation Publishing Company of America, 1991. (Second edition).

Hodges, Peter and Norman Friedman. *Destroyer Weapons of World War II.* Annapolis, MD: Naval Institute Press.

Holloway, James L. "The Holloway Plan - a summary view and commentary," *Proceedings US Naval Institute* 73(11) for 1947: 1293-1303.

Howarth, Stephen. *To Shining Sea: A History of the United States Navy, 1775-1991.* New York: Random House, 1991.

Hoyt, Edwin P. *The Pusan Perimeter.* New York: Military Heritage Press, 1984a.

Hoyt, Edwin P. *On to the Yalu.* New York: Stein and Day, 1984b.

Isenberg, Michael T. *Shield of the Republic: The United States Navy in an Era of Cold War and Violent Peace.* Vol. 1. New York: St. Martin's Press, 1993.

Jane's Fighting Ships 1947-48. (50th edition). London: Sampson Low, Marston and Co., Ltd., 1948.

Jane's Fighting Ships 1951-52. London: Sampson Low, Marston and Co., Ltd., 1952.

Jane's Fighting Ships 1965-66. London: Sampson Low, Marston and Co., Ltd., 1966.

Jane's Fighting Ships 1987-88. London: Sampson Low, Marston and Co., Ltd., 1988.

Kelly, Orr. *Brave Men, Dark Waters: The Untold Story of the Navy Seals.* Novato, CA: Presidio Press, 1992.

Kiely, CAPT Denis J., USMC (Ret.). "Are the Academies worth it?" *Proceedings US Naval Institute* June 1991: 36-39.

Kjellman, LTJG John V., USNR. "Letter response to 'UDT comes of age'," *Proceedings US Naval Institute* 91(6) for 1965: 118-119.

Love, Robert W., Jr. *History of the U. S. Navy.* Vol. II: 1942-1991. Harrisburg, PA: Stackpole Books, 1992.

MacDonald, C. A. *Korea: The War Before Vietnam.* New York: The Free Press, 1986.

Maihafer, Harry J. *From the Hudson to the Yalu: West Point '49 in the Korean War.* College Station: Texas A&M University Press Military Series, 1993.

Maloy, W. L. "The education and training of naval officers: An investment in the future," *Proceedings US Naval Institute* 101(5) for 1975: 134-149.

Martineau, David L. "The present promotion situation," *Proceedings US Naval Institute* 73(8) for 1947: 915-922.

Michener, James A. *The Bridges at Toko-Ri.* New York: Random House, 1952.

Morgan, Major John D., Jr. "Letter to US Naval Institute," *Proceedings US Naval Institute* 73(8) for 1947: 977.

Morison, Samuel Eliot. *History of United States Naval Operations in World War II.* Vol. XV. Supplement and General Index. Boston: Little, Brown, 1962.

_____. *The Two-Ocean War.* Boston: Little, Brown, 1963.

Naval History Division. *Dictionary of American Naval Fighting Ships.* Vols. 1-8. Washington: Naval History Division. Government Printing Office, 1959-1981.

Paik, General Sun Yup. *From Pusan to Panmunjom.* New York: Brassey's (US), Inc., 1992.

Polmar, Norman. *The Ships and Aircraft of the US Fleet.* (Fourteenth edition). Annapolis, MD: Naval Institute Press, 1987.

Rees, David. *Korea: The Limited War.* New York and London: St. Martin's Press, 1964.

Reilly, John C., Jr. and Frank D. Johnson (ed.). *United States Destroyers of World War II.* Dorset, England: Blandford Press, Ltd., 1983.

Ritter, LT James J., USNR. "UDT comes of age," *Proceedings US Naval Institute* 91(2) for 1965: 53-63.

Schratz, Paul R. *Submarine Commander: A Story of World War II and Korea.* Lexington, KY: The University Press of Kentucky, 1989.

Schrecker, Ellen W. *No Ivory Tower: McCarthyism and the Universities.* New York and Oxford: Oxford University Press, 1986.

Singlaub, John K., with Malcolm McConnell. *Hazardous Duty: An American Soldier in the Twentieth Century.* New York: Summit Books, 1991.

Soper, Captain M. E., USN. "Officers for the 1980s: A challenge for NROTC," *Proceedings US Naval Institute* 101(2) for 1975: 40-47.

Summers, Colonel Harry G. (Ret.). *Korean War Almanac.* New York: Facts on File Publications, 1990.

_____. *On Strategy II: A Critical Analysis of the Gulf War.* New York: Dell Publishing Co., 1992.

Thornton, CAPT John W., with John W. Thornton, Jr. *Relieved to Be Alive.* Middlebury, VT: Paul S. Eriksson Publisher, 1981.

Toland, John. *In Mortal Combat: Korea, 1950-1953.* New York: Morrow, 1991.

Watson, James and Kevin Dockery. *Point Man.* New York: Morrow, 1993.

Watts, David and James Ritter. "The combat swimmer," *Proceedings US Naval Institute,* May 1965.

Whelan, Richard. *Drawing the Line: The Korean War, 1950-1953.* Boston: Little, Brown and Company, 1990.

Index

294

F-86 ('SuperSabre,' USAF Jet fighter) 198
F4U (see 'Corsair')
F9F ('Panther,' Navy jet fighter) 198
Fankochi Point (Tungsen Got) 95, 97, 112, 178, 203; *map* 97
Far East Station, Hong Kong 8
Fargo, William CDR, USN 281
Farnam, Rob Roy, ENS, USN 219
Fast Attack Transport 229; (see also APD)
Farragut, USS (DD-348) 123
Fay, Robert, LT, USN 237, 245-6
Fifth Marine Regiment 79; Third Battalion 81; (see also US Marine Corps)
First Division (Deck Department) 154
First Marine Division 61, 107, 142; (see also US Marine Corps; X Corps; Tenth Corps)
Filipino messmen 88
fire drill 39
fire on ship 142-6
'Fireball' (voice call for USS *Oz-bourn*) 9, 87, 183
Fire-control Directors (see Director 37, 56, 63)
firerooms in a destroyer 13, 15, 70, 123-4, 140, 142-3, 149, 159, 169; (see also 'Split-plant')
Fischer's Hardware Store, Beaver 152, 196
fishing vessels 175, 192, 196, 201
fitness reports 221, 265
Fitzsimmons' Army Hospital, Denver, CO 152
five-inch ammunition 96
five-inch mounts 11-2. 14. 48. 74. 157, 169, 174-5, 179-83, 190-3, 198; (see also destroyer gunnery; three-inch batteries; 20mm batteries)
'Five-term' Program 52
'Flag' 159, 163; (see also Flag Lieutenant; LT Jerry Aachus, USNR)
Flag Lieutenant (see 'Flag')
flashless powder 175
Fleet Sonar School, San Diego, CA 211-3, 215
Fleet Training Center, San Diego, CA 46
_____ short course 212
Fletcher class destroyers 10-12, 123; (see also *Sumner*; *Gearing*; *Elly-son*; *Farragut*; *Benson* classes)

flight operations 69, 72-4
flight training 56
'Flying chairs' 158
Flying Fish Channel 79, 100-1, 111; (see also Inchon)
'Forgotten War' 211, 273
Forest Royal, USS (DD-872, Gearing class) 200
Formosa 2, 8, 118ff 141-2, 144, 162, 165; (see also Nationalist China)
_____ Foreign Persons Police 136
_____ potential invasion of 137-8
_____ Patrol 6, 114-6, 118, 134, 140; (see also Task Force 72)
_____ Straits 4, 6
Fort Pierce, FL 227
Forward Damage Control 181
Forward Officers' Quarters 48
Foul-weather Parade 154; (also see muster)
Fox Schedule 91, 127
'Four-pipers,' World War One destroyers 11
'Frammed' 281-2
Fraternal Order of UDT/SEALs 231
Fredrickson, Ronald, CAPT, USNR 276
French Foreign Legion 242
French '75,' World War One artillery piece 182
Freeman, Ross, CDR, USN 54, 62, 87
'frogman' 222-3
frost-bite 152, 258-9; (see also 'Mickey Mouse' boots)

'Gator Navy' 244
Gearing, USS (DD-710) 10-3, 281-2; (see also *Sumner*; *Fletcher*; *Oz-bourn*; 'Frammed')
General Assembly (UN) (see United Nations General Assembly)
General Quarters ('GQ') 16, 66, 71, 87, 93, 114, 159, 180, 185-6, 190, 198
'GQ' (see General Quarters)
George, Walter, US Senator (D-Georgia) 36
GI-Bill, World War Two 20
Gillespie, Robert, HMSN, USN 272; killed in action 212
Ginza, Tokyo 205
Golden Gate Bridge 40
Gombai toasts 139
Gough, *photo* 234
Gourdine, 'Flash' 88

297

Granitz, *photo* 234
Gray, Bruce 37
Greenwood, USS (DE-679, Buckley class) 274
Guadalcanal Campaign 243
Guadalope, USS (AO-57) 134, 137, 139
Guam Island ix
Guamanian messmen 88
Guantanamo Bay, Cuba 247
Gunnery Liaison Officer for Machine Gun Batteries 42
Guppy 214; (see also submarines)
Gurke, USS (DD-783) 80
gyro compass 220

Hadley, John, LTJG, USN 51, 63-9, 94, 116, 132, 139, 164, 187, 202, 213, 217, 280, 285; *photos* 51, 184
Haeju, NK 97
Hague Convention, 1907 191
Haiphong Habor, NK 117, 174
Halsey, William J., ADM, USN 123
Hampton, VA 243
Hamul, USS (AD-20) 114, 145
Hamner, USS (DD-718) 8
Han River, SK 79
'Happy Valley' 65, 161; (see also *Valley Forge*; 'Cherry Tree')
Hattie 209, 210, 217
'heating the ship' 169
Hector, USS (AR-7) 143-4
Helena, USS (CA-75) 57, 61
helicopter 73, 111, 179, 192, 196, 198, 200, 202, 204,
'Hell Week' 232, 255
helmsman 47
Henry, 'Henry,' GM1, USNR 94, 212
Henrico, USS (APA-45) 39, 42, 61
Higgins, 'Smiley,' TMC, USN 13, 182, 206
high-speed attack transport (APD) 229; (see also *Begor*; *Belknap*; *Bowers*; *Liddle*; *Ruchampkin*)
Hinzpeter, RMN1 *photo* 175
Hobby, USS (DD-610, Benson class) 62; (see also CDR Akers)
Hodge, Al, LT, USN 246; *photos* 234, 263
Hodgson, Robert E., ENS, USN 241, 256
Hokkaido Island, Japan 8
'Holiday Routine' 134
Hollis, USS (APD-86) 243

Hollister, USS (DD-788, Gearing class) 9, 45, 95, 121, 128, 134, 136, 142, 161, 193, 195, 198-201, 221
Holloway, James E., RADM, USN 20-1, 25, 27, 278, 283
_____ Plan 27-28, 278, 280, 283; (see also NROTC, US Naval Academy)
Homeward Bound Pennant 209
homosexual incident 160
Hong Kong 122, 124-5, 128, 130, 137, 158
Honolulu, HI 37, 46, 206
Hope, Bob 109, 110
Hora, LTJG *photo* 234
hospital ship 102
Hostilo, John, GM2, USN 251, 255
Hoyt, LCDR, USN 76, 237, 254
HUKs (Philippine rebels) 3, 8-9
Hungnam, NK 107-8, 110, 141-3, 146-7, 161, 175, 178
Hunter's Point 208, 216, 220; (see also San Francisco Naval Shipyard)
hurricane (see typhoon)
hypothermia 188

'I & I' (see Rest & Relaxation)
'in hack' (see confined to quarters)
Inchon, SK 61, 78ff, 107, 109, 111, 115-6, 147, 158, 203, 272; (see also 'Chromite'; Inchon Landing; Flying Fish Channel)
_____ Landing 81, 177ff; MacArthur's jacket 82-3; (see also 'Chromite'; 'Common Knowledge')
income taxes 110, 162-3, 171, 195
Indo-China 3, 76, 110-1
Inflatable Boat Small (IBS) 233-235; tug incident 256
inspections 71, 88-9, 152
interdiction 176-7, 189-91, 201
Iwo Jima 24, 231, 262
Iwon, NK 107

Jamaica, HMS (British light cruiser) 39
Japan, as a sanctuary 5
Japanese Current 161
_____ pilot 53
Jarrett, Charles, 'Tiny,' 'Charley,' USNR (Jarrett only used in text to distinguish him from 'Charley' Akers) 17, 50, 103, 116, 130-2, 156, 182-3, 186, 189, 193, 201,

298

moth-balled destroyers 10-2, 36, 145, 167
motor whaleboat (see whaleboat)
Mt. Katmai, USS (AE-16) 44-6, 56, 74
Mount Katmai, Alaska 56
Mount McKinley, USS (AGC-7) 82
Mounts 51, 52, 53 95; (see also five-inch mounts)
movies on Board 65, 74, 77, 87-94, 107, 112-4, 151, 169, 187, 207, 210
Muccio, John, US Ambassador to South Korea 3
Murphy 239
'Mustangs' (officers up from the ranks) 63; (see also Abbott; Hadley; Lockhart; Remmen)
'Mustangs' (see P-51s)
muster 43, 63, 154, 192-3; (see also foul-weather parade)
Myatt, ENS, rescue 83-6; *photo* 85; (see also *Philippine Sea*)

NAB (Naval Amhibious Base) (see Little Creek, VA; Coronado, CA)
Naktong River, SK 52, 55
Naktong River line 52, 55; (see also Pusan Perimeter)
Narragansett Bay, RI 244
National Guard, call-up 20, 94-95
Nationalist China 3, 119, 281; (see also Formosa; Taiwan)
_____ Navy, card-playing admirals 135; party 139
NATO Treaty 6
Naval Academy (see US Naval Academy)
Navy appropriations 281
_____ District Commandant 275
_____ Forces, Far East 7-8; (see also ComNavFE)
_____ officer promotions 216, 230, 235, 244-5, 265, 276
_____ officer transfers 215, 218
_____ protocol 129
_____ Reserves (USNR) 93; call-up 93-5; "saved my ass" 134
_____ Reserve Training Centers, archaic equipment 275; Springfield, MA 275; Columbus, OH 277
Navy 'black' (oil) 157; (see destroyers, refueling)
Navy Commendation Ribbon 221, 235
Navy Cross 221
Navy divers in UDT (salvage, first class and master divers) 241

NCDU (Navy Combat Demolition Unit) 227
Nehring, ENS, USN 103; (see also *Manchester*)
Netherland, Roger, ENS, USN 24-25; death 284
New Jersey, USS (BB-62) 202
New Territories (see Hong Kong)
New Year's Day, 1951 147
New York Times 112, 128, 165, 188-9, 193
Newell, GM1, USN 88, 143, 279
night vision 84, 150
Normandy 227; (see D-Day; Dimartino)
Norfolk, VA 243
_____ Naval Operating Base 244
Northwest Orient Airlines 134, 194
Norton Sound, USS (AV-11, seaplane tender) 206
NROTC 21, 23-4, 32-5, 43, 56, 66, 103, 133, 210, 217, 221, 232, 248, 283; bias 284; Class of 1951 66; competition with USNA 84; extended to three years 210; flight training 212

Obong-Ni, SK 55
O'Brien, QM1, USN 214, 221
obsolescence 10-1
OCS (Officer Candidate School, Newport, RI) 286
Officer-of-the-Deck (OOD) 40, 47, 53, 63-8, 83-4, 90, 129, 132, 150, 168; not qualified 218-9; qualified underway 222; surface warfare 285
Officer's Quarters 48
officer transfers 145, 219
Officer-in-charge 247
Ohio State University 32, 277
Okinawa 5, 11, 45, 54-7, 116, 142, 144, 233; mail 144; (see also Buckner Bay)
1-MC (shipboard public address system) 83, 144, 154
On-the-job training 46, 146, 285; (see also JOOD; OOD)
'Onion Skin' (voice call for *Philippine Sea*) 82
Onslow Beach, NC 243, 250
OOD (see Officer-of-the-deck)
Operations Division 54, 63, 88, 218, crew *photo* 208
_____ Officer 218
Operations Orders 78
Osan, SK 82
Osprey, USS (AMS-28) 103

301

304